Imposing Economic San

Imposing Economic Sanctions

Legal Remedy or Genocidal Tool?

Geoff Simons

Pluto Press

LONDON • STERLING, VIRGINIA

First published 1999 by Pluto Press
345 Archway Road, London N6 5AA
and 22883 Quicksilver Drive,
Sterling, VA 20166–2012, USA

British Library Cataloguing in Publication Data
A catalogue record for this book is available from the British Library

ISBN 0 7453 1397 3 hbk

Library of Congress Cataloging in Publication Data
Simons, G.L. (Geoffrey Leslie), 1939–
    Imposing economic sanctions: legal remedy or genocidal tool?/Geoff
Simons.
        p.   cm.
    Includes bibliographical references and index.
    ISBN 0–7453–1397–3 (hbk)
    1. Economic sanctions. 2. Sanctions (International law)
I. Title.
JZ8373.S58   1999
327.1'7—dc21   98–46772
                                                                            CIP

Designed and produced for Pluto Press by
Chase Production Services, Chadlington, OX7 3LN
Typeset from disk by Stanford DTP Services, Northampton
Printed in the EC by T.J. International, Padstow

To Leonie

Contents

List of Tables and Figures

Tables

Figures

Acknowledgements

I am grateful to the many people who have supplied information that relates directly or indirectly to the complex world of economic sanctions. Particular thanks are due to Alexandra McLeod (Librarian, United Nations Information Centre, London) who supplies copious UN documents (resolutions, letters, statements, interviews, and so on); the activists of the charity Voices in the Wilderness (Kathy Kelly, George Capaccio and others in the United States; and their colleagues in the United Kingdom, Stanhope House, 1 Hertford Road, London, N2 9BX), struggling to relieve the suffering of the beleaguered Iraqi people; Felicity Arbuthnot, journalist and Middle East specialist, who is generous with her expertise and who works tirelessly to highlight the gross injustices perpetrated by powerful states; and Christine Simons, whose substantial and growing archive is an invaluable resource, whose insights often find their way unremarked into my texts, and who helps in many other ways.

Economic sanctions, hyped by comfortable politicians and pundits as a convenient legal remedy, are too often an undiscriminating 'weapon of mass destruction'. As ever, I am grateful to the journalists, aid workers, academics and others whose efforts help to publicise the genocidal denial of food and medicine to civilian populations. Their names are given in the notes and elsewhere in this book.

Preface

Research for this book soon confirmed what I had long suspected: economic sanctions are a universe. They have always been used by contending domestic factions and exploited as a multifaceted tool in the service of foreign policy. They run through all of history and are indelibly stamped on international affairs in the modern world. In one form or another they have always been a concomitant to military action in war, and a ubiquitous and weighty element in the peacetime relations between states at times of commercial expansion and rising tensions.

Do they 'work'? Economic sanctions are so diverse – in their type, ambition and manner of application – that no general answer is possible. *International* economic sanctions, the theme of this book, are variously porous, ineffectual, counterproductive, misdirected, persuasive, effectual and devastating. They invariably have some impact, and they may achieve covert objectives quite different to those that are publicly proclaimed: the deliverers of sanctions often have hidden agendas.

Economic sanctions, in isolation, are rarely a *legal remedy* to an international crisis. They have the habit of antagonising and consolidating recalcitrant regimes which are then forced into repression and self-reliance; and of bringing immense suffering to innocent human victims. Alas, economic sanctions are more often a *genocidal tool*, subjecting helpless civilian populations – in solitary city or entire country – to comprehensive siege. And they frequently have serious consequences also for states other than the target victim.

Economic sanctions are a complex ecology – bringing minor perturbations, drastic effects and extinctions in their wake. They are seldom imposed with discriminate skill or with ethically proportionate impact. Too often, in their successes and their failures, they do no more than reflect and amplify the unjust shape of international power.

Introduction

There is no sense in which this book represents an exhaustive treatment of economic sanctions. The field is immensely complex, and space dictates that the focus must be on primary concerns and important selected examples. The entire field of trade, commerce and finance – multifaceted in modern society – invites sanctions at many different levels when states are in conflict.

A single state may take unilateral economic action in an attempt to achieve coercive affects elsewhere: as when the United States in July 1940 placed an embargo on the supply of aviation fuel and scrap iron to Japan (and so helped to 'precipitate the Japanese attack on Pearl Harbor'[1]); when Moscow in 1948 applied economic coercion in an attempt to counter the Yugoslavian struggle for independence from the Soviet bloc; and when Washington in late 1979 imposed wide-ranging sanctions (grain embargo, block on high-technology sales, curtailment of trade credits) on Moscow following the invasion of Afghanistan.[2] Alternatively, a group of states with a common interest may take concerted action: as when the Council for Mutual Economic Assistance (COMECON), created in 1949 as a response to the Marshall Plan, tried to influence international trade in Soviet interests; and when the Western importing countries imposed a boycott of Iranian oil (1951–3) following the nationalisation of the Iranian oil industry by the Mossadeq government. Or an attempt can be made to impose *universal* economic sanctions, via such organisations as the now-defunct League of Nations and its successor body, the United Nations.

Individual states can impose *de facto* or *de jure* economic sanctions against other countries as unambiguously hostile acts (for example, by attempting a blockade on the high seas), or as part of traditional trading practices (for example, in developing a protective tariff structure – which today may violate the regulations of the World Trade Organization). A group of countries acting in concert may typically have regional objectives: as when the Organization of American States (OAS), invoking Articles 6 and 8 of the Rio Treaty in August 1960, imposed economic sanctions against the Dominican Republic for committing acts of aggression against Venezuela; and when the

Arab League developed its Central Boycott Office (CBO) in 1949 to stifle the newly created Israel in the heart of Arab land.[3] Where so-called 'universal sanctions' have been imposed, with mandatory obligations stipulated by the League of Nations or the United Nations, the impression of *consensual policy* is always illusory: one or more powerful states – particularly in the UN Security Council – have been able to suborn the organisation into support for their own foreign-policy objectives.

It is clear that the instances of economic sanctions (all types taken *in toto*) in the twentieth century alone run into the thousands. Every major case of sanctions itself usually involves a hierarchy of economic prohibitions, constraints, pressures, limitations, disadvantages, and so on – variously affecting the shipment of goods, access to markets, the availability of credit, the freezing of assets, the sequestration of funds, the erection of tariffs, the withdrawal of 'most favoured trading nation' status, the blocking of aid, and many other devices to bring coercive force to bear on one or more target states. One authoritative source profiles well over a hundred major instances of economic sanctions (each discussed in detail in terms of chronology, component factors, economic effects, intended goals, and so on).[4]

The capacity to impose sanctions necessarily varies from one state to another: here, as in the rest of politics, the powerful have their perquisites. In today's post-Soviet world it is inevitably the United States that is best placed to use economic sanctions as a tool of foreign policy. Here Washington either imposes sanctions unilaterally, or coerces the UN Security Council into adopting resolutions that stipulate mandatory sanctions on selected target states. In one estimate it is suggested that today no less than '*two-thirds of the world's population is subject to some sort of US sanctions*'.[5] At the same time the one surviving superpower is able to protect recalcitrant allies from sanctions that in other circumstances would be automatically imposed: as when the Israelis broke US law in selling ballistic missile components to South Africa,[6] and when they constantly violate numerous UN resolutions.[7] But Washington is not alone in imposing sanctions or in protecting allied states from sanctions regimes. Examples of economic sanctions in the 1990s include the following.

- Limited sanctions ('sanctionettes') imposed (by Commonwealth, EU, US, UK, etc; 1992 to present) on the Nigerian military regime: mostly a limited military sales embargo; World Bank withdrawal from large natural gas project; suspension of financial credit; and various other minor measures.

- A blockade imposed on Macedonia by Greece, in violation of EC regulation 288 of 1982 on common import rules, and Article 244 of the Treaty of Rome (February 1994); Greece taken to European Court of Justice over the embargo (April 1994); Greece agreed to lift embargo after Macedonia agreed to delete ancient Greek symbol from its flag and to renounce claims on Greek territory (October 1995).
- Limited sanctions imposed on military regime in Burma; growing number of US states and cities boycott Burmese goods; Dutch beer giant, Heineken announced it was abandoning brewery-building plans for Burma (July 1996); other companies announced withdrawal plans; EU withdrew Burma's 'special trading' status (December 1996); Burma's admission to the Association of South East Asian Nations (ASEAN) in July 1997 has helped to undermine the impact of limited sanctions; Britain and the United States have continued to oppose tough sanctions on Burma.
- Tough sanctions were imposed on Burundi by African and other states in August 1996; the sanctions included a ban on oil shipments to the military regime following the *coup d'état* in July.
- A blockade of food supplies to some of the poorest regions of Afghanistan was introduced by the Taliban fundamentalist militia in May 1997; hundreds of children and the old were reportedly dying of cold and hunger; in July 1998 the EU suspended all new humanitarian aid to the Taliban regime in Kabul, principally in protest at the regime's denial of equal treatment to women; some £2.5 million of aid was suspended.

Such examples (the list could easily be extended) are accompanied by frequent *threats* of sanctions – which in itself, even without subsequent imposition, is an often effective use of economic sanctions as a coercive measure. Thus the EU was vocal in considering the imposition of economic sanctions on Russia in January 1995 in response to its genocidal war in Chechenia; in April 1998 Russia threatened to impose economic sanctions on Latvia because of 'continuing discrimination against the 700,000-strong Russian-speaking population'; and in August 1998 city and state authorities across the United States threatened sanctions against Swiss banks unless they paid more than $1 billion to Holocaust survivors from deposits made before 1939. Again the sheer complexity of the sanctions option is manifest. Coercive economic measures can be delivered in thousands of different ways, and by the various elements in a complex hierarchy: powerful individuals, small companies, large corporations, cartels, states, regional groups, international alliances, the United Nations ...

The present book, sensitive to the complexity of the field, has three main aims:

- to illustrate the historical continuity of the economic-sanctions option as a powerful means of coercion. Here the emphasis is primarily on sanctions as a means of economic warfare, a concomitant to naked violence, though it should be equally obvious that economic measures can be used to drastic effect also within a purely domestic context;
- to illustrate the character and impact of particular sanctions regimes. It is one thing to block the shipment of arms (and not much else) to an apartheid South Africa, quite another to subject a medieval city or a modern Arab country to a total years-long economic blockade. Any attempt to judge the morality or efficacy of the sanctions option must consider the range of possible measures set against the goals to be achieved;
- to indicate that the use of the sanctions option has many implications in ethics and law, not always the ones that are openly proclaimed by the sanctions deliverers. There are often hidden agendas, where powerful states can exploit the availability of the sanctions option to support undeclared aims of commercial and foreign policy (for example, US efforts to keep Iraqi oil off world markets may have more to do with regulating energy prices than with any worry about 'weapons of mass destruction').

Chapter 1 illustrates the continuity of economic sanctions from ancient to modern times. Here it is useful to note (as with the Megarian Decree) that a campaign of sanctions can be as much an incitement to war (as with the 1930s sanctions against Japan) as an actual concomitant to military action. It is significant also that the horrific ancient sieges of great cities were to find dreadful parallels through the centuries up to modern times, with all the increased suffering that larger populations and more advanced technologies made possible; and that the terrible siege of a city could be extended to the siege of an entire nation (continuing now, as I write).

The real possibility of imposing 'universal sanctions' via the mechanism of supranational bodies emerged only in the twentieth century through the formation of firstly the League of Nations and then the United Nations. Before, it was possible to arrange comprehensive sanctions through allied states acting together, but for every historical alliance there may have been a countervailing grouping with different interests. The League of Nations, despite its limited membership and obvious shortcomings, was the first significant attempt to impose a global system of order in which the systematic use of economic sanctions would serve as an effective coercive tool. The successor United Nations, with ultimately a much larger membership, was able to elevate the sanctions option to – as it proved in the 1990s – genocidal proportions. Here the principal problem was that a single state, no longer constrained by the opposing interests of a competing superpower, has been able to suborn the only focus of power in the United Nations organisation; namely the Security Council. Washington's hegemony in the world body is far from absolute: its power is limited but disproportionately weighty, a constant rebuke to Article 2(1) of the UN Charter, intended to protect the 'sovereign equality' of all UN members.

Chapter 3 considers the American approach to economic sanctions when Washington is forced to act alone. The US suborning of the Security Council in connection with Libya (Chapter 2) is paralleled by its unilateral action on Cuba (Chapter 3) – where domestic legislation with 'extraterritorial reach' demonstrated to the world the enormity of American arrogance and the hollowness of its ideological posture. Here we find a naked attempt to starve a civilian population into supine acceptance of American policy – a circumstance that invites various ethical and legal questions (Chapter 4). And this serves as a prelude to consideration of the Iraq Question, where Washington tells us to accept that the survival of a demonised tyrant justifies the genocide of a civilian population through US-contrived biological warfare, through the remorseless infliction of starvation and disease on helpless men, women and children with no control over the character of the Iraqi regime.

At the same time there were signs that Washington was beginning to doubt the value of sanctions: 'The White House and Congress have decided that, in many cases, sanctions just are not an effective way to make foreign policy.'[8] It was being reported that in recent months the United States had moved away from the imposition of sanctions on various countries to enable them to buy American wheat, that the interpretation of the Helms–Burton legislation (Chapter 3) was becoming increasingly loose to avoid antagonising the Europeans and the Canadians, and that the proposed sanctions on China were being abandoned to enable US businessmen to compete freely in that market. In part, Washington was now beginning to respond to such business groups as the Chamber of Commerce and USA Engage, a group of 676 companies working together to promote American commerce. Said Bill Lane, a Caterpillar Inc. director and the Chairman of USA Engage: 'Unilateral sanctions only make foreign rivals stronger and taint us as unreliable suppliers.'[9] In the same vein Richard Haass, a former National Security aide to President Bush, was commenting: 'The free ride for sanctions is over. Like other foreign policy tools, sanctions are now subject to greater scrutiny.'[10]

It remains to be seen whether such 'greater scrutiny' will radically affect the traditional US reliance on economic sanctions as a valuable tool of foreign policy, but it is still plain that sanctions (legal remedy or genocidal tool) can be many things and that they pose a problem – common to all exercise of power – that has yet to be answered. Those individuals and states best placed to impose them are almost invariably the ones least entitled to do so.

1

In History

The possession of economic power confers upon individuals, organisations, states and supranational bodies the capacity to exert social influence in various ways. At the most mundane level, parents may be expected to define the consumption patterns of their offspring; while on a totally different scale groups of nations acting together are sometimes able to subject a targeted country to a comprehensive and devastating economic siege. The political use of economic power can be *positive* – as in the purchase of labour and other market resources, in the effective control of law-making and judicial procedures, in the financing of socially beneficial institutions, and in the funding of commercial and political propaganda; or *negative* – as in the blocking of access to finance and raw materials, and in restricting the flow of food and medical supplies to the civilian populations of so-called 'rogue' or 'pariah' states. It is the negative use of economic power, in all its forms, that indicates the political scope of economic sanctions.

All states have at one time or another been involved in international dispute, attempts at political coercion, and war (many are so involved today); and in the vast bulk of such cases there has been resort to economic sanctions. Here the scope of the sanctions has necessarily varied according to circumstance. Thus a country that has developed food self-sufficiency may be relatively immune to an international maritime blockade; a state with little interest in international funding may not be seriously affected if it is suddenly denied access to sources of international finance. But today, with the development of the global economy, it is inevitable that concerted and comprehensive economic sanctions can drastically affect a targeted state. Even where sanctions are partial, nominally limited in scope or maintained by a single powerful state, they can have serious social and economic affects on the victim country; where the sanctions are virtually total they can function as 'weapons of mass destruction' with genocidal consequences.

The Sanctions Spectrum

Economic sanctions are typically exploited by one state or a group of states acting together to reinforce other types of pressure (for example, moral, diplomatic and military). In one delineation, hardly rigorous, at least five classes of economic sanctions 'embargoes') are recognised: '... on exports of arms, munitions, and implements of war; ... on imports; ... on raw materials; ... on technology; and ... an international boycott'.[1] Here it is noted that the terms 'boycott', 'embargo' and 'sanctions' (to which we way add the term 'blockade') are often used interchangeably, though it is sometimes important to identify particular differences.

A *boycott* is generally recognised as an action designed to achieve the economic or social isolation of an individual, group or nation to express disapproval, to coerce change, or to function as a supplement to a military campaign. This form of action takes it name from Captain Charles Boycott, an English estate manager in Mayo, Ireland, whose ruthless rent-collection policies in the 1880s so enraged the impoverished Irish tenants that they refused to harvest crops for him. Thus a boycott is typically seen as a concerted campaign of social or economic non-intercourse as a means of expressing disapproval or applying coercion. It is used as a policy in international relations, regarded (according to taste) as a synonym for 'embargo' or as distinct from this term. There are many historical examples of international boycotts; for example, the American refusal to buy British goods after the enactment of the Stamp Act of 1765, the refusal of the Chinese to buy United States products in 1905 because of the racist US immigration policies, and the Arab League's compilation of Israel-friendly foreign companies with which Arab trade is forbidden. The boycott need not be primarily economic (as with the US boycott of the Moscow Olympic Games in 1980 and the reciprocal Soviet boycott of the Los Angeles Games in 1984).

An *embargo* (Spanish, *embargar*; Latin, *imbarricare* from *barra*, 'bar') is depicted in international law as a ban on the movement of goods to a foreign country by land, sea or air. The embargo is said to be 'hostile' where the property of a foreign state is detained – for return if no war occurs and for forfeiture in the event of war; and 'civil' when domestic ships are prohibited from transporting goods to foreign territory. Embargoes can be used for many purposes; for example, to aid a war effort, to coerce another state, and to support domestic commercial activity by preventing scarce resources from leaving the country. The US Embargo Act of 1807, a famous example, was enacted to protect American shipping at a time when the British were blockading Napoleonic France and its allies and so impeding American efforts to trade with a belligerent in non-contraband goods. President Thomas Jefferson believed that the British need for American food and raw materials would force respect for US neutrality, but the embargo was opposed by American force and other commercial interests. In 1809 the Embargo Act was replaced by the Non-Intercourse Act, which allowed trade with some European countries.

A *sanction* (French, *sanction*; Latin, *sanctio* from *sancrire*, 'to render sacred or inviolable'), in international affairs, is a penalty imposed against a nation to coerce it into compliance with international law or to compel an alteration in its policies in some other respect. Originally an ecclesiastical decree, a 'sanction' may be considered to have an ethical component, encouraging moral action or serving to validate a moral judgement. Economic sanctions were imposed by the League of Nations and subsequently by the United Nations (see Chapter 3) in many different contexts; and powerful nations, particularly the United States, have found them a helpful unilateral tool of foreign policy (Chapter 4). Where a state is relatively weak it is usually unable to mount an effective challenge against internationally mandated sanctions or analogous economic measures introduced unilaterally by a powerful country.

Attempts to indicate the various elements of sanctions show the diverse ways in which economic pressure can be brought to bear against a targeted state. Some of the measures may require legislation, intended to have domestic or international affect; others may not. For example, conventional definitions imply that *boycott* does not necessarily have the force of law, signalling no more than a form of ostracism conducted on a private rather than a legislative basis. The boycott is often seen as a retaliatory act, instituted by government or private interest and intended to encourage other bodies to follow suit. *Embargo*, characteristically carrying the force of law, is a stronger measure typically implemented in time of war or threatened hostilities. Thus, in one commentary:

> embargoes in the form of export prohibitions have been undertaken individually or collectively, to force countries to cease assertedly illegal or undesirable activities or to prevent them from utilizing certain categories of goods, mostly war materials, for purposes objected to by states instigating the embargoes.[2]

A *sanction*, clearly only one element of 'economic sanctions', is generally intended to serve as a form of punishment, a practical signal that the targeted state is manifestly derelict in its ethical or legal behaviour. Here there is the obvious question of who is to judge. The much-quoted Juvenal question *quis custodiet ipsos custodes*? ('who will guard the guardians?') can be recast to highlight the problem of establishing the authority behind the imposition of a sanctions regime: *quis iudicabit ipsos iudices*? ('who will judge the judges?'). In the event the effective authority derives from power, rather than from any unassailable ethical status. States may act in concert through international bodies or unilaterally. In all cases 'sanction' is virtually synonymous with '*punitive* sanction'.

The term 'quarantine' has often been used as a synonym for 'sanction', as with Franklin Roosevelt; here 'quarantine' has been deployed as a 'euphemism for blockade, or one-sided embargo',[3] a usage that conveniently implies a containment of disease and so helps to validate the policy. In fact the language of economic sanctions can be discussed at length in considerable detail. After a significant contribution to such enquiry, two authorities propose their preferred definition:

> Economic sanctions (coercion) are actions initiated by one or more international actors (the 'senders') against one or more others (the 'targets') with either or both of two purposes: to punish the targets by depriving them of some value and/or to make the 'targets' comply with certain norms the senders deem important.[4]

There is discussion also of the relationship of economic sanctions to warfare: are sanctions in fact a type of warfare, though conventionally distinct from the 'military option'? It has been argued (before genocidal sanctions were imposed on Iraq in 1990) that economic sanctions, typically imposed in peacetime, are milder than economic warfare, an adjunct to military action. Thus Professor William Medlicott suggests that economic warfare is 'a military operation' designed 'to deprive the enemy of the material means of resistance ... It must be distinguished from coercive measures appropriate for adoption in peace to settle international differences without recourse to war, e.g., sanctions, pacific blockade, economic reprisals, etc., since unlike such measures, it has as its ultimate sanction the use of belligerent rights.'[5] (The distinction seems unconvincing, not least because 'pacific blockade' in the circumstances of the global economy can effectively deny a population the necessities of life – scarcely less drastic than a 'military operation'. It is unfortunate also that Medlicott uses the word 'sanction' in two different senses in the same sentence.)

It should be obvious that the language is less important than the practicalities of such matters: an Iraqi child starving to death because of US-contrived United Nations policies will not be overly concerned to enquire whether she is the victim of 'sanctions', 'embargo', 'boycott', blockade', 'quarantine' or 'economic warfare'. A preoccupation with terminology, a nice self-indulgence of lawyers and academics, often diverts attention – sometimes intentionally – from practical realities; here, from the scale of devastation and human suffering caused by specific economic policies. It should be remembered that economic sanctions, in depriving (usually) helpless civilians of 'some value' (food, clean water, medical supplies), can have an appalling affect on innocent populations. You cannot do more to a people than denying them food or compelling them to die from preventable diseases (see Chapter 5).

Such a consideration should tell against the 'aura of righteousness'[6] that was part of sanctions policy during the period of the Cold War; and against the idea that sanctions should be distinguished 'from violent or non-violent techniques employed specifically to further the interests of one or more states at the expense of others'.[7] In fact, sanctions are today most likely to be imposed in a brutally cynical way to support the foreign-policy objectives of powerful states; in particular, the United States, via the calculated manipulation of the United Nations and other international bodies. Before considering the use of economic sanctions in the modern world it is helpful to give examples of their historical use. Such instances, far from exhaustive, often exhibit characteristics that can be found in the modern use of sanctions. The central principle is simple and applicable in all ages: that a targeted group, society or country be deliberately deprived of the means to an effective economic life.

The Historical Frame

The use of economic sanctions, in one form or another, has characterised conflict in and between societies from the earliest times. For example, one authority notes that siege 'is the oldest form of total war'[8] (see below). Invading armies have always been keen to provision their own forces at the expense of their enemies: so crops and other supplies have been commandeered while local people, especially the civilians, have often been deprived of basic sustenance. In ancient times defending soldiers way withdraw into a garrison or citadel while the ordinary people would be left to the mercy of the aggressor. Even where the civilians were allowed into a fortress, in

Table 1.1   Selected pre-First World War examples of economic sanctions

Sender country	Target country	Active years	Background and resolution
Athens	Megara	c. 432 BC	Pericles issued decree limiting access to Megara's products – contributed to starting the Peloponnesian War
American colonies	Britain	1765	Colonies boycotted English goods – Britain repealed the Stamp Act in 1766
American colonies	Britain	1767–70	Boycott of English goods – Britain repealed Townshend Acts except on lea (tea tax led to Boston Tea Party of 1774)
Britain and France	France and Britain	1793–1815	Napoleonic Wars – economic warfare deemed inconclusive, France developed sugar beet as substitute product
United States	Britain	1812–14	US embargoed British goods in response to British economic pressure – revocation of the Acts failed to prevent war
Britain and France	Russia	1853–6	Danube blockaded – Russia defeated; Turkish partition was prevented
US North	Confederate States	1861–5	Civil War – blockade enhanced North's industrial superiority over the South; South lost
France	Germany	1870–1	Franco-Prussian War – blockade of German coast and occupied ports; Germany prevailed
France	China	1883–5	Indochina War – France declared rice contraband; China ceded to France control of the Annamese territory
United States	Spain	1898	Spanish-American War – naval blockade of Cuba and Philippines; Spain forced to cede the various territories
Britain	Dutch South Africa	1899–1902	Denial of contraband articles to the Boers – Boers eventually defeated; South Africa added to the British Empire
Russia	Japan	1904–5	Russo-Japanese War – blockade on rice, fuel, cotton, etc.; Russia defeated
Italy	Turkey	1911–12	Limited blockade – Italy acquired Libya from Ottoman Empire

Source: G. C. Hufbauer *et al.*, *Economic Sanctions Reconsidered: History and Current Policy*, Institute for International Economics, Washington, D.C., 1990.

anticipation of a siege, they would be likely to die first: the army, necessarily in control of provisions, would be unlikely to sacrifice soldiers in the interests of non-combatants (the phrase 'useless mouths' has been used in the military literature to describe non-fighting civilians).

The scope of economic sanctions has grown over time. Where in the past it was generally possible to block the flow of supplies to a fortress or town it was rarely practical to subject an entire nation to comprehensive economic siege: land borders may have been too long to police, and even in the presence of hostile forces the indigenous people may have been able to smuggle goods through difficult terrain. In modern times, with the development of technology and the increasing reliance of states on international trade, it became possible – as with Iraq (see Chapter 5) – to monitor a country's entire perimeter and to impose an economic siege, analogous to medieval castle sieges, on a whole nation.

It is easy to understand the tactical appeal of economic measures in time of civil or international conflict, or as a means of coercing a foreign state in circumstances where human casualties may not be overtly intended. In war the simple and main purpose is to crush the enemy's capacity to function as an active belligerent – by depriving him of manpower through the slaughter facilitated by a useful knowledge of physics and chemistry, or by depriving him of the means to fight (enemy forces may be denied munitions, oil, transport and other war supplies; and food, potable water and medical provisions – to facilitate a helpful extermination by indirect methods). The earliest forms of economic warfare involved no more than the presence of troops required to interdict the flow of goods to a targeted army or society. Here the enterprise may be supported by a close or distant maritime blockade, where a country's ports may be rendered useless by a ring of hostile ships or where the sea traffic in goods might be blocked in international waters or even far away at the ports of the sender countries. The use of sanctions/embargo/ blockade/siege/ quarantine/interdiction has been a common feature of conflict between states over the centuries, and also in circumstances of civil war where contending factions have striven to crush or coerce their enemies (Table 1.1).

The Megarian Decree

The most celebrated example of economic sanctions in the ancient world was the Megarian Decree in Greece, enacted by Pericles in 432 BC. The specific reasons for the Decree, one of the earliest examples of trade sanctions, are debated, but some commentators have noted that it followed the kidnapping of three Aspasian women. Thucydides gives brief attention to the enactment in *The Peloponnesian War*, emphasising how the Megarians resented the Athenian block on their trade: 'There were many who came forward and made their several accusations; among them the Megarians, in a long list of grievances, called special attention to the fact of their exclusion from the ports of the Athenian empire and the market of Athens ... .' Aristophanes, in his comedy *The Acharnians* (his earliest surviving play despite two earlier productions), considers the Decree to have been a major cause of the Peloponnesian War (431–404 BC) between Athens and Sparta:

> Then Pericles the Olympian in his wrath
> thundered, lightened, threw Hellas into confusion,
> passed laws that were written like drinking songs
> [decreeing] the Megarians shall not be on our land,
> in our market, on the sea or on the continent ...

The Decree has been seen as an unambiguous act of economic imperialism, enacted in peacetime but perhaps intended to provoke war; as a deliberate provocation to the Peloponnesian League, of which Megara was a member; and even as an actual act of war designed to establish Athenian hegemony over Sparta. The Athenians declared that the Decree was provoked by Megarian encroachment onto sacred Athenian land and other Athenian territory, and by their illicit harbouring of fugitive slaves. Some writers have suggested that Pericles was seeking to punish Megara to deter its support for Corinth in its confrontation with Athens. As with so much foreign policy, there is room for interpretation and official claims should not be taken at face value.

It does seem clear that in imposing restrictions of Megarian trade the Athenians were seeking a middle course. To have done nothing may have encouraged hostility to Athens, whereas resort to the military option would have violated treaty obligations and provoked a military response from Sparta. Pericles probably judged that the trade embargo, while having an affect on the lives of most Megarians, would be unlikely to bring catastrophe or to provoke a wider conflict. Then, as now, it was judged that economic sanctions would have a punitive impact and serve as a warning to other states without bringing the harsh consequences of military action. In reality, if we are to believe Aristophanes, the Megarians *'were starving little by little'* and in consequence

begged the Lacedaemonians to have the decree
arising from the three strumpets withdrawn.
But we were unwilling, though they asked us many times.
Then came the clash of the shields.

Then, as now, there were enough powerful individuals to insist that
civilian populations would be starved to death by economic sanctions
for trivial reasons:

Someone will say it was not right. But say then, what was?
Come, if a Lacedaemonian sailed out in a boat
and denounced and confiscated a Seriphian puppy,
would you have sat still?[9]

Perhaps the Megarian Decree was intended to be a moderate measure;
and perhaps Pericles was relying on his personal friendship with the
Spartan king, Archidamus, to avoid plunging Athens into war. But
there seems to be no doubt that the Decree brought hardship to the
civilian Megarian population and helped to create the atmosphere
in which a new war was inevitable. The Spartans went so far as to
state publicly that if the Athenians withdrew the Decree there would
be no war, relying on the judgement that the embargo had never
been intended to provoke a military response. Nonetheless Pericles
refused to compromise and cited an obscure Athenian law that
forbade him from taking down the tablet on which the decree was
inscribed. Plutarch (in *Pericles*) recorded the Spartan response: 'Then
don't take it down, turn the tablet around, for there is no law against
that.' Pericles would not budge and now was prepared for war:

Let none of you think that you are going to war over a trifle if we
do not rescind the Megarian Decree ... For this 'trifle' contains the
affirmation and the test of your resolution. If you yield to them
you will immediately be required to make another concession
which will be greater, since you will have made the first concession
out of fear.

The economic sanctions imposed by Athens on Megara, to the
dismay of Sparta and other states, would remain. Pericles affirmed
that the Athenians would 'do nothing under dictation' but were
prepared to resort to arbitration according to their existing treaty
obligations.

The opportunity for a negotiated settlement of the regional
problems had been lost, with war the inevitable consequence. The

Peloponnesian War resulted in Athens being stripped of its empire and in Sparta emerging as the unchallenged leader of the Greek world. The war had been triggered by confrontation with Athens and Corinth, a major ally of Sparta supported by Megara. The first (Archidamian) stage of the war ended in stalemate in 421 BC, following the onset of plague in Athens (430 BC) and the consequent death of Pericles (429 BC). After various reverses, including a rebellion among its allies and the emergence of Spartan sea power supported by the Persians, Athens was successfully blockaded – involving a further drastic imposition of economic sanctions – and Athenian resistance was finally crushed. Athens surrendered its fleet, was forced to witness the destruction of its fortifications, and then submitted to the oligarchy of the Thirty Tyrants. The oligarchy was overthrown in 403 BC but Athens never again emerged as a mighty imperial city. The Megarian Decree imposed by Pericles, the most famous example of peacetime economic sanctions in the ancient world, while far from the only shaping factor of the Peloponnesian War, was certainly one of the reasons for the eclipse of the mighty Athenian empire.

The Siege

The siege – in one view 'the oldest form of total war' – may be active or passive: that is, the walls of a fortress may be battered by catapult or cannon; or the surrounding army may simply camp on the surrounding plain, waiting for the defenders' provisions (essentially food and drinkable water) to be fatally depleted. It is plain that the passive siege, perhaps supplemented by military initiatives, is an obvious form of economic warfare. Here the principal aim is to starve a protected population, combatants and civilians alike, into submission. Little attention was given to the possibility that it might be immoral or illegal for an invading army to slaughter an innocent population within a citadel by denying them food and water. Indeed, ancient codes specifically urge mass slaughter; as in the Old Testament (Deuteronomy, 20:16–17): '... thou shalt save alive nothing that breatheth, but thou shalt utterly destroy them'. And when a city has been besieged for a long time, the surrounding trees that provide food for the besieging army (that is, fruit trees) shall not be destroyed: 'only the trees which thou knowest that they be not trees for meat, thou shalt destroy and cut them down; and thou shalt build bulwarks against the city ... until it be subdued' (Deuteronomy, 20: 19–20).

Some observers have suggested that this Deuteronomic code is ethically sensitive in urging the protection of food supplies during the extreme conditions of military siege, but in fact the clear aim is simply to strengthen the hand of the besiegers at the expense of the population within the garrison or fortress. Thus one authority notes: 'The propriety of attempting to reduce [a city] by starvation is not questioned.'[10] In ancient times it was long accepted that the civilian population in an encircled city must expect to perish; with the corollary that starvation and disease – manifest modes of biological warfare – were legitimate tools for securing the capture of a citadel or fortified city. We may reflect that the emergence of various modern Conventions (for example, the Geneva Convention), prohibiting the starvation of civilians in wartime represents some sort of ethical progress (see Chapter 5).

There are many descriptions of sieges, ancient and modern, where the drastic nature of economic warfare is graphically portrayed. Thus Josephus, outside the walls of Jerusalem in AD 72, described the impact of the Roman siege of the city:

> The restraint of liberty to pass in and out of the city took from the Jews all hope of safety, and the famine now increasing consumed whole households and families; and the houses were full of dead women and infants; and the streets filled with the dead bodies of old men. And the young men, swollen like dead men's shadows, walked in the market place and fell down dead where it happened.

In these dire circumstances, afflicting an entire society, there was no opportunity to afford the dead and dying proper respect. The living, soon to be dead, could do no more than contemplate the mounting catastrophe around them:

> And now the multitude of dead bodies was so great that they that were alive could not bury them; nor cared they for burying them, being now uncertain what should betide themselves. And many endeavouring to bury others fell down themselves dead upon them ... And many being yet alive went unto their graves and there died.[11]

And yet, according to Josephus, there was no weeping or lamentation, 'for famine overcame all affections'. The dying, without tears, beheld the dead; the city was silent.[12]

Again it is easy to identify the aim of the besieging armies: to compel the leadership of the beleaguered fortress or town, made to contemplate the scale of civilian suffering, into unconditional surrender. (This ploy, familiar over the centuries, is manifest in modern times: not least as with Iraq, where through the 1990s the US-orchestrated sanctions caused civilian casualties running into millions.) Sometimes the architects of siege have shown remorse for the mass killings of innocent men, women and children. But Josephus recorded that Titus, commander of the Jerusalem siege, raised his hands to heaven and called God to witness that 'it was not his doing'.[13] Thus sometimes no remorse is shown. (Madeleine Albright, then US Ambassador to the United Nations and now Secretary of State, confronted in May 1996 with the fact of half a million Iraqi children killed through sanctions, commented: '... we think the price is worth it'.[14]) Titus, like the modern organisers of harsh sanctions regimes, was keen to absolve himself from moral responsibility for the copious deaths he had wittingly caused: the obstinate Zealots who had seized control of the city were the true cause of the calamity. Titus found this a congenial view (just as the Clinton Administration, persisting in its methodical extermination of Iraqi children, was eager to blame the intransigence of the Iraqi leadership).

The character of sieges, one of the most nakedly obvious forms of economic sanctions, developed over the centuries.[15] In the earliest times military commanders devised methods of reducing the effectiveness of fortified encampments and garrisons. Later, whole towns and cities were surrounded with walls and other obstacles to attack, in turn stimulating the development of siege techniques. The early Roman architects of siege warfare learned from Greek practice, and Roman methods were influential as late as the Middle Ages. Such techniques were typically 'active'; that is, involving the use of rams, catapults and other machines to assault the defensive walls of castles and other fortifications (and using miners to erode foundations and so to cause walls to collapse). But due attention was given also to obvious provisioning requirements. The importance of an internal water supply was acknowledged as essential to the long-term defence of a fortification; whilst the Persians have been cited as recognising the importance of destroying a region's food crop before the commencement of a siege.[16] It is plain that the exhaustion of food or water supplies would make it impossible to defend a fortification. As one example, Baldwin de Redvers rebelled against King Stephen of England (1135–54) in 1138 but when, holding out behind fortifications in Exeter, his water supply dried up he was forced to negotiate. On the Isle of Wight he again defied the king, this time from Carisbrooke Castle, but when the well dried up he was yet again forced to flee. Food and water were as essential to successful rebellion as were the strongest castle walls; with patience a garrison could be starved into submission if it proved impossible to breach the fortifications.

Even an abundant food stock would be reduced over time, but in the early stages of a siege might be flaunted to taunt the poorly provisioned soldiers outside the walls. As stocks gradually became depleted, groups defending a fortress would be tempted to hoard their own secret provisions. In one celebrated example the hungry defenders of Limburg announced that they would eat the fat monks in the city rather than capitulate, whereupon the well-fed monks quickly yielded up their hidden provisions, enabling the garrison to survive its siege.[17] The importance of adequate supplies was always recognised in siege warfare, encouraging an invader to attack before the fresh harvest had been gathered in. King Stephen, as a typical campaigner, destroyed food that might be purloined by his enemies; and Helias at Le Mans carried into his castle all that could be gathered and destroyed the rest to deny 'the cruel raiders' any supplies. One Scots army was urged not to leave food that might be used by the enemy; at Belford they carried off oxen, horses, cows, ewes and lambs; and around Milan a military campaign involved the destruction of vineyards and olive groves, to encourage the spread of famine and disease.[18]

There are many cases where a fortified town has been compelled to surrender when supplies ran out. An adequate supply of munitions was of little consequence if the soldiers and protected civilians ran out of food and drinkable water. Thus the surrender of Rouen to Geoffrey of Anjou was achieved in 1144 for this reason; and Henry II forced Dol to yield through lack of provisions, having used Welsh troops to cut French supply routes.[19] Besiegers may seek to divert or contaminate the water supply to a fortress (there are cases where defenders have relied upon wine to resist a siege); for example, by putting the putrid corpses of men and animals into the water. There were no international laws and conventions to discourage such early examples of biological warfare.

While the defenders of a fortified town may have been forced, through assault or the exhaustion of their provisions, into surrender, this cannot have been a very attractive option. Surrender terms were sometimes negotiated (Chapter 5) but more typically a medieval city, once captured, was mercilessly looted and then put to the torch, its hapless citizens variously raped, tortured, mutilated and killed. Thus in March 1257 the Mongol leader Mangu, son of Tului, sent an ultimatum to the caliph Mustasim in Baghdad, demanding that he come to pay homage. Mustasim, deemed by Muslims to be the proper ruler of the world, could never accede to the demands of an animist heaven – and so the fate of Baghdad was sealed. On 18 January 1258 the vast Mongol army reached Baghdad, the heart of Islam, and within a fortnight the mangonel bombardment had reduced the city defences to ruins. At the same time the Mongol engineers were breaking the irrigation dykes, causing many of the panic-stricken inhabitants of the city to drown in the rising waters. The soldiers of the caliph were ordered to assemble on the plain outside Baghdad, where all were massacred; then the Mongol troops were allowed to plunder the city at will and to kill any surviving Muslims still struggling to hide in the rubble. One estimate suggests that some 800,000 men, women and children were slaughtered in Baghdad and on the plain over a matter of days. A special fate was reserved for the caliph Mustasim and his sons. Since the Mongols were superstitious about shedding the blood of sovereign princes, they were first rolled in carpets (or sown in sacks) before being trampled to death under the hoofs of horses. Thus the Abbasid caliphate was finally extinguished in 1258, and all the glories of medieval Baghdad were reduced to ruins.

These then were the options facing fortress defenders over many centuries – to suffer a speedy and overwhelming assault, after which the rape and slaughter would inevitably follow as the traditional practice of victorious soldiery; or a fortified garrison or town could be progressively reduced over time until the defenders exhausted their supplies of food and water. The latter option was scarcely to be preferred, though defenders were understandably reluctant to yield to a merciless besieging army: those who have never witnessed it can only imagine the horrors of a collective starvation deliberately inflicted, where parents, children, friends and lovers must helplessly watch each other slowly weaken, sicken, despair and die. To die through the impact of the harshest economic sanctions – of which the siege, ancient and modern, is the most graphic example – must be a dreadful way to perish. We need to remember that the technique of total siege was not abandoned in the Middle Ages but has had genocidal manifestations – involving vast cities and entire countries – in modern times.

Early Nineteenth Century

Centuries of siege generally involved land-based targets, though action was often taken against coastal fortifications and garrisons receiving supplies by river. In the circumstances where countries relied upon substantial seaborne trade a coastal blockade to interrupt foreign commerce could drastically affect their war capacity. Here a close blockade of enemy ports could be supplemented by a distant blockade of trading nations to deny the enemy access to foreign goods. Furthermore, belligerents would presume to intercept neutral ships to ensure by search that no 'contraband' goods were being transported to aid the enemy war effort. It may be assumed that all such efforts at close or distant blockade were porous to a greater or lesser extent but even a partial denial of supplies could have a substantial impact on a country's war-making capabilities.

The Napoleonic Wars of the early nineteenth century are generally cited as one of the first examples of economic blockade on a significant scale. Here it is judged that the affects were considerable but not decisive,[20] while important lessons were being learned about the scope of economic warfare for future international conflicts.

It was inevitable that the belligerent practice of stopping and searching neutral ships on the high seas would sometimes provoke other nations into a military response, if only to protect their own vital commerce. When, following the outbreak of the French Revolution in 1789, hostilities again developed between France and England the fresh confrontation quickly affected many other countries, including the United States. Both the main belligerents were interfering with American shipping while at the same time urging Washington to become an active participant in the mounting conflict. (At the same time Barbary pirates were attacking American shipping off the North African coast.) Such developments stimulated Congressional support for the funding of coastal fortifications and an expansion of the navy. It is interesting to reflect that it was principally the European wars of the time that encouraged the early militarisation of the United States, feeding the appetite for the subsequent imperial expansion at the expense of the Americas, Spain and others.

The American tensions with France, including interference with commercial shipping and a French attempt to bribe American diplomats (the 'XYZ Affair'), brought the two countries into a state of undeclared warfare in 1798. The US Secretary of the Navy, Benjamin Stoddert, urged a rapid and substantial expansion of American sea power. Negotiations with France helped to defuse the crisis but by now the start of the American navy had been established. Captain Thomas Truxton's *Constellation* defeated the French *Insurgente* and almost defeated the heavily gunned *Vengeance*, while Commodore Edward Preble's onslaught on Tripoli (1803–4), one of the first

American attacks on Libya, demonstrated the growing reach of US naval power.

In the early nineteenth century the United States still lacked the military power to compel the European states to observe the rights of neutral shipping on the high seas. During the later years of the Jefferson Administration (1801–9), Washington was increasingly drawn into a fresh international conflict, and by 1812 was unable to avoid involvement in naval conflict with Britain. Too weak to compel British observance of the American view of international law regarding the rights of neutral shipping, the United States resolved to attack British interests where they were most vulnerable; in the event this policy included a desultory American invasion of Canada and a fruitless naval expedition by Commodore John Rodgers in command of three frigates (*President*, *United States* and *Congress*) and two smaller vessels.

Rodgers favoured the strategy of concentrating American warships to discourage the British from dispersing their vessels for interception of American commerce. Thus three US squadrons were established and, by distracting British warships, were able to keep American ports open – but only for a matter of weeks. With the American navy in 1812 numbering a few dozen vessels and the Royal Navy comprising more than 600 ships, the contest was an unequal one. In November three American captains (Charles Stewart, Isaac Hull and Charles Morris) signed a document predicting the likely attacks on American commerce. The 'first object', of an enemy maritime power

> will be to restrain, by ships of the line, our frigates and other cruisers from departing and preying upon their commerce; their next object will be to send their smaller cruisers in pursuit of our commerce; and by having their ships of the line parading on our coast, threatening our more exposed seacoast towns, and preventing the departure of our smaller cruisers, they will be capturing what commerce may have escaped theirs, and recapturing what prizes may have fallen into our hands.

Such objectives would offer little risk to the enemy forces, by virtue of their numerical superiority:

> they can at all times consult their convenience in point of time and numbers; and will incur no expense and risk of transports for provisions and water, but can go and procure their supplies at pleasure, and return to their station ere their absence is known to use.[21]

In December 1812 the British mounted a blockade of the Delaware and the Chesapeake as a preliminary sanctions measure; five months later an effort was made to blockade the entire Atlantic and Gulf coasts (with the exception of New England opposed to the war). At the same time the Royal Navy took active steps to disrupt American commerce, looting and burning coastal defences. At the end of May 1814, immediately after signing a peace treaty with France, Britain announced a blockade of the entire American coastline. This was no more than a punitive measure: the European war was seemingly over and Britain's survival was not at stake. But now the decision to punish the United States resulted in a massive reduction in American seaborne commerce. The privateers struggled to remain active, government sloops constructed like privateers managed a few forays, and the *Constitution* attempted occasional sallies; but by now it was obvious to Congress that the United States needed to fund a much more substantial navy.

The power of economic measures in both peacetime and wartime was now abundantly plain: the lessons learned from centuries of land-based sieges had been found to be equally relevant to confrontations between widely separated maritime countries. The provisioning of combatants and noncombatants alike demanded an uninterrupted flow of supplies – not just specific war *matériel* but the food and other necessities of life required to sustain armed forces and civilian populations. It was now widely assumed that economic sanctions, of one type or another, could be used as a devastating weapon against both enemies and potential enemies.

The American Civil War

The American Civil War (1861–5) involved vigorous attempts at blockade and other economic sanctions, deemed important but not decisive. On 19 April 1861 President Abraham Lincoln ordered an economic blockade against Confederate ports to deny the seceding states access to foreign goods. Within weeks the Union had bought or chartered scores of merchant ships, armed them, and sent them off on blockade duty. The blockade, maintained for the duration of the war, seriously hampered but did not entirely prevent the supply of goods to the Confederacy.

To manage the blockade and to conduct other naval operations the Navy Department took advice from Professor Alexander D. Bache, Superintendent of the Coast Survey, who suggested that a board of conference be established. One board member, Captain S. F. Du Pont, noted in a private letter on 1 June 1861: 'It may be that I shall be ordered to Washington on some temporary duty, on a board to arrange a programme of blockade – first suggested by Professor Bache.' A later memoir (16 July) deals with the blockade of the coast from Cape Henry to Cape Romain in one section, and as far as Cape Florida in another. These locations emerged as the extent of the North and South Atlantic blockading squadrons. A further report (26 July) stresses the importance of maintaining a 'superior naval force' to command the specified parts of the coast. Yet more memoirs (9 August, 2 September and 3 September) focus on the management of the blockade on the west coast of Florida and to the Mexican border.

The early attempts at managing an effective blockade quickly revealed 'the necessity of the occupation of as many Southern ports as possible'. Thus Rear-Admiral Daniel Ammen noted: 'A blockade from within a harbor may be made effective by one or more ships without the fatigue and uncertainty attendant upon an exterior blockade which must be maintained beyond the range of the guns of an enemy in possession of the adjacent coasts. Even thirty vessels blockading the two entrances to the Cape Fear River were unable to prevent the frequent arrival and departure of blockade-runners.'[22] In these circumstances the support of the army was sought to increase the effectiveness of 'the most extended and effective blockade ever known in history'.[23] On 22 August 1861 Captain Du Pont recorded how vessels were being adapted for blockade duty: 'We drove where several of the purchased vessels were being altered, and examined the *Alabama*, *Augusta* and *Stars and Stripes*. But, alas! it is like altering a vest into a shirt to convert a trading steamer into a man-of-war. Except that there is a vessel and a steam-engine, all else is inadaptable; but there is no help for it – the exigency of the blockade demands it.'[24]

The Union had succeeded in establishing and maintaining, according to Rear-Admiral Ammen, a 'most efficient system of blockade along all the Southern coasts'. This notable success was attributed to Du Pont's 'intelligence and ability', and in particular to his experience of blockade management during the Mexican war. For his part, Du Pont had no doubt that the blockade issue deserved serious study. He had already recorded his thoughts in an early private letter (27 July 1847): 'I have exhausted Kent, Wheaton, and Vattel on the subject – a right good piece of professional work and study, which may be invaluable in the future. Three or four issues have been started not covered at all by those authorities, of which I have made notes.'[25] Du Pont's study did prove 'invaluable in the future'. The Confederate privateers struggled to break the blockade but with little success. On 3 February 1862 the Lincoln Administration announced that captured privateer crews would be treated as prisoners of war, while at the same time the Union was bringing pressure to bear on neutral states not to support Confederate trade. A few blockade runners achieved notoriety but the secessionist states were poorly equipped to counter Union naval power on the high seas or along the rivers of the South.

The Union was effectively blockading some 3500 miles of coastline with 10 major ports and around 180 inlets and bays accessible to smaller vessels. By June 1861 three dozen Union ships were on blockade patrol, with further vessels being acquired for the purpose every week and southern ports being seized to ease the burdens of a distant blockade campaign. It was inevitable that the blockade would remain porous to a degree. In June 1861 the five-gun Confederate sloop *Sumter* penetrated the blockade at the mouth of the Mississippi, captured or burned 18 Union vessels over the next six months, and in January 1862 was finally trapped at Gibraltar. Over the period of the war some 500 ships took part in blockade activities, with around 150 on patrol at any given time; 1500 vessels seeking to evade the blockade were either captured or destroyed.[26] One Union officer noted the character of blockade service: 'Day after day, day after day, we lay inactive, roll, roll'; another wrote to his mother that she would understand the burdens of blockade duty if she were to 'go to the roof on a hot summer day, talk to a half-dozen degenerates, descend to the basement, drink tepid water full of iron rust, climb to the roof again, and repeat the process at intervals until fagged out, then go to bed with everything shut tight'.[27] By contrast, the blockade runners seemingly enjoyed themselves, if one British officer was typical: 'Nothing I have ever experienced can compare with it. Hunting, pig-sticking, steeple-chasing, big-game hunting, polo – I have done a little of each – all have their thrilling moments, but none can approach running a blockade.'[28]

Nonetheless the blockaders had some compensations: crews were given half the proceeds from every captured prize – which meant about 7 per cent of the value for the captain, a smaller amount for each officer, and about 16 per cent shared among the ordinary seamen. The rare jackpot was impressive: when the gunboat *Aeolus* captured two blockade runners in the autumn of 1864 the captain netted $40,000, the officers $8–20,000, and each seaman $3000. With such inducements the blockaders, despite the burdens of their service, must often have been well motivated.

By the summer of 1862 the blockade had developed as a highly effective strategy. On 27 August 1861 a Union flotilla under Flag Officer Silas H. Stringham attacked Confederate positions at Hatteras Inlet and landed 800 troops from Fort Monroe under Major-General Benjamin F. Butler to establish a blockade base. On 7 November nine warships under Captain Du Pont overwhelmed the defensive forts at Port Royal Sound, an important inland waterway connecting Savannah and Charleston. Some 17,000 troops under Brigadier-General Thomas W. Sherman were landed, with Port Royal quickly converted into an important naval base for the Union's blockading squadrons. The pattern was established. Within a few months most of the southern ports were either occupied or sealed off, allowing the Union vessels to concentrate on the remaining active Confederate ports.

Small ships close to land would fire rockets when a blockade runner was seen trying to leave or enter harbour, whereupon all the warships in the area would converge on the vessel. A second cordon of Union ships was maintained several miles out to patrol a wider area, allowing little scope for the runners carrying contraband. Now ships were being designed and built, mainly in Britain, specifically to evade the blockaders. The most successful runners were sleek, grey and shallow-drafted, burning smokeless fuel, and equipped with collapsible smokestacks and underwater steam-escape valves to minimise visibility. On moonless or foggy nights a runner might pass close to a blockading warship without being detected.[29]

Where the blockaders had financial incentives in the form of captured prizes, the runners were offered substantial inducements. In Bermuda or Havana they would take on guns, ammunition, army blankets, salt, tea and other goods; risk the one in three chance of capture in running to the Confederacy; and then load with cotton for the return journey. A runner captain was receiving up to $5000 for a round trip, with other officers earning as much as $3500 and seamen $250; and captains might store their own cotton for later auction. One estimate suggests that the runners brought in a million pairs of shoes, half a million rifles, a thousand tons of gunpowder, several hundred cannon, and so on; and carried back half a million bales of cotton.[30] Confederate spokesmen declared that the Union effort to block its trade was no more than a 'paper blockade', while Confederate president Jefferson Davis denounced the 'so-called blockade' a 'monstrous pretension'; and in the same vein the historian Frank L. Owsley pronounced the blockade an 'absurdity', 'old Abel's ... practical joke on the world'.[31] Many southern observers saw another picture. One noted in July 1861 that the blockade was shutting ammunition out, that it was 'a stockade which hems us in'. A trader wrote of the prostration of business, while after the war a southern naval officer acknowledged that the blockade had deprived the Confederacy of Supplies and 'weakened its military and naval strength'.[32]

Paris and the Commune

By the late 1860s tensions were again developing in Europe, with France and Prussia each contemplating the likely outcome of a new confrontation. France, with a much larger population and other advantages, appeared the stronger: its armed forces had been active in the Crimea, Italy and elsewhere; the Chassepot rifle far outranged the Prussian needlegun, while the Prussian forces possessed no equivalent to the *mitrailleuse* machine-gun; the French navy was superior; and France could expect significant military support from other European forces. In July 1870 the Franco-Prussian War began – and was soon concluded with a speedy French collapse. By 4 September the demoralised French army had surrendered at Sedan; Napoleon III (nephew of the Great Napoleon) was captured ('The army is defeated and captive: I myself am a prisoner' – telegraph to the Empress, 3 September 1870); and the imperial regime had been overthrown in Paris. The French capital withstood a bitter four-month siege until, on 28 January 1871, a truce was arranged.

On 8 December 1870, in conditions of mounting desperation, the Parisian Edmond de Goncourt noted in his journal: 'People are talking only of what they eat, what they can eat, and what there is to eat. Conversation consists of this, and nothing more ... Hunger begins and famine is on the horizon.' Theophile Gautier, a friend of Goncourt, was wearing braces for the first time ('his abdomen no longer supporting his trousers'); the government-supplied salted meat was 'inedible', and Goncourt described how he had killed a chicken with a Japanese sabre ('It was terrible, the bird escaped from me and fluttered about the garden, without a head').[33] Cheese, butter, milk, fresh vegetables, the vast herds of cattle and sheep available only months before – all had disappeared. Bismark had cynically proposed that the smart Parisian bourgeoisie would be broken by 'eight days without *café au lait*'; by the end of December the siege had lasted for 100 days.[34] Now horsemeat, formerly consumed only by the poor, was being eaten by all classes; thus a banquet demonstratively attended by the Commission *Centrale d'Hygiène et do Salubrité* included a number of horse dishes (*consommé de cheval, culotte de cheval, à la mode, filet de cheval rôti,* and so on).[35] The famous journalist Henry Labouchere reported that he had consumed 'a slice of spaniel the other day'; and that one acquaintance intended to eat a large cat ('surrounded with mice, like sausages') on Christmas Day.[36]

For a time domestic animals were fed to carnivores in the city's zoos, but later human needs took precedence. While cats and dogs were being eaten by an increasingly desperate population, the zoo animals themselves became vulnerable. Carcases of bear, deer, antelope, kangaroo and wolf were made available to the hungry Parisians; though reportedly the lions, tigers, monkeys and a hippopotamus from the Jardin des Plantes survived. Two elephants, Castor and Pollux from the Jardin d'Acclimatation, were messily despatched after several attempts with explosive bullets. Parisians variously recorded their consumption of crows, larks, camel hump and rats ('brewery' and sewer rats were priced differently). Scientists worked to synthesise substitute foodstuffs (for example, the *osseine* concoction made out of bones and gelatine), while the authorities attempted in desultory fashion to fix food prices and to organise a rationing system (rumours of bread rationing provoked riots). A few pockets of affluence, where food had been successfully stocked, were largely oblivious to the near-famine conditions in much of Paris. For example, the American Legation, some Parisian officials and many restaurants seemed relatively untroubled by the chronic food shortages beyond their doors. After the siege Goncourt and his friends offered to *Chez Brébant* a medallion bearing words that drew attention to the indifference of the restaurant clientele 'dining in a city of two million besieged souls'.[37]

The siege produced the inevitable toll of fatalities (Table 1.2), pneumonia in particular helping to swell the mortality figures. As with all sieges, it was the vulnerable that suffered most – infants, the sick, the old. But even this dreadful toll of disease and death was relatively mild compared with later sieges. The Prussian siege of Paris had lasted four months – compared with the 900-day siege of Leningrad (1941–4), where for many months people were dying at the rate of 9000 a day; and the decade-long siege of Iraq (1990–), where by 1999 more than one million children had been killed by sanctions-induced starvation and disease. The 1870–1 siege of Paris was bad enough, but immediately after the January capitulation and the lifting of the siege there was worse to come.

The truce arranged on 28 January 1871 did not yield an immediate peace with the provisional French government. On 8 February a

National Assembly was chosen by universal manhood suffrage to determine whether the war should continue and, if not, what peace terms should be sought. The new assembly comprised 400 monarchists (popular in the country because of their pro-peace sentiments), 200 Republicans, and a residue of 30 Bonapartists. Now the majority of the French people wanted to avoid another hopeless struggle and to resume a normal national life, to which end they were prepared to sacrifice some territory to the Prussians; the Republicans, unwilling to contemplate a diminished France, were prepared to fight to the bitter end. From 13 February to 10 March the National Assembly convened at Bordeaux, the question of a permanent form of government was adjourned, and Bismarck's terms for peace were considered. Before any terms could be agreed civil war had broken out between Paris and the National Assembly. Observed Vicomte de Meaux, a newly elected deputy: 'We provincials were unable to come to an understanding with the Parisians. It seemed as if we did not even speak the same language ...'; and a left-wing chronicler noted the Republican faith of the Parisians: '... they found themselves confronted by forty years of greedy hatreds, provincial notables, obtuse *châtelains*, grainless musketeers, clerical dandies ... a completely unsuspected world of towns ranged in battle against Paris; the atheistic, the revolutionary city which had created three Republics and shattered so many idols'.[38]

Table 1.2   Prussian siege of Paris (1870–1) – fatalities

Cause	1st week of Siege	10th week	18th week (14–21 January)
Smallpox	158	386	380
Typhoid	45	103	375
Respiratory ailments	123	170	1,084
All causes	1,266	1,927	4,444

Source: A. Horne, *The Fall of Paris: The Siege and the Commune 1870–71*, Macmillan, London, 1965, p. 221.

By mid-March the revolutionary Parisians, unwilling to contemplate the prospect of war against the National Assembly, were focusing on the election of a municipal council (the 'Commune') and on the scope for political reform. On the evening of 18 March 1871 the garrison withdrew from the Mont-Valerien fortress, which remained unoccupied for three days. Then regular troops moved back to occupy the fortress that dominated the western approaches to Paris, so signalling that the rebels had lost the initiative. Ten days later the

Commune de Paris, having secured through election (26 March) a four-to-one preponderance of 'Reds', officially installed itself in the Hôtel de Ville. To the sounds of celebratory cannon fire and cries of '*Vive la Commune!*' the scene was now set for war between Paris and Versailles.

The Parisians now faced a new siege, a fresh bloody defeat, and punitive post-defeat massacres; the Commune lasted two months. In London *The Times* (29 May 1871) commented: 'The laws of war! They are mild and Christian compared with the inhuman laws of revenge under which the Versailles troops have been shooting, bayonetting, ripping up prisoners, women and children during the last six days.' Estimates of the scale of the slaughter range from 6500 to 40,000, with the French government itself revealing that the Municipality of Paris alone had funded the disposal of 17,000 corpses. Perhaps as many as 25,000 Parisians, most of them helpless civilians, were killed by the government troops – more French fatalities than in any battle of the Franco-Prussian War.

The Prussian siege of Paris had produced fewer than 5000 fatalities. The Versailles siege of (Communard) Paris had prepared the ground for perhaps five times as many deaths. Again the potent role of economic measures, here as a supplement to or part of war, was manifest.

The First World War

The centuries-long use of economic sanctions as an element in both domestic and international conflict is easily signalled: it had long been obvious that even the most resolute enemy, once deprived of essential supplies, would be unable to sustain a military confrontation. The Napoleonic Wars, the American Civil War, the Prussian onslaught on France – all had advertised the potentially decisive power of siege/blockade/embargo in bringing victory in war. This in turn helped to stimulate the theoretical assessment of economic sanctions in planning for the possibility of future conflicts between states. For example, even before the First World War the United States was framing various strategies for war with other nations, with economic measures having a primary function in such schemes. Notable among these plans was the so-called War Plan Orange, the US Navy's strategy to defeat Japan in a future war.[39]

The plan required 'the final and complete commercial isolation of Japan'.[40] The principle of a total commercial blockade, proposed in 1906, was detailed in the 1911 version of War Plan Orange. Neutral ships would be intercepted and searched for US-defined contraband on the high seas, though it was acknowledged that such a measure would have only limited success. Japan might still be able to import goods through Korea, Manchuria, North China and Siberia. Even the most stringent maritime blockade would have only partial success in eroding the war-making capacity of a nation able to acquire essential supplies by other routes. (At the same time little attention was given to the provocative and possibly counterproductive character of any blockade initiative. In 1941 Harold L. Ickes, Roosevelt's Interior Secretary, commented that the president 'was still unwilling to draw the noose tight' around Japan; that he thought 'it might be better to slip the noose around Japan's neck and give it a jerk now and then'.[41] The tentative Roosevelt blockade was later judged to be one of the contributing causes to the bombing of Pearl Harbor on 7 December 1941.)

The outbreak of war between Germany and Britain in 1914 was immediately followed by wide-ranging economic sanctions. Between August and October the United Kingdom published successively longer lists of goods judged to be contraband (that is, goods that might aid the German war effort), at the same time progressively reducing the trading privileges of neutral vessels.[42] On 26 December the United States lodged the first in a series of protests concerning British attempts to restrict the scope of American trade, while on 4 February 1915 Germany announced that the safety of neutral ships around the British Isles, a declared war zone, could not be guaranteed.[43] On 11 March the United Kingdom, ignoring US protests, instituted a complete blockade of Germany as a declared reprisal for German submarine warfare. Again the vital importance of economic measures in a war situation was widely recognised: 'Apart from the traditional use of the methods of blockade and contraband, the efforts of the belligerents to cripple their opponents by curtailing their economic resources were reinforced by other practices ... On the British side, new devices were evolved with the object of preventing supplies from reaching enemy destinations through adjacent neutral territory.'[44] By January 1915 the economic life of Germany had not been seriously affected, though there was mounting concern as Britain redoubled its efforts to stem the flow of goods to enemy ports; Germany 'was still breathing normally but was haunted by fears of suffocation; she beheld herself as it were a fortress, already beset, a state of mind which was itself becoming an obsession'.[45] For its part Germany expanded the scope of the submarine campaign in an attempt 'to disorganise radically the maritime trade of the Allies'.[46] The United States was now raising repeated objections to the shipping restrictions imposed by the British, with London rejecting the US proposal that the Declaration of London (1909) should apply to the trading rights of neutrals. After entering the war in 1917, the United States reversed its earlier objections and worked with Britain to enforce the blockade against Germany.[47]

The blockade had a substantial affect on the German economy. Between 1913 and 1918 exports (in millions of marks) fell from 10,900 to 3000, with imports falling from 11,600 to 5900. Over the same period the receipts from German customs fell from 850 million marks to 133 million; cereal consumption dropped by 36 per cent, meat consumption by 82 per cent, and fats by 88 per cent; imports of oleaginous grain were entirely stopped by the end of 1914 (oil from this source was replaced from other sources but there was a 90 per cent cut in the output of the leather and soap industries). British coal and cotton exports (£175 million in 1913) were reduced by a half, and imports declined from 55 million tons in 1913 to 35 million tons in 1918. In 1915 US shipments of cotton to Scandinavia were 17 times normal (cotton, essential to the manufacture of explosives, was left off the contraband list as a concession to the United States).

The economic warfare developed during the First World War evolved as a strategy 'vastly different from anything that had been known before, with a new range of effectiveness'.[48] The British blockade was countered by German submarine attacks on merchant shipping, though with less overall success, while a bureaucratic administrative system was established to address the complex question of neutral shipping. Neutral vessels were examined at suitable 'control ports', which led to considerable delays and inconvenience, until a system of 'navicerts' documents issued at source was introduced to certify the neutral destination. The British negotiated with neutral governments and trade associations to reduce the level of trade with Germany; and blacklists were compiled of countries with perceived sympathies with Germany. The technique of economic warfare had reached a new level of sophistication: 'This was a new kind of blockade, enforced at long range through control of contraband and by agreement with neutrals, and bearing little resemblance to the old-style direct naval blockade of the enemy coast.'[49] An official British statement summarised some of the main features of the blockade:

1. German exports to overseas countries have been almost entirely stopped. Such exceptions as have been made are in cases where a refusal to allow the export of the goods would hurt the neutral concerned without inflicting any injury upon Germany.

2. All shipments to neutral countries adjacent to Germany are carefully scrutinised with a view to the detection of a concealed enemy destination. Wherever there is reasonable ground for suspecting such a destination the goods are placed in the prize court. Doubtful consignments are detained until satisfactory guarantees are produced.
3. Under agreements in force with bodies of representative merchants in several countries adjacent to Germany, stringent guarantees are exacted from importers, and so far as possible all trade between the neutral country and Germany ... is restricted.
4. By agreements with shipping lines and by a vigorous use of the power to refuse bunker coal, a large proportion of the neutral mercantile marine which carries on trade with Scandinavia and Holland has been induced to agree to conditions designed to prevent goods carried in these ships from reaching the enemy.
5. Every effort is being made to introduce a system of rationing which will ensure that the neutral countries concerned only import such quantities of the articles specified as are normally imported for their own consumption.

In such a fashion a comprehensive system with international weight was established and evolved over the period of the war. Many countries were forced to comply with British demands, if not already happy to do so. Many of Germany's most vital imports (cotton, wool, rubber and others) were blocked, while shortages of many other products (fats, oils, dairy produce and meat) had caused rocketing price inflation. Massive discontent surfaced in many German towns, leading to food riots and other serious dislocations. Commentators later acknowledged the drastic impact of sanctions on the German economy. Thus Mitrany quoted Lord Curzon, a member of the British War Cabinet: 'I doubt very much whether, if Germany had anticipated when she plunged into war the consequences, commercial, financial, and otherwise, which would be entailed upon her by two, three, or four years of war, she would not have been eager to plunger in as she was.'[50] In the same vein the analyst Margaret Doxy noted that the blockade 'was undoubtedly a factor in Germany's eventual defeat'.[51] And the historian Liddell Hart depicted the German High Command haunted by 'the spectre of slow enfeeblement ending in eventual collapse',[52] a prospect that pushed Germany into its disastrous 1918 offensive.

The management of the blockade was a complicated affair, compelled as it was to address the sensitivities of neutral trading powers, the state of current international law, the disposition of naval forces, and many other matters. The Hague Convention had sought to regulate the conduct of war on land, but as yet there was nothing comparable for the control of naval vessels in time of war. The 1908 London conference – considering such issues as blockade, contraband, search, the position of neutrals, and so on – yielded the Declaration of London (1909), but this agreement had no legal power. On 20 August 1914 Britain put the Declaration into force, though excluding the defined lists of contraband and subsequently introducing other modifications. Other powers similarly ignored the Declaration when it suited them, just as other agreements – such as the Declaration of Paris (1856) and The Hague Convention (1907) – could be ignored, even though their stipulations on such matters as blockade, the use of armed merchantmen, and so on, were nominally binding on all states.

The issue of stipulated contraband was particularly contentious (just as it would be a highly controversial question during the economic siege of Iraq in the 1990s). The Declaration of Paris referred to 'contraband' but did not define it. Precisely what goods were to be seized? Was it prudent to deny an enemy state *all* supplies? Food and medicines were clearly important to a war effort. Should these be seized also or allowed through as a gesture to innocent civilian populations? With some items there was no dispute: arms, ammunition, military supplies of all sorts – such were obvious contraband and could legitimately be seized, destroyed or exploited. About such 'absolute' contraband no discussion was required. But what of 'conditional' contraband that might not be intended for war but which might be so used in extreme conditions? Was it even possible to make a distinction between *absolute* and *conditional* contraband? And there were further problems about the destination of possibly contraband items. Material might be shipped to a neutral port and then conveyed further, to a belligerent. The British government, like the other involved parties, judged such matters as best it might, and provoked many protests.

The Germans alleged that the United Kingdom was treating all food as contraband – supposedly legitimate where food was intended for enemy armed forces but unlawful when intended for a civilian population. Who was to judge? (Food and medical supplies were nominally exempted from the US-orchestrated sanctions on Iraq through the 1990s, but a *de facto* blockade was maintained, with genocidal consequences.) At the end of January 1915 the German government announced its intention to take over all the foodstuffs in the Reich – which immediately made it possible for Britain to prohibit all food shipments to Germany. The German government, increasingly desperate, agreed to abandon the submarine campaign if Britain rescinded the blockade of foodstuffs. Britain declined and quickly reaffirmed its commitment to the blockade: a government statement (1 March 1915) announced that in view of German disregard for international law 'her opponents were driven to frame retaliatory measures, in order, in their turn, to prevent commodities of any kind from reaching or leaving Germany ... The British and French Governments will therefore hold themselves free to detain and take into port ships carrying goods of presumed enemy destination, ownership, or origin.'[53]

Throughout the period of the war the British navy had faced no serious challenge from German warships. Enemy cruisers had been swept away, German commerce had been drastically reduced by the comprehensive blockade, and the remaining German colonies had been exposed to inevitable conquest. The United States, having decided to support Britain with active military involvement, reversed its earlier blockade policies and helped to deprive Germany of the means to continue the war. Frank Polk of the US State Department declared: 'It took Britain three years to reach a point where it was prepared to violate all the laws of blockade. You will find that it will take us only two months to become as great criminals as you are.'[54] Here was the tacit admission that *in extremis*, in the desperate circumstances of a bitter war, agreements, conventions and international law counted for little: the aim was victory.

The circumstances of the blockade have been discussed by many historians in great detail.[55] Few can doubt that the experience gained came to shape the prosecution of later periods of economic warfare – primarily in the Second World War and through many of the conflicts of the Cold War. The importance of blockade measures grew in magnitude through the period of the conflict. In February 1916 the British government even deemed it worth while to appoint a Minister of Blockade with a seat in the Cabinet; Lord Robert Cecil, a barrister who had practised in international law, was appointed to the new position. Now it was plain that Britain saw the blockade 'no longer as an auxiliary but as a main weapon of war'.[56] Nor should it be forgotten that in 1917–18 the United States was running a blockade for the containment of Japan, doubtless drawing on the War Plan Orange strategy; and that the United States, Britain and other states were running an anti-Bolshevik blockade against the newly hatched Soviet Union.[57]

The effectiveness of a comprehensive maritime blockade, like a land-based siege, was not in question; but, throughout the nineteenth century and after the legal and moral propriety of economic warfare was continuously debated. The central ethical point was encapsulated in the issue of contraband. In short, was food to be included to the extent that vast suffering was caused among civilian populations? But sometimes the ethical question was submerged in mere practicalities. Thus Captain John Bigelow argued in *The Principles of Strategy* (1894) that the American Civil War had demonstrated 'that the most effective blockade should not be expected to prove decisive in itself. An entire country can hardly be starved like a city into surrendering'[58] (the point might be debated, particularly in view of sanctions experience accumulated through the 1990s – see Chapter 5). It was well known that the medieval siege of castle or fortified town had caused immense suffering among nominally innocent men, women and children. Should this be a legitimate aim of blockade managers in the circumstances of international conflict in the modern world?

On 7 May 1919 the defeated Germans were presented with the peace terms and told that they would be allowed fifteen days in which to submit their comments. There would be no discussion of the Treaty of Versailles: the Allies were dealing with a beaten enemy, the German government was humiliated, and the German people were continuing to suffer immense privation. When the text of the treaty was handed to Count Brockdorff-Rantzau, the leader of the German delegation, he declared while seated and with evident hatred that the Allies were killing 'with cold deliberation' hundreds of thousands of non-combatants through the continuing imposition of the blockade. (One historian deemed this charge 'outrageous' in view of both the food negotiations that had taken place and the fact that the Germans were still refusing to surrender merchant ships in Spanish ports.[59]) The Brockdorff-Rantzau contribution did no more than stiffen the Allied hostility to the German case.

The Germans had no doubt that as the defeated belligerent they were being punished in a vindictive and heartless fashion, that they were being 'deliberately reduced to beggary'.[60] The comprehensive Allied blockade was sustained for months after the armistice, despite protests from the American government and elsewhere: 'the vindictive nature of the terms was plain to see, and so was the risk, thus created, of another war'.[61] The British Cabinet claimed to have planned only a 'limited economic war', directed 'against the armed forces of the enemy'; but the German government had responded 'by interposing the German people between the armies and the economic weapons that had been leveled against them and by making the civil populace bear the suffering inflicted'.[62] The British claim was predictable: if the blockade was punishing the German people it was the fault of the German government; just as if economic sanctions were killing Iraqi civilians by the hundreds of thousands through the 1990s it was not the fault of the United States but of Saddam Hussein. Those who knowingly implement policies that will produce millions of human casualties are equally adept at placing the blame elsewhere. To preserve British virtue intact in the context of the First World War it has to be assumed 'that the British did not in fact aim at the benefits they won from the slow starvation of German civilians' – a 'fortunate blindness ... though finally unacceptable'.[63] The vital question of the effects of economic warfare on civilian populations is one that the architects and managers of sanctions/blockades/ embargoes should not be allowed to ignore (Chapter 4).

Attitudes

The power of economic warfare had been demonstrated over centuries: the obvious proposition that people need supplies in order to survive and to perform any task in the real world had been reinforced time and time again by all the instances of domestic and international conflict over the ages. At a theoretical level the option of economic sanctions has encouraged discussion in terms of Kuhnian paradigm theory,[64] where the so-called Genevan School of Thought (GST), with roots preceding the First World War, is seen to embody a number of discrete statements: for example,

> By the establishment of international economic sanctions [an international organisation can enforce the law without military conflicts]. This weapon is powerful, effective, relatively cheap, bloodless, and, moreover, easy to use to bring any aggressor to his knees. Economic sanctions have a moral power. They enjoy universal public support. States are innately rational. With the economic threat hanging over their heads, they will not find it worthwhile to deliberately wage wars of aggression.[65]

This represents an essentially benign view of economic sanctions: they are perceived as effective but relatively painless. So viewed, they became embodied in the Covenant of the League of Nations and in the Charter of the United Nations (Chapter 2 of present book). The popularity of the GST paradigm over a period of decades has been illustrated in a substantial amount of commentary:[66]

the League [of Nations] will sever all relations of trade and finance with the lawbreaker ... and also prevent as far as possible all commercial and financial intercourse between the subjects of the law-breaker and those of any other state ... The effect of such a complete automatic trade and financial boycott will necessarily be enormous (J. C. Smuts, 1918);

the economic weapon is the most powerful in the varied armoury of the Allies ... no human power can prevent it from ultimately ... bringing victory, final and decisive, to the Allied cause (A. E. Zimmern, 1918);

Article 16 [of the Covenant] allows us, as far as possible, to avert wars and to settle international disputes by peaceful means (Signor Schanzer, 1918);

The 'economic sanction', if simultaneously directed by all the world against a State which is not itself economically self-sufficing, would be a weapon of incalculable power (Austen Chamberlain, 1925);

The world has concluded ... that this blockade weapon is more indivisible and far more deadly than had formerly been supposed ... an instrument so atrocious ought not to be left in the power of any private belligerent ... blockade involves so intolerable an interference with neutral commerce, and especially so intolerable an injury to the belligerents' civil life, that it stands on a different footing from the others [boycott, the general strike, non-cooperation] (W. Arnold Forster, 1925);

The peace of Europe today depends in a large measure upon the obligation to use economic sanctions against a treaty breaker ... to interrupt its trade with neutral powers (Philip Kerr, 1929);

It is possible to attain real security, the reduction of armaments, and an objective attitude towards treaty revision and other political problems only with the establishment of an international organisation, in which international sanctions play a fundamental part (Raymond Leslie Buell, 1932);

Collective intervention manifested through a boycott is a powerful weapon of self-help ... It marks the welding together of economic power to crush or penalise a weaker adversary ... It is the expression of conflict by forces that may be as relentless and effective as the sword or the submarine (Charles Cheney Hyde, 1933);

It seems that coercion will continue to hold a place in international relations. If, as we hope, the accepted form of coercion is no longer to be war, the boycott in some form will, no doubt, find an important place (C. F. Remer, 1933);

These developments, which have enabled the United States to assume effective leadership of the free world and to accept responsibility in a manner few thought possible in 1944, could not have occurred unless a universal system of sanctions by combined forces had first been set up (Charles Webster, 1956);

The great advantage of economic sanctions is that on the one hand they can be very potent, while on the other hand they do not involve that resort to force which is repugnant to our objective of peace (John Foster Dulles, 1932);

It seems to be unfortunately true that the epidemic of world lawlessness is spreading. When an epidemic of physical disease starts to spread, the community approves and joins in a 'quarantine' of the patients in order to protect the health of the community against the spread of disease (Franklin D. Roosevelt, 1937).

The enthusiasm for economic sanctions has never been universal (see Forster, above): some have criticised the sanctions option because it is necessarily *ineffective*, bound to concede a degree of porosity to trade and the supply of goods; some because it is *too* effective, likely to have drastic consequences for (often) innocent civilian populations. Thus J. M. Spaight emphasised the problem of organising effective sanctions: 'The provision for penalties can never be made complete, the circle can never be closed ... in the international community your criminal and your policeman have a way of exchanging roles.' In the same vein John Dewey denounced sanctions as 'impracticable', likely to distract attention from more effective measures; moreover, 'enforcement of peace' ... 'combines two contradictory ideas'. And General H. Rowan-Robinson recommended the elimination of the sanctions provisions from the Covenant of the League of Nations.[67]

Many objections to economic sanctions have been noted: sanctions tend to generalise war rather than to isolate it; aggression is difficult to define, blame difficult to assess; nations can rarely be singled out as criminal; sanctions tend to perpetuate international injustices and to divert attention from measures more likely to solve international disputes; sanctions are more likely to be imposed against weak countries rather than strong ones; sanctions distract attention from efforts to resolve the underlying cause of tension; sanctions are likely to cause resentment and bitterness, with incalculable consequences for the future.[68] To such objections can be added the perception that economic sanctions are likely to bear most heavily on innocent civilian populations. This last point was graphically demonstrated by the maintenance of post-armistice sanctions in 1919; and today (late 1998) is shown by the decades-long imposition of US sanctions against Cuba and the years-long imposition of US-contrived sanctions against Iraq. Thus Ramsey Clark, former US Attorney-General, has emphasised that economic sanctions, when comprehensively maintained against civilians, are far from benign:

> As a lawyer ... I see the blockade clearly as a crime against humanity, in the Nuremburg sense, as a weapon of mass destruction ... a weapon for the destruction of the masses ... it attacks those segments of the society that are the most vulnerable ... infants and children, the chronically ill, the elderly and emergency medical cases.

The character of sanctions means that they are often limited and unfocused in their affects: they may have devastating consequences but may not achieve their declared objectives. Throughout the nineteenth century and the First World War economic sanctions, in their many manifestations, frequently had an inevitable international impact. In the twentieth century, with the formation of first the League of Nations and then its successor United Nations organisation, a fresh boost was given to the internationalisation of economic warfare. Now one of the principal objections to the sanctions option was thrown into stark relief: weak states were highly vulnerable to concerted economic measures while powerful states were relatively immune to external economic pressure.

Throughout the period of the Cold War a crude balance of power was maintained in the UN Security Council: both the United States and the Soviet Union, along with the other three Permanent Members, were able to veto the imposition of sanctions allowed under Article 41 (Chapter VII) of the Charter. But with the collapse of the Soviet Union in 1991, coupled with the illegal assumption by the Russian Federation of the Soviet seat in the Security Council, the crude balance of power was destroyed. Now the one surviving superpower could exploit the UN sanctions option as a tool of American foreign policy – with a massively reduced chance of a hostile veto in the Council. The American scope for imposing international sanctions under a UN 'flag of convenience', while not unlimited, remains substantial; and where the Council members cannot be bribed or intimidated into support for US foreign policy the United States always has the option of imposing unilateral sanctions. Power has many prerogatives.

2

From League to United Nations

There have always been dreams of an *international order* rooted in the peaceful solution of disputes between people and nations. Isaiah (2:4) has been endlessly quoted: '*And he shall judge among the nations, and shall rebuke many people: and they shall beat their swords into plowshares, and their spears into pruning hooks; nation shall not lift up sword against nation, neither shall they learn war any more.*' (Elsewhere in the Old Testament there is immense rejoicing at the slaughter of vanquished enemies; and in the New Testament the alleged Son of God urges anyone without a sword to acquire one – Luke 22:36.) The phenomenon of *internationalism*, peacefully mediated or not, did not begin in the twentieth century. Ancient empires, like their modern equivalents, always had internationalist ambitions; and other forms of internationalism have been well represented by the centuries of commercial expansion (for example, consider the growth of Ulrich Fugger & Bros, founded by Jacob Fugger (1459–1525) and soon to develop subsidiaries all over Europe); the many treaty-based alliances between states; and the countless attempts – common in the nineteenth century – to evolve rules and protocols for the regulation of international behaviour between countries.

A principal theme in the formation of the League of Nations and the subsequent United Nations organisation was the perceived importance of settling international disputes without the recourse to military action (thus the UN Charter preamble includes the words: 'We the peoples of the United Nations determined to save succeeding generations from the scourge of war ...'). Neither the League nor the United Nations ruled out the military option (the UN Charter defines how it should be used), but attention was given also to the pacific solution of international disputes. In this context the role of economic sanctions – long perceived as a powerful international weapon of coercion – was assigned a central role.

The League of Nations

Origins

Ambitious conquerors, proselytisers and entrepreneurs have long wanted to extend their sway over humanity by means of military adventure, ideology and commercial initiative. Such ambitions have always implied the development of an international order of one type or another. Thus the Dutch humanist Erasmus (1466–1536) envisaged kingdoms 'united in a Christian league'; Maximilien de Béthune, Duc de Sully (1560–1641), Henry VI's Chief Minister, recommended a Christian Commonwealth of Europe, equipped to settle disputes that threatened the peace and to sustain a stable order; the Dutch jurist and theologian Hugo Grotius (1583–1645) published *De Jure Belli et Pacis* (On the Law of War and Peace) in 1625, laying a basis for international law that would influence the shaping of the League Covenant three centuries later; William Penn (1644–1718), the Quaker founder of Pennsylvania, published *An Essay Towards the Present and Future Peace of Europe* in 1693, showing how a recalcitrant sovereign might be forced to submit a dispute to an international assembly by other sovereignties, 'united as one strength'; and other schemes for the pacific settlement of international disputes were proposed by the Abbé de Saint-Pierre in his *Project for Settling Perpetual Peace in Europe* (1713), by Jean Jacques Rousseau in his *Judgement on a Plan for Perpetual Peace* (1761) and Immanuel Kant in *Perpetual Peace* (1795). In this last the German philosopher declared that every state would come to feel the 'ever-growing burden of armaments' and that eventually they would be forced

> to do what reason could have taught them at once without so many bitter experiences, namely to give up their lawless life of savages and enter a League of Nations, an organisation where every state, even the smallest, can expect security and peace, not from its own power or its own decision as to what is right in its own cause, but from this great Society of Nations.

In 1816 the London-based Peace Society was founded, following the efforts of the Quaker William Allen, but quickly ran into Christian opposition. When a branch of the Society was formed in 1827 in Birmingham under the Quaker Joseph Sturge, many Christian commentators expressed the doubts that had been so graphically conveyed in the *Northumberland Monthly* (1819): 'Will holding out the idea that war is inconsistent with Christianity restrain the Turks, the pirates of Algiers, or the savage Indians of North America? Nothing could be more gratifying to Turkish and heathen nations than to hear that Christians had abolished war; in this case every European kingdom would soon be deluged with blood, and every Christian community exterminated.' But such denunciations did little to erode the activist initiatives of Quakers and other pacifists. In 1828 the American Peace Society was founded by William Ladd who advanced ideas that would later influence the building of the League and the United Nations (for example, he urged the creation of an international court and the development of international law).

Peace conferences were held throughout the nineteenth century, often attracting international participation with delegates from many countries. Now various themes (the peaceful settlement of disputes, sanctions against recalcitrant states, the growing importance of international law, and so on) were being considered that together would prepare the way for the establishment of international bodies that would symbolise the community of nations. Free trade was being recommended, rightly or wrongly, as a route to international peace; while various international organs were being created with powers over national administrations: for example, the Danube Commission (1856), the International Telegraphic Union (1865), the International Institute of Agriculture (1905), and the International Health Office (1907). At the same time various bodies (for example, the Brussels-based *Institut de Droit International*, founded in 1873) were working on the development of international law. In 1936 Bertrand Russell reminded us that his father, Lord Amberley, had in 1871 advocated a version of the League of Nations, 'with the whole apparatus of economic and military sanctions'.[1] Conferences at The Hague (1899 and 1907), attended (respectively) by 26 and 44 nations addressed questions relating to weapons usage, arms limitation, the rights of neutral shipping (highly relevant to the issue of economic warfare) and other matters. A third Hague conference was aborted by the onset of the First World War, but by now the ground had been well prepared for the creation of the League of Nations.

One of the main architects of the League was Thomas Woodrow Wilson (1856–1924), a law professor and the twenty-eighth President of the United States. On 8 January 1918 he announced to the US Congress the conditions that should govern the peace at the end of the Great War. After a preamble in which he emphasised the importance of peace and self-determination, he outlined the celebrated Fourteen Points[2] and declared: 'A general association of nations must be formed under specific covenants for the purpose of affording mutual guarantees of political independence and territorial integrity to great and small states alike.' Wilson then worked to establish the Covenant of the League as part of the Paris Peace agreement; and then – without success – to sell the spirit and letter of the League to a sceptical United States. The objective, asserted by Wilson on 30 May 1919 at the American graveyard at Suresnes near Paris, was that the immense human sacrifice made in the Great War should never have to be made again: 'This can be done. It must be done, and it will be done. The great thing that these men [the war casualties] left us ... is the great instrument of the League of Nations.' Wilson then placed a wreath, donated by the Boy Scouts of America, by the graves; a Frenchwoman added her own flowers.

Wilson was successful in securing the League Covenant as part of the 15-section Peace Treaty (the Treaty of Versailles); he had stated that he could not see 'how a treaty of peace could be drawn up or how both elasticity and security could be obtained save under a League of Nations, with the only alternative the traditional balance of power between the Great Powers that had only produced aggression and war ('the people are heartily sick of such a course and want the peace conference and the powers to take an entirely new course of action'). But it was inevitable, since the Covenant was part of the Treaty, that German hostility to Versailles would at the same time affect German attitudes to the League. In this context it has been argued that the League – designed as it was to secure a 'peace of the peoples' merely paved the way for Adolf Hitler and the most destructive war in the whole of human history.

The League was largely defined by its structure and powers, as defined by the Covenant; its performance by its shifting membership (Table 2.1) and by the range of political and administrative problems it was forced to confront. Many specific institutions were created to support the League Assembly, the Council and the Secretariat: the main supplementary bodies established for this purpose were the International Court, two Commissions for military and disarmament affairs, the Mandates Commission (see Table 2.2), and the Minorities Committee. In addition to these legal/political bodies a number of social/economic and humanitarian bodies were also created: the International Labour Organization, the Economic and Financial Organization, the Organization for Communications and Transit, the Health Organization, the Committee of the Drug Traffic, the Committee on the Traffic in Women, the Committee on the Protection of Children, the Committee on Slavery, and the Committee on Intellectual Co-operation.

Table 2.1   *Membership of the League of Nations*

Member	Date of entry	Notice of withdrawal (effective after two years)
Afghanistan	September 1934	
*Union of South Africa		
Albania	December 1920	(†)
*Argentine Republic		
*Australia		
Austria	December 1920	(††)
*Belgium		
*Bolivia		
*Brazil		June 1926
*United Kingdom of Great Britain and Northern Ireland	December 1920	
Bulgaria	December 1920	
*Canada		
*Chile		June 1938
*China		
*Colombia		
Costa Rica	December 1920	January 1925
*Cuba		
*Czechoslovakia		
*Denmark		
Dominican Republic	September 1924	
Ecuador	September 1934	
Egypt	May 1937	
Estonia	September 1921	
Ethiopia	September 1923	
Finland	December 1920	
*France		
Germany	September 1926	October 1933
*Greece		
*Guatemala		May 1936
*Haiti		April 1942
*Honduras		July 1936
Hungary	September 1922	April 1939
*India		
Iraq	October 1932	
Ireland	September 1923	
*Italy		December 1937
*Japan		March 1933
Latvia	September 1921	
*Liberia		
Lithuania	September 1921	
Luxembourg	December 1920	
Mexico	September 1931	

continued

Table 2.1   continued

Member	Date of entry	Notice of withdrawal (effective after two years)
*Netherlands		
*New Zealand		
*Nicaragua		June 1936
*Norway		
*Panama		
*Paraguay		February 1935
*Persia		
*Peru		April 1939
*Poland		
*Portugal		
*Romania		July 1940
*Salvador		August 1937
*Siam		
*Spain		May 1939
*Sweden		
*Switzerland		
Turkey	July 1932	
Union of Soviet Socialist Republics	September 1934	(§)
*Uruguay		
*Venezuela		July 1938
*Yugoslavia		

Notes:
*   Original members
(†)   Annexed by Italy, April 1939
(††) Annexed by Germany, March 1938
(§)   Declared no longer a Member, by Council Resolution, 14 December 1939

Source: F. P. Walters, *A History of the League of Nations*, London, Oxford University Press, 1960.

The focused interests of the individual supplementary bodies were reinforced by the League's primary commitment to peace among nations. Thus the preamble to the Covenant begins with the words: '*The High Contracting Parties – In order to promote international co-operation and to achieve international peace and security by the acceptance of obligations not to resort to war ...*'; and concludes '*Agree to this Covenant of the League of Nations*', after which the 26 Articles defining the structure of the League and the responsibilities of League members are given. Articles 10–15 address such issues as external aggression, war and the threat of war; here the roles of the Secretary-General, the Assembly and the Council are indicated, with emphasis given to the rights of members, arbitration and judicial settlement of disputes between states. Throughout the period leading up to the drafting of the Covenant, and throughout the life of the League, the issue of enforcement evoked continuing discussion. All the deliberations and decisions of the Secretary-General, the Assembly and the Council were worthless if the League had no powers to coerce states that were in manifest breach of the Covenant. It was recognised that economic measures, applied in a concerted fashion against any recalcitrant state, could represent a powerful coercive tool. So it was that the sanctions option was explicitly incorporated into the Covenant of the League of Nations.

Table 2.2   Mandatories and mandated territories*

Mandatory power	Territory	Area (sq. km)	Population (1938)
UK	Tanganyika	932,304	5,287,929
	Togoland	33,772	370,327
	Cameroons	88,266	857,675
	Palestine	27,009	1,435,341
	Transjordan	Declared independent, 1946	
	Iraq	Declared independent, 1932	
France	Cameroons	429,750	2,609,508
	Togoland	52,000	780,699
	Syria and Lebanon	Declared independent, 1944	
Belgium	Ruanda-Urundi	53,200	3,752,742
South Africa	South-west Africa	822,909	292,079
Australia	New Guinea	240,864	587,625
New Zealand	Western Samoa	2,934	57,759
British Empire	Nauru (administered by Australia)	2,929	3,400
Japan	Caroline, Mariana and Marshall Islands	2,149	121,128

* The table is true to the source. All the listed territories are now independent of the mandatories stipulated by the League.

Source: H. Duncan Hall, *Mandates, Dependencies and Trusteeship*, London, 1948, Annex II.

The Sanctions Option

The question of how the League's decisions were to be enforced was endlessly discussed prior to the drafting of the Covenant and through the entire period of the League's existence. The failure to reach a consensual view on this central issue was a principal reason for the collapse of the League: '... no satisfactory answer to which all member-nations could agree was ever found'.[3]

In December 1916 Lord Robert Cecil, the Minister of Blockade in the Lloyd George Administration, proposed to Foreign Secretary A. J. Balfour the creation of a committee to inquire, 'particularly from a juridical and historical point of view, into the various schemes for establishing by means of a League of Nations, or other device, some alternative to war as a means of settling international disputes', and, if necessary, 'to elaborate a further scheme'. The committee, appointed in February 1918 under the chairmanship of Sir Walter (later Lord) Phillimore, presented its conclusions ('conservative, orthodox and minimal'[4]) on 20 March. The Committee rejected the idea of an international court, whose decisions would be enforced by some mechanism; and instead proposed that international pressure on a recalcitrant state should be applied only by a conference that would aim at the peaceful settlement of any dispute. Lord Curzon, with others, felt that the Phillimore Report had raised 'many difficult points' but had failed to answer key questions. How were the decisions of the recommended conference to be enforced? Would there be scope for concerted pressure against any state found to be violating the requirements of international order? Would such pressure be military or economic? Would it be applied on an international basis? Such questions were being addressed in various ways, not least by Jan Christian Smuts, one-time supreme commander of the Boer forces in Cape Colony and in 1917 a member of the Imperial War Cabinet in London. In a highly influential pamphlet Smuts argued that the League could not rely on even a complete trade and financial boycott. In the last resort military enforcement should be an option: 'I do not think the League is likely to prove a success unless in the last resort the moratorium [against an aggressor nation] is guaranteed by force. The obligation of the members of the League to use force for this purpose should therefore be absolute, but the amount of the force and the contribution from the members should be left to the recommendation of the Council to the respective Governments.'[5]

In the event, the League, as an international body with no historical precedent, embodied the concept of collective security reinforced by a range of collective sanctions – (in the final draft Convention) diplomatic, legal, economic, and military. The proposed text declared that the League would be able 'to exercise an efficient control' over a recalcitrant state 'by various measures which may extend to placing it under an absolute commercial, industrial or financial ban'. Here the principal measures would be: *blockade* (using force to prevent commercial intercourse with the state in question); *embargo* (seizure and sequestration of the state's ships and cargoes and of goods destined for the state); *prohibition of supply* of raw materials and foodstuffs; *prohibition* of loans to and stock quotations of the state in question. It was plain that the drafters of the Covenant, with its framework of sanctions, had been impressed by the effectiveness of the Allied blockade against the Central Powers. But would such a mechanism, reinforced by a range of other economic sanctions, provide an effective deterrent to war?

The final draft of the Covenant makes no reference to 'economic sanctions' as an explicit phrase, but the relevant text, Article 16 (Paragraphs 1 and 3) is clear:

1. Should any Member of the League resort to war in disregard of its covenants under Articles 12, 13 or 15, it shall, *ipso facto*, be deemed to have committed an act of war against all other Members of the League, which hereby undertake immediately to subject it to the severance of all trade or financial relations, ... and the prevention of all financial, commercial or personal intercourse between the nationals of the Covenant-breaking State and the nationals of any other State ...
2. The Members of the League agree, further, that they will mutually support one another in the financial and economic measures which are taken under this article, in order to minimise the loss and inconvenience resulting from the above measures ...

This emphasises the 'chief object for which the League of Nations was created'[6] the prevention of war. Of the various tools that the League was notionally able to use to deter or repel aggression, the 'economic sanction', designed 'to bring about the economic isolation of a defaulting state by denying to it all commercial, financial, and trade facilities so far as these are within the control of members of the League', was judged by many commentators to be the most important.[7] Woodrow Wilson himself declared that the League would remove the need to raise an army to fight an aggressor: 'We shut their doors and lock them in. They are absolutely boycotted by the rest of mankind. I do not think that after that remedy it will be necessary to do any fighting at all.'[8] But throughout the life of the League the sanctions issue, like much else in the Covenant, remained controversial. Some of the League members resented the obligation to become commited to a sanctions regime in circumstances where they had no nominal involvement; others thought that the sanctions weapon was poorly defined and should be strengthened.

It is significant that the Covenant did not offer a blanket prohibition of war. In fact Article 12 provides tacit approval for a state's resort to war providing the defined procedures had been observed: 'The Members of the League agree that if there should arise between them any dispute likely to lead to a rupture they will submit the matter either to arbitration or judicial settlement or to enquiry by the Council, and they agree in no case to resort to war until three months after the award by the arbitrators or the judicial decision or the report by the Council ... the award of the arbiters or the judicial decision shall be made within a reasonable time, and the report of the Council shall be made within six months after the submission of the dispute.' Moreover, Article 16 itself, offering the option of economic sanctions, notes also (Paragraph 2) the duty of the Council to recommend how military force should be used 'to protect the covenants of the League'. It is arguable that the Covenant was realistic in acknowledging that states would on occasion feel compelled to resort to war; but arguable equally that cynical and ambitious governments would be quick to exploit Covenant loopholes in attempts to justify aggression.

There were problems also in judging whether a state was in violation of the Covenant: defences, however spurious, can always be mounted in mitigation of the moot blatant derelictions. But Article 16, authorising both economic sanctions and military action, provides no route to an authoritative judgement. The Covenant as a whole provided no 'centralised locus where such a judicial decision would be rendered'.[9] Commentators recognised also that League members may have an interest in delaying a decision, not least because the limited membership of the League (Table 2.1) meant that economic sanctions might have a drastic affect on some innocent but commercially vulnerable states. These various factors – elements of looseness and ambiguity in the Covenant, the limited and shifting League membership, the conflicting interests of individual members, the unprecedented nature of international obligation that League membership implied, and so on – made it unlikely that the specified sanctions options would provide an adequate deterrent to war. In the event the enforcement provisions of the Covenant were a failure; and in consequence the League of Nations was doomed.

The Sanctions Failure

The League, equipped with the sanctions option, proved itself reluctant to implement economic measures in times of crisis. Sanctions were applied to resolve only one crisis during the lifetime of the League; and here, used with little commitment and soon abandoned, they were unsuccessful.

There were many significant challenges to the authority of the League, but – with its internal divisions and limited membership – it was impossible to achieve, let alone sustain, a robust consensual approach to any international crisis. One of the earliest challenges arose in November 1921 when the use of armed force by Yugoslavia against Albania focused attention on the possible relevance of Article 16 of the Covenant. With the Council set to meet, under British prompting, Yugoslavia admitted that the prospect of international economic pressure gave it no option but to withdraw its troops. The Yugoslav government failed to secure an intended loan; the currency exchange rate fell;[10] and it seemed plain that the mere threat of League sanctions had secured the expulsion of occupation forces.

The sanctions threat proved to be equally successful on two other occasions. Thus in 1933 Turkey, under threat of international economic pressure, acceded to all the League demands that it act to suppress the illicit export of drugs. In the same way the Bulgarian government was pressured into suppressing its production of heroin. In these three cases, rarely signalled as League successes, the mere existence of Article 16 had proved decisive: 'The sanctions power in the background has been sufficient to produce effective results.'[11] However, the countries involved were relatively small. When more powerful states were seen to be in manifest violation of the Covenant the League's management of the sanctions option was ineffective.

On 18 September 1931, in a blatant challenge to the League, Japan invaded Manchuria, created the puppet state of Manchukuo on 9 March 1932, and announced on 15 September that Manchukuo had a sovereign identity independent of China. Now Great Power interests were combining to frustrate China's appeal for the implementation of economic sanctions by the League. France and Britain, not wishing to antagonise Japan, were reluctant to invoke Article 16; while the United States, though outside the League, was convinced that the only sanction that should be applied against Japan was 'the force of international public opinion'.[12] President Herbert Hoover declared that whatever action the League took the American Government 'would not impose sanctions' of its own.[13] Japan, keen to prevent any international response to its aggression, was quick to exploit divisions within the League and to encourage external opposition to practical economic measures. Japan, through representative Yoshizawa on the League Council, emphasised the importance of Manchukuo to the Japanese people, cited alleged broken promises of China, and stressed that any international interference would only make matters worse. Yoshizawa pointed out that there were one million Japanese nationals in Manchuria and massive investments – all of which had been constantly under threat in various ways. Dr Alfred Sze, the Chinese delegate, responded by snatching up a pile of telegrams that had reached him that day (22 September), reporting 'revolting acts' and proving that the situation was deteriorating. The Spanish president of the Council urged *both* sides to refrain from further aggression, urged Japan to withdraw its forces, and proposed that the United States be kept informed.[14]

At this stage, despite the unambiguous Japanese invasion (18 September), the League was not even prepared to affirm unilateral Japanese guilt. On 30 September the Council adopted an inconsequential resolution that optimistically indicated the desire for restraint and good intent on both sides. A week later (8 October) the Japanese bombed Chinchow, providing further unambiguous evidence of Japan's aggressive ambitions. The Chinese generalissimo Chiang Kai-shek responded with a dramatic affirmation of Chinese resolve: 'China respects the Covenant and the Kellogg Pact,[15] but, if the League and the Kellogg Pact signatories fail to uphold their sacred duties, China will not hesitate to make the supreme sacrifice of bankrupting the country for half a century to go to war in order to uphold the dignity and sacred rights on international agreements and to safeguard world peace.'[16] The US Secretary of State Henry L. Stimson signalled a minor shift in American policy, declaring that the United States 'would endeavour to reinforce what the League does', while efforts to bring a representative of the (non-member) United States to attend Council meetings were denounced by the Japanese delegate as unconstitutional. In the event Prentiss Gilbert, the United States consul in Geneva, was allowed to sit at the Council table – where he did no more than convey the extent to which the United States was still opposed to any practical measures against Japan.

The British government was soon echoing the policy of the United States. At the next meeting of the Council, Sir John Simon, the new Foreign Secretary, was keen to emphasise that any resort to Article 16 would adversely affect British trade; and so every effort had to be made to prevent unrealistic Chinese emphasis on the implementation of the sanctions option. Simon went so far as to declare, in the Cabinet meeting of 11 November, that the Chinese delegate 'must assist the League and not throw the responsibility on the other members of the Council' – and yet a concerted opposition to aggression was exactly what the Covenant had been framed to achieve. The French, with their eye on trade also, were keen to support British procrastination. Perhaps a commission of enquiry could be sent out to Manchuria, if the Council could only agree its terms of reference. Professor Gilbert Murray aptly summed up the situation: 'The League Covenant can apparently be ignored with impunity. Japan has ignored it by invading Manchuria; the nations represented on the League Council have ignored it ... The Covenant has failed to save China from aggression ... the Great Powers, despite all their fine pacifist gestures, have to their great shame not even seriously protested against, let alone resisted, such a state of affairs.'[17]

On 24 February 1933 a special meeting of the League Assembly was held to consider the report of Lord Lytton on the Manchuria crisis. The Lytton recommendations, reinforced by the subsequent Committee of 19 findings, proposed essentially that the League should not recognise Manchukuo either *de jure* or *de facto* and that the parties should negotiate a settlement that acknowledged Chinese sovereignty over Manchuria. The Lytton Committee conclusions were adopted in the Assembly by 42 votes to 1 (Japan), with Siam abstaining; whereupon the Japanese delegation immediately left the hall. A month later (27 March), Japan formally withdrew from the League of Nations.

The League had finally united in condemning the Japanese aggression but nothing had been done to prevent it. Henry Stimson and McGeorge Bundy subsequently noted: 'There is a direct and significant interconnection between the actions of the Japanese militarists and those others, in Ethiopia, the Rhineland, Spain, China, Austria, Czechoslovakia, and Albania, which culminated in general war in Europe.'[18] In the same vein Gaetano Salvemini commented that the 1931/2 Manchurian crisis was the 'dress rehearsal' for the 1935 Italian invasion of Abyssinia (today Ethiopia): 'In this later crisis Mussolini was to take a position identical with that of Japan towards China in 1931–1932.'[19] It is easy to argue that the failure of the League to respond adequately to Japanese aggression serve to encourage the imperial ambitions of the Italian militarists; and that the League failure to act robustly against the Italian invasion of Abyssinia led directly to the outbreak of the Second World War.

In October 1922 the Fascist Benito Mussolini marched on Rome and became head of the Italian government, giving commentators and politicians in the West the opportunity to applaud this new bulwark against Communism. Richard Washburn Child, the American ambassador in Rome, went so far as to boast that he had influenced Mussolini's decision to seize power; and when Child was satisfied that Mussolini's hold on the country was secure he discussed the possibility of a formal diplomatic alliance with the United States. Child was duly rebuked by the State Department, though his successor, Henry P. Fletcher, continued to praise Il Duce as the only source of strong leadership in Italy: 'If Mussolini should be assassinated, which God forbid, there would be a reign of terror. Authorities would be powerless to preserve order for some time.'[20] Later, Secretary of State Stimson came to praise Mussolini as a 'sound and useful leader'.[21] President Herbert Hoover declared that he was 'delighted' by the visit of Mussolini's foreign minister Dino Grandi to the White House in 1931. And Wilbur Carr, Under-Secretary of State in the Franklin Roosevelt Administration, proclaimed Mussolini Italy's 'only one first-class mind'.[22]

The Italian invasion of Abyssinia in 1935 did not immediately affect Mussolini's popularity in the West. In the same year a Cole Porter hit song included the line: 'You're the tops – you're Musso-li-ni'; and the *Chicago Tribune* applauded Mussolini's aggression in Africa on the grounds of 'commercial, evangelical, scientific, and humanitarian purposes';[23] while the *New Republic* noted that since capitalist expansion is 'the primary impulse towards conquest', and since Fascism is only 'one of the latest disguises of capitalism', it would be 'naive to place the blame on the personal wickedness of the fascist dictators in Germany and Italy'.[24] But now, where it had been possible for the United States to ignore the abuses of human rights in Italy, it was becoming increasingly difficult to defend Italy's naked aggression against a helpless African state.[25]

It was plain that the League of Nations would be forced to address the matter of the Italian invasion. Mussolini had laid his plans in 1933. Funds were provided to support dissident groups in Abyssinia and to aid road-making in Eritrea to facilitate the planned aggression; and at the same time Mussolini gave speeches to stimulate the imperial ambitions of the Italian people. The aim was clear: to achieve a rapid expansion of the colonial possessions of Italy by attacking a relatively poor country that would be powerless to resist.

On 29 September 1924 Mussolini had assured the Abyssinian chargé d'affaires in Rome that Italy had no aggressive intentions. A decade later, on 5 December 1934, the armed forces of Italian

Somaliland and the Ogaden province of Abyssinia came into conflict at Wal-Wal, a clash in a disputed area that resulted in the deaths of 100 Abyssinians and some 30 Italian native troops. Predictably, Emperor Haile Selassie claimed that the disputed area was part of Abyssinia while the Italians insisted that it belonged to Italian Somaliland. Italian troops were ordered to mass near the Abyssinian border post of Gerlogubi, Italian aircraft were flying over the region, and fresh encounters produced more Abyssinian casualties. Haile Selassie then appealed to the League of Nations to take action to safeguard the peace; while Dino Grandi, the then Italian ambassador to London, was declaring the situation in Abyssinia 'a cancer which had to be cut out' and indicating to Sir John Simon, the British Foreign Secretary, 'in veiled though unmistakable terms that Senor Mussolini was contemplating a forward policy of the most serious dimensions'. On 21 May Il Duce declared to Sir Eric Drummond, British ambassador to Rome, that Italy might have to go to war to clarify the situation; and subsequently commented to Sir Anthony Eden that in the event of war his aim would be 'to wipe the name of Abyssinia from the map'.[26]

The Council of the League of Nations then met to address the situation; and, as with the Manchurian crisis, urged the two sides to negotiate. The recommendation was ignored. Haile Selassie was powerless and Mussolini wanted nothing less than the annexation of Abyssinia. Then the Italians made absurd demands for Abyssinia to pay reparations for the Wal-Wal incident, and when these were not met launched an invasion of Abyssinia on 3 October 1935. The Council (unanimous apart from the Italian delegate) ruled that in resorting to war Italy had violated the Covenant with the clear implication that the League was now obliged, under the terms of Article 16, to impose sanctions. Baron Aloisi, speaking for Italy on 10 October, insisted that Abyssinia had no government capable of exercising authority, that its frontiers were unclear, and that it exploited conquered people ('subjects them to slavery and destroys them'). Sanctions, Aloisi pointed out, had not been invoked to settle the dispute between Bolivia and Paraguay; and in any case Italy was only acting in self-defence, so the Kellogg Pact (1928) was not relevant.

There was some argument within the League about whether to impose sanctions, but on 11 October 1935, observing the terms of Article 16, the Council recommended various measures, 'including a prohibition of arms shipments to Italy, of the floating abroad of Italian public and private loans, of an extension of credit to Italian agencies or corporations, a prohibition on the importation of goods from territory under Italian control, and an embargo on the exports of specified goods, mostly in the category of war materials'.[27] The declared aims were to uphold the Covenant and to force Italy into proper negotiations. It was assumed that concerted economic measures would be adequate to the task, and that in consequence no resort to League-mandated military action would be necessary. On 2 November the League members resolved that the economic sanctions must begin on 18 November, a milestone decision in the long struggle to develop an international system of global security. The League, cumbersome and ineffectual in the past, had now acted, impressing some commentators but raising doubts in others. The French and the British were concerned that the sanctions might cause a European conflict in which Germany would find 'a pretext for satisfying its territorial ambitions'.[28] Even now, some imagined the possibility of an alliance between Italy and an expansionist Nazi Germany, to the obvious disadvantage of the other European powers. The anxieties were such that the French and British delegates to the League held a secret meeting at which they agreed *to limit the scope of the sanctions against Italy*. What many had applauded as an historic League decision in the interest of collective security was already being covertly undermined by powerful states. It soon became apparent just how the mandated sanctions would be constrained, nominally to prevent war but also to the point that they would be rendered ineffectual.

In the event the League rejected many of the most potent sanctions. No restrictions were placed on Italy's access to food, coal, steel and oil; no attempt was made to blockade the Italian mainland; Italy was allowed continued access to the Suez canal; and no impediment was put in the way of normal diplomatic relations. A number of commodities essential to the Italian war effort continued to arrive at Italian ports: in allowing Italy access to vital commodities such as rubber, coal, nickel, oil and tin, Britain, for example, was conducting a policy of unambiguous appeasement.[29] The British government 'had no desire to see economic sanctions produce any results',[30] since, had they been successful, there would have been an unwelcome moral obligation to use them again in the future.[31] It has been judged that a block on Italian access to oil would have been decisive; without oil the Italian army would have been forced to withdraw. But here there was no guarantee that a League ban would not have been circumvented by American companies. Thus US Secretary of State Cordell Hull expressed his concern 'that if the League of Nations imposed sanctions on the export of oil to Italy, American business would step in to supply the petroleum that Italy needed to continue waging war'.[32] Britain and France, keen to avoid a wider war, assured Mussolini that no 'military' (as opposed to 'economic') sanctions would be imposed, whereupon Mussolini declared that he would regard oil sanctions as an act of war. All the League members who had formerly supplied oil to Italy – most notably, Britain, Venezuela, Romania and the Soviet Union – continued to do so. Some countries (Switzerland, Austria and Hungary) never agreed to apply *any* sanctions; though Germany, having resigned from the League in October 1933, placed an embargo on the sale of arms, oil, textiles, iron, steel and other commodities to both belligerents. It was an obvious paradox that the members of the League, under the obligation of Article 16 to impose sanctions, were less likely to do so than at least one country *outside* the League.

So it was that the League action against Italy proved to be totally ineffective. The sanctions nominally agreed by League members were partial and divisive (France and Britain were often at odds with the weaker members); and states outside the League showed little interest in the affair. When League proposals were sent out to non-members Saudi Arabia, Brazil, Costa Rica, Egypt, Germany, Iceland, Japan, Liechtenstein, Monaco and the United States, only Egypt and the United States troubled to reply (with Roosevelt indicating that he could do no more than make moral appeals to American oil producers). France was more concerned about Hitler's remilitarisation of the Rhineland, and it was increasingly recognised that harsh sanctions against Italy would end all chances of retaining an ally against Germany. And Samuel Hoare, British Foreign Secretary, and Pierre Laval, French premier, had even agreed the odious Hoare–Laval Pact (1935), whereby parts of Abyssinia would be coded to Italy as a means of resolving the dispute. Public outcry at this manifest reward for aggression led to a British repudiation of the Pact and Hoare's resignation. Such developments did nothing to strengthen sanctions against Mussolini or to bolster the general campaign against the Italian annexation of a sovereign African state.

On 30 June 1936 Haile Selassie began to address the League Assembly (to be greeted by whistles, catcalls and shouts of 'murderer', 'slaver' and 'bandit' from what *The Times* called a 'brawling claque of Italian journalists'[33]). His speech, delivered in Amharic (understood by none of the other delegations) and translated into French and English, was heard in silence. He declared:

> I ask the 52 nations not to forget today the policy on which they embarked eight months ago and on the face of which I directed

the resistance of my people against the aggressor whom they had denounced to the world ... The Ethiopian Government never expected other governments to shed their soldiers' blood to defend the Covenant when their own immediate personal interests were not at stake. Ethiopian warriors asked only for means to defend themselves. On many occasions I have asked for financial assistance for the purchase of arms. That assistance has been constantly refused me ... the problem submitted to the Assembly is a much wider one than that of the situation created by Italy's aggression ... It is the very existence of the League of Nations ... it is international morality that is at stake ... .

In his conclusion Haile Selassie commented: 'God and history will remember your judgement ... Placed by the aggressor face to face with the accomplished fact, are states going to set up a terrible precedent of bowing before force? Representatives of the world, I have come to Geneva to discharge in your midst the most painful of the duties of a head of state. What reply shall I have to take back to my people?'[34] He did not have to wait long for an answer.

Addis Ababa had fallen to Italian troops on 6 May 1936, and by then Eden was admitting that the sanctions – such as they were – had failed. Britain and France were prepared to take no effective action against the aggression, and all that remained was for the League to extricate itself from an embarrassing involvement that was producing no useful results. On 9 May Mussolini proclaimed the formal annexation of Abyssinia and announced that King Victor Emmanuel III was that country's new emperor. Haile Selassie decided to seek exile, whereupon Eden let him know that he could come to Britain – *provided he did not expect British help with his travel beyond Gibraltar, provided he travelled incognito in Britain, and provided he limited his entourage to six persons.* The ousted leader of a sovereign state was treated with scant respect while Britain and France sought pragmatic and shameless accommodations with Mussolini. By the time Haile Selassie journeyed to address the League Assembly at the end of June, Britain was considering how sanctions might be abandoned. It would have helped the British government if Mussolini had been prepared to declare his good intent and his willingness to join a united front against Nazi Germany. Now there was a shift in the French position: Leon Blum's Popular Front had taken power and could not be relied upon to support the anti-sanctions posture of the British Cabinet; but France remained hostile to any League resolution that would complicate future relations with Italy. Abyssinia was one issue but there were more momentous events taking place in the world.

Haile Selassie delivered his dignified and despairing speech to the Assembly (30 June), after which – in direct opposition to his ethical appeal – the League set out the formal task of ending the partial and ineffectual sanctions against Italy. Now Britain and France were unwilling even to sign a League declaration pledging non-recognition of the Italian annexation of a sovereign state. The League had demonstrated its 'moral sickness ... a sickness to which Britain had contributed'.[35] On 4 July the League adopted a resolution to end the economic sanctions against Italy: to its shame the Assembly voted unanimously, with one exception – Abyssinia. It has been argued that Assembly members were seeking to avoid thrusting Italy into the arms of Nazi Germany, though accommodations between those two countries were already being made (in June an Italo-German air pact was negotiated and Italy expressed open approval of the Austro-German agreement announced on 12 July).

It had emerged through the instances of Japanese and Italian aggression that some states were more prepared to violate the League system of collective security than were the League members to defend the Covenant. The failure of the sanctions option had reduced the likelihood that collective sanctions would be imposed in the future, and so had contributed to the increasing irrelevance of the League: its impotence – even when able to agree to the imposition of a sanctions regime against an aggressor state – had been advertised for all to see. The wound would never heal.

The League had been humiliated over the invasions of Manchuria and Abyssinia, soon followed by the Spanish Civil War – a conflict that quickly assumed an international dimension and so attracted the attention of the League. Nazi Germany was quick to perceive an interest in aiding the Franco Fascists, by means of aerial bombardment and other measures, against the legal Republican government. Britain, keen to support a right-wing authoritarian regime, resisted pressure from other League members for an international response; and welcomed the creation of the odious Non-intervention Committee, set 'to graduate from equivocation to hypocrisy and humiliation, and which was to last out the Civil War'.[36] Thus the British government argued that intervention in a civil war was inappropriate, while prepared to tolerate German and Italian involvement in the conflict. On 24 September 1936, two months after the start of the war, Eden pledged support for the League but was keen to proclaim Britain's non-interventionist policy. There was no prospect that Article 16 of the Covenant would be invoked as a response to German aggression – so offering a 'green light' to Hitler's expansionist ambitions.

The League members were in no doubt about what was happening. For example, Sir Denys Bray and Laurence Webster had reported that the civilian population of the Republic were living on minimum rations, which in any case were often not being distributed. In Barcelona a million refugees, under *de facto* siege, faced appalling privation. The Fascist revolt that had begun the civil war was soon receiving help from Germany, Italy and Portugal, with the Soviet Union supplying help on a much smaller scale to the legitimate Republican government. The Spanish government made an early request to the League Secretary-General to invite the Council to consider the flagrant external aggressions against Spain – and was answered with indifference and delay. When the Council eventually convened on 12 December, none of the principal foreign ministers were present and more than half the Council members had already pledged support for the Non-intervention Committee. Thus a majority of Council members were already committed to a policy that violated an essential element in the Covenant. The Committee, in absurdly resolving to treat both sides – Fascist rebels and legitimate democratic government – equally had already undermined any initiatives that the League might have otherwise decided to take. There were Italian troops in Spain, the Germans were bombing Guernica, and Italian submarines and destroyers were sinking Spanish merchant ships. The League, despite repeated appeals from the legitimate Spanish government, was prepared to take no action. In March 1939 the Fascist rebels, enjoying massive support from the Axis powers, overthrew the Republican government and consigned the Spanish people to decades of brutal dictatorship.

The legitimate needs of Manchuria, Abyssinia and Spain had been ignored by the League. Manifest aggressions had either been ignored or addressed only with a weak and temporary response: the League, having failed to establish a system of collective security, had thus sacrificed all its claims to international authority. The League's limited membership, the narrow interests of key members, the ambiguous role of the non-member United States, the accumulation of successive international crises, the seismic outbreak of the Second World War – all had combined to consign the League to oblivion. The League had managed to settle a few minor disputes, idealistic themes were enshrined in debates and declarations, and for the first time the ideal of the pacific settlement of disputes was established in a body that enjoyed international recognition. National sovereignties were left largely intact, but governments did not enjoy coming under the critical spotlight of the League Commission. For a time the League represented a powerful moral pressure, though largely impotent in practical affairs. It remained rooted in the convulsions of the First World War, just as the United Nations Organisation was in the to remain rooted in the convulsions of the Second.

The League Secretary-General Eric Drummond declared in his last year of service that *if the League 'were to disappear today, nearly every treaty of a political character which has been concluded during these 13 years would vanish with it ... A state of chaos would result ... the first task which would confront the statesmen on the League's disappearance would be to reinvent the League'*. These words, spoken in 1933, were prophetic: the moribund League was only allowed to die when its spirit and functions could be transferred to another international body.

The United Nations

Origins

Soon after the start of the Second World War, before the final collapse of the League of Nations, the Allied powers began to plan a new international body that would keep the peace in the post-war world. The humiliated League, with limited membership and viewed with suspicion in the United States, was doomed. The League Covenant embodied in the Treaty of Versailles inevitably gave the League a European focus. Soon the focus of a system for collective security would shift to the United States.

In June 1941 representatives of Great Britain (and its Dominions), France, Belgium, Greece, the Netherlands, Luxembourg, Norway, Poland, Yugoslavia and Czechoslovakia met in London to frame the Inter-Allied Declaration (12 June), pledging all the signatories to strive for a world in which all peoples could live in peace and security. Two months later Roosevelt and Churchill, meeting secretly off Newfoundland, agreed the Atlantic Charter, designed to outline the principles that should govern settlements in the post-war world; the Charter was later signed by the Soviet Union and 14 other states fighting against the Axis alliance.

The principles of this historic agreement came to influence the subsequent drafting of the Charter of the United Nations. The Charter, enshrined as a key Declaration, was approved on 1 January 1942 in Washington D.C. by representatives of 26 nations via the mechanism of a United Nations Declaration (Roosevelt had always dubbed the Allies the 'United Nations'); now the option of a United Nations organisation, able to supplant the League of Nations, was on the political agenda. On 30 October 1943 these developments received a further boost when representatives of Britain, the United States, the Soviet Union and China agreed the Moscow Declaration on General Security, developing the idea of a new international body for the preservation of peace in the post-war world. Now the United States had a dominant role in the shaping of the new organisation. There had always been American doubts about the role and character of the League, just as many influential American pundits and politicians would come to harbour suspicions about the potential power of the United Nations to constrain the implementation of US foreign policy; but now, with America a key player in the framing of UN plans (and with the new international body likely to be sited in the United States), it seemed probable that the United Nations organisation would have a global and sustainable influence, whatever its nature.

The Roosevelt Administration worked to cultivate support for the United Nations concept: it was important that there be no rerun of the League fiasco where a sceptical Congress, after all the efforts of Woodrow Wilson, had blocked the possibility of American membership. The League Covenant, carried in the Treaty of Versailles, had inevitably been associated with the punitive treatment of Germany. By contrast the Charter of the United Nations, while enshrining the concept of the 'enemy state ... any state which during the Second World War has been an enemy of any signatory of the present Charter' (Article 53), is not associated with the terms of a punitive treaty. Thus it was hoped that the UN Charter, unlike the League Covenant, would not antagonise certain states from the outset.

At the same time a number of important international organisations were being created to address the perceived needs of the post-war world, but in a context where the United States clearly intended to be the principal player. At the Bretton Woods Conference (New Hampshire, 1–22 July 1944) the International Monetary Fund (IMF) and the International Bank for Reconstruction and Development (the World Bank) were created, so helping to consolidate US influence over most of the capitalist world. By the time the Third World peoples had gained their independence from colonialism they had no opportunity to reshape the powerful financial institutions to which they were now in thrall. At the Dumbarton Oaks Conference (Washington D.C., 21 August 1944), dominated by the United States, a framework was established for the United Nations organisation; and at Yalta (4–11 February 1945) Roosevelt, Stalin and Churchill laid plans for the Great-Power management of the post-war world – with particular attention to the US-orchestrated Dumbarton Oaks proposals and the forthcoming conference in San Francisco for the establishment of the United Nations.

On 25 April 1945 the representatives of nearly 50 nations convened in the San Francisco Opera House and accepted by acclamation that the new international body would be called the 'United Nations' (Roosevelt's favoured term). President Truman, speaking from Washington, wished the Conference well, whereupon the delegates were divided up into 4 main commissions and 12 technical committees to consider 547 amendments to the Dumbarton Oaks proposals. The Conference emerged as 'a mixed bag of power politics, muddy thinking, official hypocrisy, high idealism, keen good sense, legalistic nonsense, compromise and false hopes'. The range of contributions from many disparate states, set against the (scarcely) invisible hand of American power politics, yielded tensions and ambiguities: 'Men could take from it almost anything they wanted.'[37] On 26 June the Conference concluded with the signing of the Charter. By now it seemed plain that the United States, having laboured at Dumbarton Oaks and Yalta to define the UN framework, had broadly succeeded in shaping the form of a new international organisation that could be made to work in ways that were helpful to the development of American interests. Things did not always run smoothly for the United States, particularly as many former colonial territories came to gain their independence and a seat in the General Assembly; but in the main the establishment of the United Nations Organisation and the many associated bodies did little to disrupt, and much to aid, the cynical prosecution of American foreign policy: '... the UN Charter implied the American Way of Life writ large'.[38] This circumstance would come to affect how the United Nations came to use its enforcement powers – including economic sanctions against recalcitrant states.

The siting of the United Nations headquarters became a matter of intense debate before a decision was taken. According to Trygve Lie, the first UN Secretary-General, the new organisation would become the 'political centre of gravity' of the world.[39] The Americans were keen that this should be established within the borders of the United States – an idea that soon achieved general acceptance. The Russians raised no objection, which surprised the Europeans; and it was widely conceded that Geneva – as a site favoured by some – was inevitably associated with the failures of the doomed League of Nations. Considering the option of a Europe-based United Nations, Trygve Lie noted that 'the world cross-roads of determinative political forces ... had moved farther west' and that it was now necessary 'to settle on new shores'.[40] The UN Preparatory Commission's Committee Eight duly voted (30 to 14) that the permanent headquarters of the United Nations should be located in the United States of America; and, despite further debate and some opposition, so it was.[41]

There remained only one important task to complete, before the newly hatched United Nations organisation assumed its world role and began its work. On 8 April 1946 the Assembly of the League of Nations convened in the *Palais des Nations* in Geneva to transfer power to the new international body. The reserve funds were distributed among the donor nations; the Palace itself, with all its associated possessions, was handed over to the new organisation; and in particular the League library and its invaluable archive were assigned to the new UN Secretariat. The Assembly resolved that on 19 April 1946 the League would cease to exist. At the last meeting of the General Assembly of the League of Nations Sir Robert Cecil declared:

> Let us boldly state that aggression wherever it occurs and however it may be defended, is an international crime, that it is the duty of every peace-loving state to resent it and employ whatever force is necessary to crush it, that the machinery of the [UN] Charter, no less than the machinery of the [League] Covenant, is sufficient for this purpose if properly used, and that every well-disposed citizen of every state should be ready to undergo any sacrifice in order to maintain peace ...
>
> I venture to impress upon my hearers that the great work of peace is resting not only on the narrow interests of our own nations, but even more on those great principles of right and wrong on which nations, like individuals depend.
>
> The League is dead. Long live the United Nations.[42]

The question of how to enforce United Nations decisions had been and continued to be considered in detail. Cecil emphasised that the UN Charter was sufficient for the task of crushing aggression ('whatever force is necessary'), but the implication that aggression would necessarily have to be countered by an international military response was only part of the picture. The Charter, like the Covenant, gave scope also for the collective imposition of economic sanctions. It would be found that this option could prove as destructive to the flesh and fabric of a sovereign state as any military initiative.

The Sanctions Option

The English and American drafters of the UN Charter were well aware of the power of economic sanctions throughout history in general and the Second World War in particular. In the face of Japanese imperial expansion in the 1930s the League of Nations had failed to take economic measures against Japan, but by 1940, with American interests increasingly at stake, the sanctions issue became a matter of primary concern.

In October 1940 Joseph Grew, the American ambassador in Japan informed the America-Japan Society, in a speech approved by Roosevelt, that the United States objected to Japanese aggression in China and was considering economic retaliation to prevent further threats to American interests. At the same time the United States was continuing to supply Japan with oil to meet its military and other needs. The Japanese navy depended on American fuel oil; just as the Japanese used American high-octane aviation gasoline. As one observer noted, the arsenal of democracy was also the filling station of fascism; in due course 'American boys would face Jap battleships propelled by American fuel oil, their drive shafts turning on American grease'.[43] In such circumstances it seemed plain to many observers, American and other, that an American oil embargo on Japan would be highly effective in curtailing its expansionist ambitions. Lord Lothian, the British ambassador to the United States, urged Henry Morgenthau, one of the hawks of the Roosevelt Cabinet, that it was time to stop shipping fuel to Japan: 'If you will stop shipping aviation gasoline to Japan, we will blow up the oil wells in the Dutch East Indies so that the Japanese can't come down and get that ... .'[44] On 22 July 1940 he proposed to Roosevelt that petroleum products and scrap metal be added to the list of strategic materials subject to the embargo. In the event, pressure from the State Department yielded export control orders limiting the embargo to high-octane gas and steel scrap. Debate continued within the Roosevelt Cabinet on how far the embargo should extend – with the result that American gasoline continued to be shipped to Japan during the first six months of 1941, while the Japanese militarists prosecuted their expansionist plans. On 26 July, when the deteriorating international situation was plain for all to see, the American government moved to freeze all Japanese funds, effectively removing the Japanese capacity to buy further quantities of American oil.

At the same time Roosevelt was keen not to goad Japan into retaliatory military action against the United States. He went so far as to explain personally to Ambassador Nomura that, despite the freezing of funds, he was not ordering a total ban on oil exports but emphasised that an 'exceedingly serious situation would immediately result' if Japan moved to seize the Dutch East Indies oilfields. But the partial American blockade had provided the hardliners in both

Washington and Tokyo with the opportunity to represent the Roosevelt initiative as a draconian measure, 'the most drastic blow short of war' (according to the *New York Times*). Washington was now also pressuring the Australian government not to allow Japan access to its abundant supplies of iron ore. It was an easy matter for the ambitious Japanese military leadership to depict the escalating embargo as immensely hostile, a threat to the very survival of the Imperial Navy. In Tokyo there was renewed pressure for military expansion to the south to secure the oil resources in the East Indies. The limited Roosevelt blockade, with the attendant pressure on other states to comply, was seen later as one of the contributing causes of the bombing of Pearl Harbor on 7 December 1941.

Many of the techniques of economic warfare introduced in the First World War themselves derived from nineteenth-century experience – were soon being developed and refined to meet the circumstances of the new international conflict. Again the compulsory navicerts were employed to block the shipment of contraband; ship warrants were issued to signal compliance with British regulations; and blacklists were compiled. Key raw materials were purchased on a pre-emptive basis; neutrals were subjected to import rationing; and diplomacy was exercised to discourage such states from supporting the Axis powers. Germany, with allies and much conquered territory, was able to resist what might have proved to be a decisive blockade; but nonetheless the effects of the Allied economic warfare were considerable. German imports (in particular, the access to vital raw materials) were severely curtailed; Axis manpower and transportation deployments were seriously affected; neutral resistance to Axis pressure was stiffened by Allied economic aid; and what has been dubbed a 'blockade neurosis' impacted heavily on German strategy.[45]

In addition to the general economic strategies devised by both the Allied and Axis blocs, particular events and campaigns in the Second World War emphasised the potentially decisive power of economic measures. We need only recall the collapse of Singapore (15 February 1942) – the so-called 'impregnable citadel' that became one of Britain's greatest humiliations – where an effective siege led to the rapid depletion of food stocks and the water supply;[46] the German submarine campaign against vital merchant shipping; the Battle of Stalingrad (September 1942 to February 1943), where the seeming success of the German General von Paulus was converted by General Zhukov into the encirclement and surrender of vast German armies, a turning point of the war; and the 900-day siege of Leningrad (September 1941 to January 1944), where 200,000 civilians were killed by German shelling and bombing, and another 630,000 by cold and starvation (on Christmas Day 1941, 3700 people starved to death; in the one month of April 1942 some 102,497 people – men, women, children, babies – died of starvation).[47] Such events, appalling in their magnitude and human cost, emphasised to the architects of the United Nations organisation – if further emphasis were needed – that the option of economic sanctions must be available to the international community for the enforcement of Security Council decisions.

Two specific punishments for recalcitrant states are included in the Charter of the United Nations, with other possible punitive actions left to the discretion of the Security Council. Thus a UN member who has 'persistently violated' the principles of the Charter may be expelled from the General Assembly upon the recommendation of the Security Council (Article 6); and a UN member in financial arrears may not be allowed to vote in the General Assembly, unless the failure to pay is beyond the member's control (Article 19). These provisions have been criticised on the ground of their general vagueness. How is a Charter 'principle' to be recognised? What does 'persistently' mean? Who is to say whether a state is able to pay its dues? And so on and so forth.

At the same time many obligations are placed upon signatory states to the Charter: for example, all UN members shall refrain 'from the threat or use of force against the territorial integrity or political independence of any state' (Article 2(4)). The issue of whether a state is in violation of the Charter is for the Security Council to judge – which immediately confers immense power on a few leading states (the Permanent Members: the United States, Britain, France, China and Russia) that are usually able to intimidate or bribe other Council members into support for this or that judgement. Thus the Permanent Members effectively decide whether a state is violating the Charter and what action should thereby be taken by the United Nations.

Article 41 of the Charter specifically provides for the option of economic sanctions, under the discretion of the Security Council:

> The Security Council may decide what measures not involving the use of armed force are to be employed to give effect to its decisions, and it may call upon the Members of the United Nations to apply such measures. These may include complete or partial interruption of economic relations and of rail, sea, air, postal, telegraphic, radio, and other means of communication, and the severance of diplomatic relations.

Later Articles in Chapter VII provide the option of military force if the Council judges that the actions permitted under Article 41 'would be inadequate or have proved to be inadequate' (Article 42). Thus the Security Council is empowered by the Charter (Article 39) to judge whether there is a threat to the peace or an actual aggression; and to recommend non-military sanctions (Article 41) or a military response (Articles 43–47) under specified control.[48]

There has been much debate about the relationship between legalism and politics in the UN Charter. The inclusion of only minimal juristic sanctions in the Charter, as compared with the League Covenant, has been taken as acknowledgement that the demand for universal sanctions resting on 'a framework of legalism are, quite simply, ineffective'.[49] The failure of the League to adequately punish Japanese and Italian aggression has been sited as a collapse of the intended relationship between 'obligation, delict and sanction'.[50] Thus the framers of the UN Charter – arguably acting in a more realistic or chastened mood – have tried to shift the emphasis from legal compulsion to political obligation on member states when collective action is authorised by the Security Council. The relevance of this shift of emphasis to the punishment of recalcitrant states can be debated, but some argue that the perceived importance of achieving political 'consensus before proceeding [to punitive action] has no doubt contributed to the continuing relevance of that organisation in international politics'.[51]

The shift in emphasis has been depicted another way. Thus the approach of the United Nations, against that of the League, 'is contingent upon the formulation of a number of principles, findings, and determinations by organs of the United Nations which provide the legitimate basis for UN action'.[52] In this context a gradual escalation of sanctions, based on agreement among the five Permanent Members of the Security Council, is envisaged 'from selective optional sanctions through an intermediate stage of selective mandatory sanctions reaching "comprehensive" mandatory sanctions'.[53] Thus a distinction is drawn between voluntary and mandatory sanctions. If voluntary sanctions follow a Security Council recommendation they may be assumed to have only moral and political weight; by contrast, if the Council chooses to urge mandatory sanctions (under the authority assigned by Article 39) then the proposed measures are binding and have the force of law. Thus, while the explicit wording of the Charter implies a *political* rather than a *legal* emphasis, decisions by the Council can convert a political judgement into a legal obligation. However, debate continues about the precise legal status of decisions made by the Security Council, if only because Permanent Members and ordinary members outside the Council are scarcely *equal before the law* (a primary requirement of licit statute).

Other problems have arisen about how to ensure the participation of non-members in the enforcement of sanctions measures. Thus Daoudi and Dajani, writing in the early 1980s, pointed out that various states (Switzerland, West Germany, East Germany, North Korea and South Korea) were not members of the United Nations, and emphasised that it was hard enough to ensure the good faith of members. Should non-members be obligated to observe sanctions resolutions made by a body in which they have no voice? Different international lawyers have given different answers.[54] And it was found also that the availability of the veto to Permanent Members could erode the power of the Security Council to discipline recalcitrant members. Powerful states (typically the Permanent Members) have never been challenged by the threat of UN sanctions; and regional bodies (such as the Organization of African Unity, the Organization of American States and the Arab League) have always felt free to impose their own sanctions regimes outside the deliberations of the UN Security Council.

The UN Charter carries no automatic sanctions provision equivalent to Article 16 of the League Covenant (a difference that has been represented as both strength and weakness). The power of a few UN Security Council members to impose sanctions on almost any targeted state arguably serves the *realpolitik* ambitions of the powerful against the weak, rather than providing a genuine basis for collective security. And in the post-Soviet world it is easy to see that the Security Council (lacking a strong counterweight to US power) has been suborned to a large extent into doing little beyond what the US State Department wants. A global organisation working for collective security seems manifestly desirable; but only if all UN members enjoy genuine 'sovereign equality' (according to Article 2 of the Charter), and where the Security Council is more than a convenient tool serving the commercial and strategic interests of the one surviving superpower.

It is useful to glance at UN involvement – minimal, appropriate or excessive – in some of the major international crises over the last half century. In all these cases the powerful option of economic sanctions was considered and then rejected or imposed (sometimes with genocidal consequences). The UN imposition of economic sanctions has always generated controversy, highlighting the disparate interests of different states. The disinterested international body striving for collective security which the United Nations may eventually become – does not yet exist.

The Berlin Blockade (1948–9)

In this crisis, one of the first significant events of the Cold War, the United Nations had minimal involvement. The issue was essentially about economic sanctions and Great-Power rivalries. It quickly illustrated UN impotence in circumstances when powerful states were reluctant to submit to its judgement.

In early 1948 the four-power Allied Control Council for Germany began negotiations about the introduction of a new currency in Germany, to restrain inflation and to reduce unemployment. On 20 March, with the talks in deadlock, the Soviet delegates withdrew after being denied a report on three-power talks in London. Ten days later, General Clay – without attempting to secure Soviet approval – announced a plan for currency reform. When the Russians were then refused permission to inspect Western military trains passing through Soviet-controlled territory to Berlin, they stopped all railway and river traffic and at the same time imposed comprehensive road blockades. The crisis escalated. On 20 May the American authorities closed its zonal borders to Soviet traffic; a month later, the new currency was introduced into the western parts of Berlin, whereupon the Russians halted all the remaining traffic into the city, including food supplies for the civilian population; on 28 June the famous air lift began, though many observers doubted that it would be able to carry enough supplies to keep the city alive; on 6 July the Russians offered to feed the entire population of Berlin[55] – an offer which the Western powers, sensing the opportunity for a great propaganda *coup* – rejected.

Now the Western powers (the United States, Britain and France) were busy organising an effective counter-blockade. Reparations deliveries to the Soviet Union were suspended; the United States and Britain blocked the shipment of goods to the Soviet zone of Berlin, and halted all rail traffic from non-German countries to the zone through the American and British zones; on 4 February the West stopped all the residual truck traffic to the Soviet zone; and on 20 March announced that the West mark would be the only legal tender in West Berlin. Subsequent talks between Soviet and Western representatives, including discussions with Stalin, achieved little, whereupon the pressures mounted for a UN involvement.

The Western powers were reluctant to refer the issue to the Security Council: a settlement under Chapter 6 of the Charter, stipulating a pacific resolution of the dispute, was unlikely since four of the five Permanent Members of the Council were parties to the crisis and able to exercise the veto. The option of imposing UN sanctions against the Soviet Union would clearly have been attractive to the West, but the Soviet power of veto obviously ruled out this course. For such reasons France and Britain saw little value in taking the matter to the Security Council but the United States was keen to achieve a substantial propaganda victory in the world forum.[56] There would be no attempt to invoke sanctions but a minor power on the Council would be encouraged to table a resolution urging the Soviet Union to lift the blockade: it was hoped that the use of the Soviet veto would expose the Russians in their true light.

In the event the small (non-Permanent) states on the Council, reluctant to serve American propaganda interests, tabled their own resolution. This was duly vetoed by the Soviet Union, affording the United States the hoped-for propaganda advantage. But this was a petty success. On 13 November President Herbert Evatt of the General Assembly and Secretary-General Trygve Lie urged the four powers to begin fresh negotiations. The appeal was rebuffed: Washington was enjoying the propaganda success of the Berlin air lift ('a striking psychological and political success for the West'[57]), though by early 1949 there were clear signs that the Soviet Union wanted an end to the affair. On 4 May the four-power representatives to the Security Council finally announced that the blockade and counterblockade would be ended; on 12 May 1949 this duly happened. The Berlin air lift continued until 30 September, when the first dangerous confrontation of the Cold War was brought to an end.

The Berlin blockade represented a classic case of economic sanctions – another city under siege. Here the sanctions were imposed by the decisions of sovereign states, with consideration and no more given to the possibility that the UN Security Council might be asked to impose economic sanctions of its own. The crisis (in particular, the air lift) is now generally recorded – in the true spirit of victors' history[58] – as a triumph for the West against the forces of evil. There is only rare mention of the provocation of a withheld report, the paradox of a Berlin 125 miles inside a Soviet zone agreed by the West, the refused Soviet offer to supply food, and American procrastination for propaganda advantage. The Security Council was unable to impose sanctions against the Soviet Union because of the Russian veto; but the West would have welcomed such a use of UN power. Washington scarcely knew in 1949 that the time would come when the Soviet veto was no more.

The Korea Question (1945–53)

The involvement of the United Nations in the Korea Question did not begin with the Korean War. Washington had encouraged a

Soviet incursion into North Korea as a strategic gambit in the Second World War, but with the collapse of the Japanese war effort in Asia the Soviet presence in the Korean peninsula was an embarrassment to the American strategists. Thus on 10–11 August 1945, during a night-long session of the State-War-Navy Co-ordinating Committee in Washington D.C., John J. McCloy, the Assistant Secretary of War, ordered two young colonels, Dean Rusk and Charles H. Bonesteel, to withdraw to an adjoining room and to decide where to draw a line on the map to divide Korea. This line, drawn arbitrarily at the 38th parallel, put Seoul in the southern (US) zone, and set the scene for a succession of repressive US-sustained dictatorships in the years that followed. The Korean War (1949–53), in which the North enjoyed substantial civilian support in the South, was essentially a conflict between Korean nationalists seeking to unify their country and Western imperialists determined to protect strategic outposts in Asia.[59]

The United States, maintaining a permanent military presence in South Korea, was keen to see the reunification of the peninsula under a pro-Western government. On 17 September 1947 the US State Department informed the Russians that the matter would be referred to the UN General Assembly (in which at that time Washington could rely on overwhelming support). The Assembly voted 41 to 6 (7 abstentions) to refer the issue to committee consideration, whereupon Moscow recommended that all foreign troops should be withdrawn from the peninsula to enable the Korean people to settle their differences. The proposal alarmed Washington: it was well known that the southern regime, massively unpopular, would quickly collapse without the support of American troops. On 14 November the Assembly voted (43 to 9, with 6 abstentions) for the creation of a UN Temporary Commission on Korea (UNTCOK) for the supervision of nationwide elections – which, in the event, were rigged to secure the appointment of the US-backed tyrant Syngman Rhee.

Clashes between the popular regime in the North and the tyranny in the South produced some 100,000 casualties in 1949 (the year in which the war began). On 25 June 1950, in a dramatic escalation of hostilities, Kim Il-sung's armies swept into the South. The United States, having split the country and installed a dictator, was now determined to protect its strategic position: Washington resolved to respond immediately and to seek United Nations support for American foreign policy. Thus Roy Jenkins (now Lord Jenkins of Hillhead) acknowledges that Truman 'authorised United States naval and air action sixteen hours in advance of the second UN resolution which gave him the authority of international legality'.[60] The Soviet

Union, boycotting the Security Council for its failure to seat the legitimate representatives of the People's Republic of China, was not present to veto crucial US-devised resolutions. In addition to the authorisation for military action (Resolutions 82 and 83; 25 and 27 June 1950, respectively), the Security Council stipulated a range of economic and other sanctions against North Korea.

On 30 June President Truman ordered a naval blockade of the Korean coast, at the same time imposing a total trade embargo against the North; on 16 December he invoked the Trading with the Enemy Act to terminate all US economic contracts with North Korea; and he took action to freeze the negligible North Korean assets in the United States. In addition, noting the Chinese involvement in the conflict – provoked by US threats to the border (Yalu River) – Truman also imposed an embargo against China and froze all Chinese assets in the United States. On 18 May 1951 the UN General Assembly voted 47 to 0 (8 abstentions: Afghanistan, Egypt, Burma, India, Indonesia, Pakistan, Sweden and Syria), with Soviet bloc countries not participating, to recommend that member states impose an arms embargo against the North (to include arms, ammunition, implements of war, and associated production items: atomic energy materials, oil, transportation materials of strategic value, etc). On 1–5 July, of the 55 replies to the UN concerning the implementation of the May resolution, 35 nations (including 5 non-members: West Germany, Italy, Spain, Vietnam and Laos) pledged complete support, while 8 Soviet bloc countries rejected the resolution as illegal In September 1952 the North Atlantic Treaty Organization (NATO) set up a second co-ordinating committee (CHINCOM), supplementing the original Co-ordinating Committee (COCOM), to deny North Korea access to industrial equipment and raw materials, and to impose new restraints on the North's use of shipping and bunkering. On 27 July 1953 an armistice was reached to bring the Korean War to an uncertain end – but the United States continued to prohibit all economic contact with North Korea in the interest of American Cold War policy.

The general UN embargo (Assembly Resolution 500, 18 May 1951) had added little to the strategic embargoes already set in place by the Western powers in their Cold War confrontation with the communist bloc, and the UN contribution – in terms of effective economic sanctions – has been judged to have been far from decisive:

The first United Nations experiment with collective measures of an economic nature was therefore incomplete, indecisive and inconclusive. The embargoes were not formally authorised by the

UN, were ancillary to the military effort and could be of only limited effect since China could, at that time, obtain military equipment from the Soviet Union and other Communist countries. The Korean armistice in July 1953 brought an end to all United Nations measures, though not to the Western embargoes.[61]

In the case of China, in the context of a powerful Soviet bloc, the American economic embargo signalled no more than the 'futility' of 'economic ostracism'. But a pattern had emerged that would evolve in the years ahead: UN economic sanctions would often operate in concert with economic measures adopted unilaterally by individual states or regional groups. The United Nations has never been able to supplant powerful nations and international alliances in seeking to protect their own perceived interests, often through the mechanism of economic measures.

South Africa and Apartheid (1948–94)

South Africa attracted the attention of the United Nations on two separate but related grounds. Most importantly, there was the issue of racist apartheid: the complex of white attitude, prejudice and law that worked for the permanent suppression of the black majority. Apartheid, having international consequences for the continent of Africa and elsewhere, clearly came within the scope of Article 39[62] of the UN Charter: 'The Security Council shall determine the existence of any threat to the peace, breach of the peace, or act of aggression and shall make recommendations, or decide what measures shall be taken ... to maintain or restore international peace and security.' It was unhelpful that racist attitudes were not absent from the UN Security Council: for example, Britain and France, both Permanent Members of the Council, were not prepared to support a 1960 resolution condemning the Sharpeville massacre.

The second ground for United Nations interest was the South African behaviour in South West Africa (later Namibia). Again the relevance of Article 39 was plain. As early as 1916 South West Africa had come under South African control when South African troops active in the First World War invaded the German colony on behalf of the British Empire. In 1920 the League of Nations, noting that the territory had been taken from Germany by the Treaty of Versailles, assigned South Africa with a mandate over South West Africa. Hence, in its wisdom, the League had extended the sway of an increasingly racist state over a vast area (822,909 sq. km). (It is important to recall how Britain helped to lay the basis for a racist South Africa. In

1899 Lord Milner declared that the 'ultimate end' of British policy in the area 'is a self-governing white community supported by well-treated and justly-governed black labour'. King Edward VII signed the South Africa Act in September 1909, so enshrining white racism in law. In 1911 the Union Parliament, building on the many British racist initiatives, passed the Mine and Works Act, blocking the access of black workers to skilled jobs. White South African racism, at least partly aired by British colonial prejudice, was well entrenched in attitude and law by the time the overtly racist Nationalist Party assumed power in 1948 and began to apply the odious policy of apartheid on a rigid basis.)

In April 1960 some 64 Africans were shot dead by the essentially white police force in Sharpeville, an event that provoked worldwide outrage. If anyone had doubted the brutal character of apartheid it was now plain for all to see. And the event was far from isolated. Other demonstrations were being mercilessly suppressed throughout South Africa, with the black casualties running into thousands. Majority opinion in the UN Security Council blamed the government's racial policies for the mounting toll of black African fatalities, recognised that the situation might endanger international peace, and urged the South African government to abandon apartheid. Britain and France refused to support the ensuing resolution (134, 1 April 1960), providing an unambiguous demonstration of their easy tolerance of the racist status quo. Soon the African states, with mounting international support, were demanding economic sanctions against the South African regime. In 1961, after emerging as a republic, South Africa withdrew from the Commonwealth, was increasingly being regarded as a pariah state (though covertly and overtly supported by powerful Western interests), and was progressively excluded from specialised UN agencies.

The UN General Assembly, with majority opinion increasingly incensed by the horrors of racist apartheid, began calling for economic sanctions against South Africa in 1962. Members were requested 'separately or collectively, in conformity with the Charter'

- to break diplomatic relations with South Africa or refrain from establishing them;
- to close ports to shipping flying the South African flag;
- to forbid their ships to enter South African ports;
- to boycott South African trade;
- to refuse landing or passage facilities to aircraft belonging to the government or to companies registered in that country.

The Assembly resolution (1761, XVII, 6 November 1962) established also the Special Committee on Apartheid for continuous review of South African racist policies, and urged the Security Council to respond to apartheid with economic sanctions and, if necessary, the expulsion of South Africa from the United Nations. On 19 October 1962 Francis T. P. Plimpton, the US representative to the United Nations, had already criticised the efficacy of economic sanctions against South Africa, at the same time declaring that the United States 'will continue to oppose' specific sanctions.[63] In this spirit the United States, Britain, the 'old' Commonwealth and Japan voted against Resolution 1761; most Latin American and Scandinavian countries abstained; and the Afro-Asians and the Soviet bloc voted in favour.

In June 1963 the Organization of African Unity was established – and immediately urged that economic sanctions be imposed on South Africa, that diplomatic links be severed, that overflight rights be denied, and that the United States make an overt choice between the emerging African states and the colonial powers. On 2 August Adlai E. Stevenson, the US ambassador to the United Nations, responded by confirming Washington's continued opposition to mandatory sanctions measures: 'The application of sanctions in this situation is not likely to bring about the practical result that we seek ... Punitive measures would only provoke intransigence and harden the existing situation ... .' But now the United States, pressured by world opinion, was being forced to shift its policies: by the end of 1963 there would be no fresh shipments of US-manufactured arms to the South African regime. On 7 August the Security Council adopted Resolution 181 (with United States support; Britain and France abstaining), calling on all states to voluntarily cease the shipment of arms to South Africa. Now the Council had acknowledged that the situation in South Africa was 'seriously disturbing' international peace and security. There were no votes against Resolution 181; but, significantly enough, a proposal for a trade boycott was defeated. The Special Committee on Apartheid continued to report the incidents of unrest and suppression in South Africa.

On 4 December 1963 the Security Council (with support from the United States, Britain and France) adopted Resolution 182 unanimously, calling for a ban on arms shipments (and on equipment for making arms) to South Africa. The Council unanimity was unprecedented, but Britain and France qualified their position by stating that they would distinguish between weapons that might be used for internal oppression and those that might be used for external defence. The United States, Britain and France continued to oppose the imposition of economic sanctions. In October 1964 the newly elected Labour government in Britain, seeking to strengthen the arms embargo, removed the Tory distinction between arms for internal suppression and national defence: as far as Britain was concerned, there would now be a total arms embargo.

It was now plain that the United States would continue to oppose any international pressure for economic sanctions, not least because the US had important commercial and strategic interests that weighed heavily against any mere ethical constraint. For example, by the end of 1963 the United States was negotiating the terms of future uranium purchases from South Africa: in comparison with the desirable capacity to incinerate millions of civilians the need to put economic pressure on a racist regime was a trivial matter. But many states were continuing to press for economic sanctions. In April 1964 a Group of Experts appointed by the UN Secretary-General urged South Africa to convene a National Convention 'fully representative of the whole population' to chart a new political way forward for South Africa – a proposal that the government immediately rejected. The Group also recommended that the option of economic sanctions be considered. By now the United States, while continuing to oppose any movement towards a comprehensive economic blockade, was increasingly sensitive to the mounting international pressure for economic action against racist apartheid. Washington resolved to act, but not in a way that would seriously undermine the South African regime: loans from the US Export-Import Bank (Eximbank) were restricted; the US voting power in the IMF was used to block the purchase of South African gold; and moves were taken to restrict capital flows into South Africa. By contrast, India was now imposing a total trade embargo.

The unwillingness of South Africa to place the mandated South West Africa (in 1968 renamed Namibia by the UN) under international trusteeship or to allow the territory an independent status was also attracting international criticism. (At the same time South Africa was refusing to apply the mandatory UN sanctions on Rhodesia – see below.) On 21 October 1966 the UN General Assembly passed Resolution 2145 (114 to 2; 3 abstentions) to end the South African mandate for South West Africa, so nominally placing the territory under UN administration.[64] The international pressure on South Africa continued, though always falling short of full economic sanctions. In June 1968 the IMF, under US pressure, refused to purchase gold from South Africa at prices in excess of $35 per ounce – a form of economic sanction, albeit limited.[65] The voluntary arms embargo was extended on 23 July 1970, via the mechanism of Security Council Resolution 282, again signalling the extent of the international hostility to apartheid; but the world opposition to institutionalised racism remained mixed. In November 1973 the Organization of Arab Petroleum-Exporting Countries (OAPEC) imposed an oil embargo, whereupon Iran, unwilling to comply, became South Africa's major oil supplier.

In 1976 riots in Soweto and elsewhere throughout South Africa led to hundreds of black casualties; but even now it proved impossible to secure a mandatory UN resolution for economic sanctions. On 4 November 1977 the Security Council passed Resolution 418, declaring that the arms trade with South Africa – but not apartheid *per se* – was a threat to peace under Article 39 of the UN Charter. France, formerly hostile to UN constraints on its arms trade, announced that existing contracts would be honoured but that no further arms sales would be permitted. On 13 December the UN General Assembly recommended to the Security Council that a mandatory oil embargo be imposed; but the abstentions of the United States, Britain, France and other countries denied the Council resolution its necessary majority. Efforts to deny the South African security forces access to arms received a mild boost when President Jimmy Carter issued regulations (22 February 1978) prohibiting the export or re-export of any item to South Africa or Namibia if the exporter 'knows ' or has reason to know' that the item will be 'sold to or used by or for' the police or the military in South Africa.

Through the 1980s the UN General Assembly continued to agitate for an effective Security Council response to the continued abuses of the black majorities of South Africa and Namibia; but was continually frustrated by the residual and unambiguous racism of the United States, Britain, France and other countries. Premier Margaret Thatcher in Britain remained steadfastly hostile to the imposition of effective sanctions against white racism (and was later enthusiastic about the genocidal sanctions on the Iraqi civilian population after the 1990 invasion of Kuwait – itself largely indistinguishable in ethics and law from the continued South African occupation and abuse of Namibia). President Ronald Reagan continued to provide *de facto* support for the South African regime, linking the South African withdrawal from Namibia to the withdrawal of Cuban troops from Angola: 'Washington thereby dismantled collective Western diplomatic pressure on Pretoria and provided the issue of Cuban troops as a rationale for a prolonged South African military presence in Namibia.'[66] Now Reagan was urging a policy of 'constructive engagement' with South Africa – a euphemism for the continued American tolerance for institutionalised racism.

On 13 December 1984 the Security Council reaffirmed the mandatory embargo (1977) of arms exports to South Africa, unanimously requesting that 'all states refrain from importing arms ammunition of all types and military vehicles produced in South Africa'. Again the option of further steps was being discussed by the UN Special Committee against Apartheid: in June 1986, fearing that the Committee was moving to propose radical measures – possibly even an effective economic response to the continuation of apartheid – the United States, Britain, West Germany and other states boycotted the Committee proceedings. On 28 February 1987 the United States, Britain and West Germany voted in the Security Council against mandatory sanctions. There was still no prospect of effective economic sanctions that would have hurt Pretoria. On 10 September 1989 a UN panel on sanctions called for tightened financial sanctions, supplementing the various unilateral actions taken by many US and UK companies. On 21 March 1990 Sam Nujoma, the former leader of the South West Africa People's Organization (SWAPO), was inaugurated as president of an independent Namibia.

By the end of the 1980s it was clear that South African apartheid was doomed. Despite the failure of the UN Security Council to impose mandatory economic sanctions on the racist regime a *de facto* worldwide embargo had gained strength over the years, inspired in part by ethical awareness and in part by a cynical calculation of likely commercial advantage in a future black-governed state. In February 1990, after President F. W. de Klerk had unbanned the African National Congress (ANC), Nelson Mandela was released from jail (to be elected the ANC president in 1991). In April Mandela condemned Thatcher's opposition to sanctions and emphasised that the economic and other sanctions that had been maintained by the EC, despite the failure of the United Nations, 'have given us tremendous strength'.[67] The mandatory UN arms embargo against South Africa had been porous,[68] but – allied to the robust indigenous struggle – had helped to end the illicit occupation of Namibia. At the beginning of 1993 Mandela told a news conference that he would recommend the ending of international sanctions against South Africa in return for job creation: if agreement could be reached on early non-racial elections, 'I would say to my organisation [the ANC] Let's lift sanctions now.' Within a year, before the scheduled elections had taken place, the sanctions were nominally at an end, though capital was still flowing out of the country.[69] The long-anticipated non-racial elections took place over three days (26–28 April 1994), with the African National Congress securing nearly two-thirds of the seats in the National Assembly. On 25 May the UN Security Council passed Resolution 919, lifting the mandatory arms embargo and other restrictions on South Africa; dissolving the Special Committee on

Apartheid; and stressing the urgent need to facilitate South Africa's reintegration into the international community.

The United Nations had failed to impose comprehensive economic sanctions on the apartheid regime, though the mandatory arms embargo had a substantial affect. The international sanctions imposed unilaterally by various companies, factions and states had an impact, though there is debate about its scale and significance.[70] In one assessment, South Africa became skilful in circumventing economic sanctions (which in any case were 'relatively mild and enforced only loosely'). The OAPEC embargo on oil was undercut by Iran's willingness to continue supplying Pretoria, and South Africa had stockpiled, developed nuclear energy, and invested in synthetic fuels. The block on arms shipments was successful: 'However, the arms embargo did prevent South Africa from obtaining highly sophisticated weapons systems, particularly fighter planes, and seems to have contributed to South Africa's willingness to withdraw from Namibia. Thus, we conclude that the UN sanctions ... made a modest contribution to a partially positive outcome.'[71]

Portugal and Colonialism (1960–74)

On 15 December 1960 the UN General Assembly voted to classify Portugal's African colonies as 'non-self-governing' territories, thus rendering them subject to the provisions of the UN Charter on decolonisation. The Resolution (1542, XV) notes an earlier resolution (742, VIII, 27 November 1953) in which there is approval of factors to be used 'as a guide in determining whether any particular territory falls within the scope of Chapter XI of the UN Charter'.[72] The Resolution also recognises 'that the desire for independence is the rightful aspiration of peoples under colonial subjugation and that the denial of their right to self-determination constitutes a threat to the well-being of humanity and to international peace'; and subsequently lists the territories under Portuguese administration that could be properly regarded as 'Non-Self-Governing Territories within the meaning of Chapter XI': The Cape Verde Archipelago, Portuguese Guinea, São Tomé and Principe, São João Batista de Ajudá, Angola, Mozambique, Goa, Macau and Timor. Resolution 1542 declared the obligation on Portugal to provide information concerning the listed territories, and requested the Portuguese government to provide such information to the UN Secretary-General.

The Portuguese response to the UN charges was a familiar one in the history of colonial apologetics: the listed territories were not 'colonies' but inherent parts of the Portuguese state.[73] On 4 February

1961 an armed rebellion broke out in Angola, to be followed two months later by a similar revolt in Guinea. Such events, linked to international awareness of Portugal's colonial history, induced the UN General Assembly to begin passing a series of resolutions calling for the imposition of economic sanctions against Portugal to force recognition of the principle of self-determination for its African territories. On 25 September 1964 an armed revolt broke out in Mozambique, compounding the growing insecurity in the far-flung Portuguese empire. By 1971 estimates suggested that Portugal was spending more than $400 million on a war on several fronts.

In 1963 the Organization of African Unity (OAU) adopted a resolution declaring an economic and diplomatic boycott of Portugal, and calling on the Western powers (particular the United States and Britain) 'to cease all direct and indirect support to Portugal'. On 21 December 1965 the General Assembly passed a resolution (66 to 25) calling for an economic and arms boycott against Portugal until the African colonies were freed; the same resolution was passed by large margins in every subsequent session until December 1973. As usual, the Security Council, with Permanent Members sympathetic to Portugal, refused to endorse the Assembly views. Instead, the Council passed two recommendatory resolutions (180, 31 July 1963; 218, 23 November 1965) calling for a ban on arms and equipment for manufacturing military *matériel* that could be used for the suppression of indigenous peoples. The Council gestures were empty: 'For Western countries, strategic and trade links with a fellow member of NATO took precedence over concern about Portugal's colonial policy.'[74] The colonial territories would be liberated by the mounting guerrilla war, if at all, and not by economic pressure exerted by the United States and the other Western powers. On 29 August 1970 the OAU adopted a resolution condemning the United States, Britain, France and West Germany for their 'massive support' of Portugal.

On 14 December the General Assembly adopted a resolution requesting withdrawal of international support for the construction of the Cabora Bassa dam in Mozambique (Sweden had already withdrawn support in 1969; Italy had followed suit by the end of 1970). The Assembly resolution, sensitive to the plight of colonial peoples, noted that the project was intended 'to perpetuate the domination, exploitation and oppression of the people of this part of Africa by the Government of Portugal'. In May 1971 the US State Department expressed its opposition, supported by anti-apartheid Congressmen, to the Cabora Bassa project; while at the same time General Electric, formerly interested in the scheme, withdrew its application for an associated Export-Import Bank loan. West Germany continued to support the project. On 22 May 1973 the United States and Britain vetoed a Security Council resolution to extend the trade sanctions already in place against the rebellious regime in Rhodesia (see below) to South Africa and the Portuguese lands In Africa. Again, nothing was being accomplished through the Council: radical opinion in the Assembly could always be blocked by the pro-Portugal states in the Security Council.

On 21 November 1973 the OAU adopted a resolution appealing to all member states of the organisation and all friendly countries to 'impose a total economic embargo, and in particular an oil embargo, against Israel, Portugal, South Africa and the minority regime in Rhodesia'. Three days later, some OAU ministers threatened to take 'diplomatic and economic measures' against the United States and some European countries if they continued to support the white regimes in Africa and elsewhere. In April 1974 a *coup d' état* brought an end to the Salazar regime in Portugal; and independence for Angola and Mozambique followed in 1975.

The Portuguese episode again illustrated the failure of the UN Security Council to address the essence of an issue well covered by the terms of the Charter. The pro-Portugal Permanent Members on the Council continued to block the majority Assembly opinion to the end, not least because Portugal had been admitted to NATO in 1949 and so provided the United States and Britain with strategic access to African territories: 'At the same time, the economic potential of the Portugese African possessions ... represented vast raw-material resources for the industries of the NATO countries, so there was even more reason to give military support to Portugal despite the growing disapproval of public opinion in the NATO countries themselves.'[75]

The United Nations had again proved largely ineffectual. No attempt was made to impose comprehensive economic sanctions on a plainly recalcitrant state. On the contrary, the most powerful members of the Security Council were directly supporting Portugal in its struggle to maintain colonial control. Sanctions imposed by the OAU and other factions had some affect, but the independence of the colonial territories was purchased largely by the blood of indigenous peoples: 'The OAU did not itself vigorously claim that its sanctions had, to a significant degree, contributed ... most observers would agree that the liberation struggles in the Portuguese possessions of Angola, Guinea and Mozambique were more instrumental in ousting the regime.'[76] The United Nations had not yet succeeded in saving people 'from the scourge of war'.

Rhodesia and UDI (1962–79)

In 1962 the UN General Assembly affirmed that South Rhodesia was a 'non-self-governing territory', and called upon Britain to convene a constitutional conference at which all the political parties would be represented. The United Kingdom was required also 'to take immediate steps to restore all rights to the non-European population ...'. However, elections were staged in November under the racist 1961 constitution, with Ian Smith's Rhodesian Front Party supplanting the United Federal Party. The UN Security Council then voted on a resolution requiring the United Kingdom not to transfer sovereignty to South Rhodesia until 'fully representative government had been established'. Britain, like any colonial power keen to prevent any external interference in its affairs, vetoed the resolution on the ground that British acquiescence would prevent an 'orderly devolution' of power to the artificial Federation of Rhodesia and Nyasaland (doomed to collapse at the end of 1963).

The Rhodesian Front Party had declared its aim of independence. A rigged referendum in November 1964 (with 60 per cent of the predominantly white electorate going to vote) yielded 89 per cent in favour of independence, whereupon the new Labour government in Britain warned that a Unilateral Declaration of Independence (UDI) would be illegal, would turn Southern Rhodesia into a pariah state, and would bring immediate economic retaliation. The former British government had negotiated with Ian Smith for months, seeking to secure a compromise between the interests of the 250,000 whites and the 4 million blacks: Smith had long demanded a constitution that would enshrine white minority rule for an indefinite period, while the black Africans were insisting that 'one person, one vote' was the only option. It had seemed for some time that the two positions, albeit extremes, could be reconciled but when Harold Wilson's Labour government was elected in October no agreement had been reached.

On 11 November 1965 Ian Smith announced his UDI, an illegal Proclamation of Independence couched in convoluted language reminiscent of the eighteenth-century American Declaration of Independence. On the same day, Wilson condemned the act as illegal, a rebellion against the Crown; and instructed the Governor of Rhodesia to inform Ian Smith and his colleagues that they no longer held office. There now followed the progressive imposition of economic sanctions by Britain and other states, which after a year would be reinforced by mandatory UN sanctions. In the event various companies (in particular, key oil suppliers – see Figure 2.1) and various Rhodesia-friendly states (mainly South Africa and Portugal, with possible British connivance[77]) conspired to circumvent sanctions and to sustain the racist Smith regime.

Premier Wilson had already declared to the British House of Commons that there would be no use of force to end the illegal seizure of power in Rhodesia – an obvious 'green light' encouragement to the Smith government contemplating UDI. Now Wilson had no option but to confront the rebellion with economic sanctions that over the following months and years would prove to be porous and ineffectual. The British sanctions were applied progressively over the three months that followed the UDI announcement, a protracted campaign that suggested little prior UK planning to counter the UDI

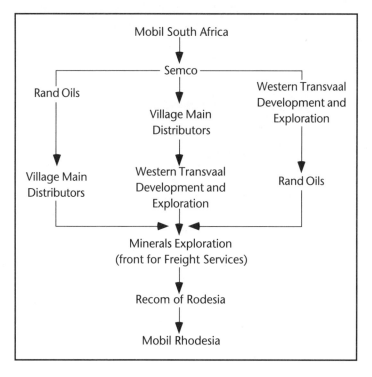

Figure 2.1   Mobil paper-chase to defeat sanctions on Rhodesia

Note: Semco, on receiving lubricants from Mobil, would feed them through three different routes to disguise the sale. Lubricants, fed through five 'paper' companies, finally reached Mobil Rhodesia.

Source: Martin Bailey, *Oilgate*, London, 1979, p. 29.

contingency. All British aid to Rhodesia was stopped; Rhodesian sterling assets in London were frozen; Rhodesia was excluded from the sterling area; the export of capital to Rhodesia was prohibited; and the London capital market for Rhodesian dealings was closed. The governor and directors of the Rhodesian Reserve Bank (with its frozen £10 million) were suspended and a new board appointed. On 11 November British territories were prohibited from importing Rhodesian tobacco and sugar; on 17 December oil exports to Rhodesia were banned; by 30 January 1966 a total ban on exports was imposed; and by the end of February a total ban on imports.[78]

Commonwealth and many other countries quickly followed Britain's lead. In December 1965 the OAU imposed a total economic boycott, a ban on communication, and a denial of overflying rights. At the same time the United States and France were imposing oil embargoes, with the United States banning all exports to Rhodesia in March 1966.[79] On 20 November 1965 the unilateral initiatives by individual states were reinforced by Security Council Resolution 217, calling on UN members to withhold recognition of the new Rhodesian regime, to offer no aid or support, to sever all economic relations with Rhodesia, and to embargo all oil exports to that country. In February 1966 the British navy began its blockade of the Mozambique port of Beira in a nominal attempt to deny Rhodesia access to oil (as noted, an essentially futile and duplicitous exercise[80]).

On 16 December 1966 the Security Council passed Resolution 232, imposing mandatory but selective sanctions covering imports of Rhodesian asbestos, iron ore, chrome, pig iron, sugar, tobacco, copper, meat, hides and skins, and leather goods; and covering also exports to Rhodesia of arms, equipment for the manufacture of arms, aircraft, oil and motor vehicles. It was significant that the worth of Resolution 232 depended entirely on enabling legislation by UN member states; and that only new contracts were affected.[81] On 29 May 1968 Council Resolution 253 imposed further mandatory sanctions on Rhodesian imports and exports, as well as banning air transport and withdrawing consular and trade representatives. It was subsequently found that sanctions were being violated about 50 times a year, with a few important cases exposed by investigative journalists. Council Resolution 333 (1973) called upon member states to punish any of their citizens dealing with clients in South Africa, Mozambique, Angola, Guinea and Namibia if it became known that such clients 'were shipping goods to or from Rhodesia'.[82] Council Resolution 388 (1976) aimed to forbid the insuring of commodities in Rhodesia and exports to and imports from that country.

It was now clear that the days of white minority rule in Rhodesia were coming to a close – not so much because of international sanctions, which were being widely circumvented by Rhodesia-friendly companies and states, but because of the growing successes of radical movements in the region. Portugal was losing control in its African colonies (Angola and Mozambique) and South Africa was being forced to confront an increasingly confident indigenous rebellion. The United States and Britain, perceiving that Western interests might soon be swept away in a tide of black radicalism, sought to limit the damage. In August 1976 the South African premier B. J. Vorster, under heavy American pressure, imposed economic sanctions on the Smith regime to force Rhodesian acceptance of a plan hatched by US Secretary of State Henry Kissinger for a transition to majority rule over two years; sanctions would be lifted and a $1 billion development fund made available. Black leaders rejected the plan since it involved continued white control during the transitional period.

Now Ian Smith himself was being compelled to accept that 'whites only' rule was no longer an option. In March 1978 his 'Internal Settlement' plan, supported by three major black leaders, produced a black majority in the Rhodesian parliament and a black Prime Minister (Bishop Muzorewa). But Smith's so-called 'Settlement', contrived to secure a pliant white-friendly administration, was rejected by the two principal black radical parties: the Zimbabwe African People's Union (ZAPU) and the Zimbabwe African Nationalist Union (ZANU). The guerrilla war continued (12,000 dead by the end of 1978) – involving attacks on agricultural regions, the shooting down of Air Rhodesia planes and the bombing of the Salisbury oil depot (the damage cost around £10 million in foreign exchange). Robert Mugabe's ZANU and Joshua Nkomo's ZAPU, now loosely united in the Patriotic Front, were pledged to secure unqualified black majority rule.

Now Britain's pro-Smith premier Thatcher was reluctantly convinced that the 'Internal Settlement' was impractical. At the Lancaster House Conference (December 1979) an agreement was signed between the radical black leaders and representatives of the white minority, acceding to black majority rule in Rhodesia. It was finally possible for the international sanctions to be lifted. Rhodesia reverted to colonial rule by a British governor until the long-imagined elections under universal suffrage could be held. The sanctions – unilateral or UN-mandated – had been comprehensively violated by Portugal, South Africa and other states; and many British companies (perhaps with the connivance of the British authorities) had helped the racist Smith regime to survive over the long and bloody years. Wilson, seen by many as having betrayed the black cause, faced a walk-out by the bulk of the African delegates at the United Nations. Black Africans, through armed struggle, had eventually managed to overthrow the white racist government – despite all the sanctions-busting, the illegal support provided to Smith by other racist regimes, and all the procrastination at the United Nations. On 18 April 1980 Robert Gabriel Mugabe became the first black Prime Minister of a truly independent Zimbabwe.

On 21 December 1979 the Security Council had already passed Resolution 460, lifting sanctions – a decision anticipated by Britain (12 December) and the United States (16 December).[83] The sanctions against Rhodesia, 'while not bringing an immediate result, contributed to the process of undermining white rule ... but the guerrilla war, the independence of Angola and Mozambique, and pressure from South Africa for a settlement were probably of greater direct significance'.[84] In the short term the sanctions promoted 'self-reliance in the economy'; over the long term 'the economic and moral weight of sanctions ... contributed to a negotiated settlement'.[85] Again the contribution of economic and other sanctions had proved ambiguous. Perhaps at best they had served to strengthen the mounting people's resistance to a racist regime that continued throughout its history to enjoy the support of powerful foreign factions, companies and governments. When Rhodesia became Zimbabwe it was plain above all that a national people had won a significant victory. But would they be allowed to build on their success?

Libya and Lockerbie (1991–)

A distinction should be made between unilateral US sanctions against Libya (see Chapter 3) and those nominally authorised by the United Nations (that is, by a US-dominated Security Council): the same distinction applies to a number of other countries. The underlying principle upheld by Washington is that unilateral action can be taken against states that threaten perceived American interests, but that the imprimatur of UN 'authority' is helpful whenever it can be secured. The US task in this regard was eased by the 1991 collapse of the Soviet Union (and the consequent removal of the Soviet veto in the Security Council), but still there remained important constraints on American international hegemony: US efforts to suborn the Security Council are not always successful.

On 21 December 1988 a Pan Am jet, Flight PA 103, was flying high over the Scottish borders; the Boeing 747–121, *Maid of the Seas*, was travelling from London's Heathrow to New York's John F. Kennedy airport. At about 7.03 p.m. a small terrorist bomb exploded in the cargo hold, tearing a hole in the fuselage and blasting debris into the void. The plane's electrical power supply was severed and there was no chance of even sending a distress call. Wreckage and human victims were scattered over Lockerbie and the surrounding countryside. When the wings, carrying more than 200,000 pounds of aviation fuel, crashed into Sherwood Crescent, a small street adjoining the main A74 Glasgow–England road, the resulting blast registered 1.6 at a nearby seismic monitoring station and the fireball was visible more than six miles away.

On 19 September 1989 a French DC-10 airliner, UTA 772, left Brazzaville in the Congo, stopped briefly in Chad, and then flew north across the Sahara. At about 1.00 p.m. a terrorist bomb ripped the aircraft apart, killing all the passengers and crew. Debris and mutilated passengers were spewed over 640 square kilometres in the Niger Ténéré desert, the result of the worst terrorist outrage that France had suffered.

The two terrorist outrages, in which several hundred people died, followed a number of American terrorist acts – which may or may not have motivated vengeance seekers. On 15 April 1986 American aircraft flew from Britain bases and carriers in the Mediterranean to bomb Libyan targets in Tripoli and Benghazi. There were several hundred Libyan casualties, including Colonel Gaddafi's wife Safia, three of the couple's children (all of whom suffered pressure shock from a 2000 lb bomb that hit their house), and Gaddafi's 16-month-old adopted daughter, Hanna, who died from her brain injuries.[86] The US National Security Council (NSC) had prepared a prior statement describing Gaddafi's death as 'fortuitous'; and an official who had helped plan the bombing raids admitted that 'We hoped to get him.'[87] The assassination attempt had failed but Washington, soon to be happy with the results of the UN-authorised onslaught on Iraq (Chapter 5), would be quick to exploit its dominance of the UN Security Council in the post-Soviet world.

The United States decided in mid-1991 that Libya was to be charged with full responsibility for the Lockerbie and UTA DC-10 bombing outrages – a strategic ploy that introduced the option of UN-mandated sanctions against the Gaddafi regime. Many observers noted the blatant American 'U-turn': formerly Washington had been keen to point the finger of blame at other likely suspect countries and factions (primarily Iran, Syria and various Palestinian groups), but was now keen to transfer the guilt away from states that had been usefully supportive of US strategy in the 1991 Gulf War. Libya was ordered to hand over two suspects, Amin Fhimah and Abdelbaset al-Megrahi, for trial in the United States or Scotland – with the threat of sanctions if Libya refused to comply. Already there was talk in the United States and Britain of involving the United Nations. Washington had bribed and intimidated the Security Council into supporting its Iraq policy; now the same might be done over Libya.

London and Washington were soon floating the idea of a worldwide trade embargo on Libya, and declaring that the option of military force could not be ruled out – so violating Article 2(4) of the UN Charter (All Members shall refrain in their international relations from the threat or use of force against the territorial integrity or political independence of any state'). On 20 January 1992, after Western charges against Libya had been lodged with the United Nations, the Security Council unanimously passed Resolution 731 in which the Council

1. Condemns the destruction of Pan Am flight 103 and UTA flight 772 and the resultant loss of hundreds of lives;
2. Strongly deplores the fact that the Libyan Government has not yet responded effectively to the above requests to cooperate fully in establishing responsibility for the terrorist acts ...
3. Urges the Libyan Government immediately to provide a full and effective response to those requests so as to contribute to the elimination of international terrorism ...

Then the UN Secretary-General Boutros Boutros-Ghali, in his own report on the mounting crisis, suggested that a 'certain evolution' in the Libyan position should be recognised before any further action was taken; this procrastination 'irritated London and Washington'.[88] Washington, reliably supported by a supine Britain, was now striving to achieve UN-mandated sanctions against Libya – a posture that was in direct violation of relevant international law, the 1971 Montreal Convention.[89]

This Convention, enacted under the auspices of the International Civil Aviation Organization (ICAO) and properly lodged with the United Nations (according to Article 102 of the Charter), was the proper legal instrument for addressing the Lockerbie and UTA DC-10 outrages. The United States, Britain and Libya were all signatories to the Convention but *its explicit wording did not serve the cynical strategic posture of the Western powers*. In particular, while placing obligations on Libya, the Convention protected the Libyan right *not* to extradite the two suspects:

Article 7: The Contracting State in the territory of which the alleged offender is found shall, if it does not extradite him, be obliged, without exception whatsoever and whether or not the offence was committed in its territory, to submit the case to its competent authorities for the purpose of prosecution ...

Article 8(2): If a Contracting State which makes extradition conditional on the existence of a treaty receives a request for extradition from another Contracting State with which it has no extradition treaty, it may *at its option* consider this Convention as the legal basis for extradition ... . (my italics)

In short, since Libya had no extradition treaty with either the United States or Britain it was under no legal obligation to surrender the two suspects for trial. It *was* under obligation to observe the terms of the Convention – which in fact it did: in deliberately ignoring the demands of the Convention *in toto*, the United States and Britain were blatantly violating relevant international law.[90]

Washington and London, well aware of the inconvenient terms of the Montreal Convention, knew that they stood a better chance of punishing Libya if they were to rely on the US-dominated UN Security Council. After a slight delay, to allow time for appropriate arm-twisting, Washington secured Resolution 748 (31 March 1992), the first of the UN sanctions resolutions against Libya. The Resolution, passed by a vote of 10 to 0 (5 abstentions: China, Cape Verde, India, Morocco and Zimbabwe), gave Colonel Gaddafi until the end of Ramadan on 15 April to hand over the accused men. If he failed to do so, the Security Council (under the terms of 748) 'decides that all States shall'

– deny aircraft overflight permission if 'destined to land in or has taken off from the territory of Libya, unless ... approved on grounds of significant humanitarian need ...'
– prohibit 'the supply of any aircraft or aircraft components to Libya, the provision of engineering and maintenance servicing of Libyan aircraft or aircraft components, the certification of airworthiness ... the payment of new claims against existing insurance contracts, and the provision of new direct insurance for Libyan aircraft ...'
– prohibit the supply of arms to Libya, including 'weapons and ammunition, military vehicles and equipment, paramilitary police equipment, and spare parts ... any types of equipment, supplies and grants of licensing arrangements' for arms manufacture.

In addition, Resolution 748 was intended to prohibit the training of Libyans in military and related areas, to ensure the withdrawal of military advisors, to reduce the staff quotas at Libyan diplomatic missions and consular posts, and to prevent the operation of all Libyan Arab Airlines offices. Such measures, while not without a significant impact on the conduct of Libyan affairs, fell far short of comprehensive economic sanctions. Washington was now preparing the ground for tougher measures.

On 11 November 1993 the Security Council passed Resolution 883 by a vote of 11 to 0 (4 abstentions: China, Djibouti, Morocco and Pakistan), a substantial blow against the Libyan economy. Washington had still not succeeded in blocking Libyan oil sales, that would have crippled the economy and eroded Gaddafi's power base, but 883 was clearly intended to strike at Libyan oil refining and exports. Paragraph 3 of the resolution prohibits the exporting to Libya of a wide range of equipment (listed in the 883 Annex) that is essential to the oil industry:

– Pumps of medium or large capacity (capacity equal to or larger than 350 cubic metres per hour);
– Gas turbines and electric motors (use to aid transportation of crude oil and natural gas);
– Loading buoys, single point moorings, flexible hoses and anchor chains (all used in crude oil export terminals);
– Large loading pumps, boosting pumps, pipe inspection tools, pipe cleaning devices and large-capacity metering equipment ('not specifically designed for use on crude oil export terminals but which ... can be used for this purpose');
– Boilers, furnaces, fractionation columns, catalytic reactors and prepared catalysts (all used for oil refining);
– Spare parts (for all the listed items).

The obvious aim of 883 was to achieve a progressive crippling of the Libyan oil industry: as equipment fell into disrepair it would be difficult to replace, so producing a gradual erosion of oil-producing capacity. It was possible to argue also that the prohibition on the supply of pumps and other equipment might strike at Gaddafi's most ambitious project, the Great Man-Made River, designed to vastly extend Libyan irrigation and to contribute to national food self-sufficiency. The United States had not been able to achieve a ban on the purchase of Libyan oil, not least because the European powers had been unwilling to agree an embargo that would have seriously damaged their own energy-hungry economies. Washington had therefore been forced to accept a compromise package: one that would progressively affect Libyan oil production (and so Libyan revenues) and perhaps hit also at food production.[91]

Libya responded by denouncing the hostile Western policies that were now embellished by nominal UN authority. The Libyan Foreign Ministry expressed its 'displeasure and deep regret' at the new UN sanctions and reaffirmed 'the serious and sincere will of Libya to reach a solution to this artificial crisis as soon as possible'. Opinion in the West was split: some commentators suggested that the new sanctions would have little impact, with other observers predicting tougher measures to come. One pundit, Mehdi Varzi of Kleinwort Benson, noted: 'This won't hurt their output today, but the US is sending a warning to the Libyans that if these sanctions don't work, the next lot are really going to affect their oil industry.'[92] Few commentators were prepared to argue that the new sanctions were a genuinely UN, rather than an American, initiative.

The United States continued to agitate for a strengthening of sanctions, while international opinion outside America and Europe became increasingly hostile to the years-long punishment of Libya. Washington, with a weak case in argument and in continuous violation of international law,[93] found itself in growing isolation on the Libya Question. For example, at the opening session of the African Congress (April 1994) in Kampala, Yuri Museveni, the Ugandan President, condemned the unjust measures imposed by the Security Council and called for a lifting of sanctions. (At the same Congress there were calls for compensation for Libya to be paid by the former colonisers.) In May 1994 a Libyan health minister highlighted the suffering being inflicted on the Libyan people by the US-sustained sanctions: by mid-1995 it was estimated that some 2000 Libyans and others, prevented from flying abroad for desperately needed medical attention, had died because of sanctions (the six-year-old Safaa Abdel Rasoul was one of the many Libyans, Egyptians and Palestinians who had died for this reason). On 29 June 1994 the Algerian President, Al Amin Al Zirwal, condemned the sanctions regime as an unjust manipulation of the Security Council by Western countries. In November Radio Tehran reported that Iran was keen to develop its technical and industrial co-operation with Libya, so flouting the spirit of the UN sanctions; and a month later a committee of international lawyers declared in New York that the sanctions imposed on Libya by the Security Council should be lifted and that attention should be given to the Libyan proposals adopted by the Arab League, the Non-Aligned Movement, the Islamic Conference Organization and the Organization of African Unity.

In the face of mounting international opinion, Washington worked to toughen the sanctions regime, but with little support from its Western allies. In March 1995 the White House proposed a worldwide ban on Libyan oil to force the surrender of the two Libyan suspects; America's European allies were reportedly 'surprised' at the move and treated the proposal with 'scepticism'. It was soon obvious that the United States would be unable to impose a comprehensive oil embargo. In April the sanctions were breached when Libyan pilgrims ('ready for martyrdom') flew to Mecca in Saudi Arabia. Six months later, at the 50th session of the UN General Assembly (12–13 October 1995), extensive calls were made for the lifting of sanctions. The American efforts to toughen sanctions had come to nothing, with Washington forced to admit that there was no international support for a comprehensive oil embargo. Said one American diplomat: 'Soundings from the highest level of the British government have not been encouraging. Their political judgement was that opening the issue at this time might even weaken the consensus rather than strengthen it.' A principal consideration was that Italy, Germany and Spain were currently buying nearly 80 per cent of their oil imports from Libya; and that even Britain over the previous year had sold around £195 million worth of goods to the Gaddafi regime. In this context there was a growing *de facto* and *de jure* rupture of the sanctions regime, even to the extent that aircraft parts were being smuggled to Libya from the United States, Britain and Germany.[94] In early September 1996 an Iranian ship carrying arms and explosives was reportedly about to arrive in Libya in violation of UN sanctions. Two months later, the UN General Assembly adopted a Libyan resolution (by a vote of 56 to 4, with 76 abstentions) calling for a repeal of US laws that impose penalties on companies and citizens of other countries.

In September 1997 the Arab League explicitly called on its 21 members to ease the UN-imposed air embargo on Libya, so provoking the wrath of the Western powers on the Security Council. A British diplomat commented: 'If groups of countries are encouraged to take actions to defy the United Nations and measures which have been agreed collectively, it will gradually turn the UN into a body with no influence.' A month later, Washington was incensed to learn that Nelson Mandela planned to visit President Gaddafi, so lending the Libyan regime an unwelcome respectability. The US State Department commented that it would be 'disappointed' if the visit went ahead. Mandela responded in Johannesburg by declaring that he was 'master of his own fate'; and added: 'Libya was one of those countries that supported us during our struggle when others were working with the apartheid regime. Now they have the arrogance to dictate to us where we should go.' At the same time reports from government sources in Rome indicated that Italy was seeking to restore diplomatic relations with the Gaddafi regime.

The United States was now forced to confront a further challenge to its policy on Libya. In February 1998 the International Court of Justice at The Hague (the World Court) ruled that, contrary to the claims of Washington and London, it had jurisdiction in the Lockerbie case. Now there was a real chance that the relevance of the 1971 Montreal Convention would be given an authoritative Court recognition for the first time, so undermining the entire case for sanctions. The World Court ruling immediately stimulated an international chorus for an end to the sanctions regime. For example, at the 34th summit of the Organization of African Unity (OAU) an important statement was issued on the sanctions question. It included the following points:

The Conference

- welcomes the ICJ's ruling of 27 February 1998 which confirms that it has jurisdiction in the case;

- welcomes the favourable response of family victims to the efforts exerted to find a quick settlement to the dispute;

- expresses its deep concern for the vast human and material losses inflicted on the Libyan people and OAU member states;

- expresses its dismay at the lack of a response from America and Britain to international and regional efforts exerted towards finding a settlement to the dispute on the basis of international law.

The Conference then called on the Security Council to adopt a resolution to lift the 'unfair sanctions' until the World Court issued its ruling; and '*Decides on the noncontinuation of compliance with the sanctions ... from next September if America and Britain do not respond to the proposal of holding a trial for the suspects in a third neutral country by the time of the sanctions review in July 1998*'. Now there was a serious challenge to the continuation of the sanctions regime, a threat which the United States, Britain and France immediately sought to address with characteristic intimidation: OAU members were formally told that relations would suffer if they observed the declaration issued by the Conference.

Soon there was a further blow to the US/UK efforts to hold the line on sanctions. On 9 July 1998 President Hosni Mubarak of Egypt and a team of doctors flew into Libya to examine Gaddafi's broken hip. Washington and London had little choice but to grant Mubarak and his team permission to fly to Tripoli. Said one diplomat: 'Of course it's a scam, but there's simply no way we could have opposed it.' The Gaddafi regime was quick to broadcast the Mubarak arrival as a political triumph, with Gaddafi offering a televised welcome from his wheelchair. A Tunisian medical team sent by President Zine al-Abidine Ben Ali also arrived, soon after the presidents of Chad and Niger had defied an Anglo-American warning and flown in to join Gaddafi for celebrations of the Prophet Mohammed's birthday.

There was now an obvious groundswell of activity in opposition to the sanctions regime, with UN Secretary-General Kofi Annan declaring that he would seek to find a solution to the Lockerbie issue as a matter of priority. Washington and London, clearly bending under the mounting international pressure, were now reportedly considering a dramatic U-turn: perhaps, against all that they had argued since the start of the affair (mid-1991), it might be possible to bring the two Libyan suspects to trial in some country other than the United States or Scotland.[95] In the absence of any US/UK initiative it seemed likely that sanctions would gradually melt away to the humiliation of Washington and London. If, following the U-turn, Gaddafi refused to release the suspects for trial it might prove possible to keep the sanctions regime intact; but if the suspects were surrendered, tried in an independent court (most likely The Hague) and then acquitted Libya would seem to have a powerful compensation claim for the substantial damage done to the Libyan people and the national economy since the imposition of the first UN sanctions resolution (748, 31 March 1992).

As with many other states (Cuba, Bosnia, Haiti, Iraq, and so on) it was soon obvious that the sanctions regime was striking at the most vulnerable members of society. The UN Libyan Sanctions Committee, heeding the ban on air flights across Libyan borders, has gone so far as to prohibit air ambulances – desperately needed to fly criticially ill patients for urgent treatment overseas. This has contributed to the deaths of more than 2000 Libyans and others since the start of the sanctions regime. Today (late 1998) the sanctions-induced fatalities continue to mount in Libya.

A report (S/1998/201) issued in the name of the UN Secretary-General on 15 January 1998, following a fact-finding mission, revealed the impact of sanctions on Libyan society:

> The sectors that have been most affected include health and social services, agriculture and transportation ... the level of poverty in the country had increased overall ... they [Libyan officials] attributed the problems experienced in the health and social sectors directly to the air embargo ... It has restricted and complicated emergency medical evacuation ... some patients have died while waiting for permission [from the Sanctions Committee] to be granted ... It has also led to inordinate delays in the arrival of urgently needed vaccines, serums and drugs ... Because of the air embargo, road transportation has increased in volume significantly and has led to sharp increases in the number of road accidents and casualties ... The suspension ... has also hampered the work of animal health inspectors and caused delays in the delivery of veterinary supplies needed to protect farm animals and poultry from diseases.

The Libyan officials urged the mission to request Security Council modifications to the sanctions regime that was impacting so harshly on innocent civilians. The requested changes included: 'permission to operate flights to carry medicines, vaccines and blood specimens; an increase in the number of countries where patients may be taken by Libyan medical evacuation aircraft for treatment; permission to purchase aircraft for use in medical evacuation ... permission to operate direct flights for humanitarian and religious purposes ... '. It was important, said the officials, that the UN Secretary-General be given an impartial, first-hand account of the impact of sanctions on the social and economic life of the country 'particularly regarding the deteriorating situation in the health, social and agricultural sectors ... '.

Again the consequences of the US-mandated sanctions regime was plain to anyone who cared to notice. The worst effects were being felt by the most vulnerable members of Libyan society: the young, the sick, the old. Morbidity and mortality rates were increasing (and continue to increase) with the restriction of access to medical supplies. The politically motivated plan, hatched in Washington, is a familiar one: punish innocent civilians to put pressure on regimes that refuse to acquiesce in American hegemony.

Yugoslavia – Balkanisation (1991–)

The seismic conflict in what used to be Yugoslavia broke out in August 1990, soon after multiparty elections had ended Communist rule in Croatia and Slovenia. The fresh turmoil derived from the historical circumstances of nineteenth-century Balkanisation, the territorial rivalries of external powers, the Second World War, the general collapse of Eastern Europe, and the traditionally explosive cauldron of many mutually hostile ethnic groups living in close proximity or uneasily mixed in the same communities. It is significant that the dreadful term 'ethnic cleansing' was not invented in the 1990s: the celebrated journalist Robert Fisk has drawn attention to German and Croatian Ustasha files abandoned by the retreating Wehrmacht in 1945: as the Croatians appropriated the homes and property of Serbs for donation to their loyal followers they used the word 'cleansing' to describe their odious practices.[96]

As the conflict in the region mounted, the UN Security Council unanimously adopted Resolution 713 (25 September 1991), calling on all states to implement a 'general and complete embargo on all deliveries of weapons and military equipment to Yugoslavia'. So began a tumultuous period of UN involvement, including the imposition of a range of sanctions measures, that was destined to have little impact on the course of the conflict (not least because the United States systematically violated the terms of the arms embargo) and which generated deep divisions among the Permanent Members of the Security Council.

On 8 October 1991 UN Secretary-General Perez de Cuellar appointed Cyrus Vance, a former US Secretary of State, as his Personal Envoy for Yugoslavia. A week later, Bosnia-Herzegovina declared itself a sovereign state. On 27 November the Security Council, via Resolution 721, approved the efforts being made towards the establishment of a UN peacekeeping operation in the region; a development later confirmed by Resolution 724 (15 December 1991). Subsequent resolutions came thick and fast: for example, Resolution 727 (welcoming the Secretary-General's intention to despatch up to 50 military liaison officers to support a ceasefire), 740 (reaffirming support for the peacekeeping plan), 743 (establishing the UN Protection Force, UNPROFOR), 753 (recommending that the General Assembly admit the Republic of Croatia to membership of the United Nations), 755 (recommending the admission of Bosnia and Herzegovina), and so on.

Now the Security Council was moving to toughen the sanctions regime. Declaring that an earlier resolution (752, including the placing of weapons under international control) had not been properly observed by the Federal Republic of Yugoslavia (Serbia and Montenegro), the Council passed Resolution 757 (30 May 1992) to impose *comprehensive mandatory sanctions* against that country; a subsequent resolution (760, 18 June 1992) affirmed that the simplified and accelerated 'no objection' procedure (established by Resolution 724) would allow the country access to 'commodities and products for essential humanitarian need'. Subsequent resolutions, while placing a range of obligations on the various parties to the conflict, sometimes reaffirmed the embargo terms enshrined in former resolutions. For example, Resolution 762 (30 June 1992) declares (as Paragraph 8) that the Security Council *'Reaffirms* the embargo applied in paragraph 6 of resolution 713 (1991), paragraph 5 of resolution 724 (1991) and paragraph 6 of resolution 727 (1992)'. And sometimes the Council felt it necessary to protect the flow of humanitarian supplies to regions affected by sanctions. Thus Resolution 770 (13 August 1992) *'Calls upon* States to take all measures necessary to facilitate ... the delivery ... of humanitarian assistance to Sarajevo and wherever needed in other parts of Bosnia and Herzegovina' (Paragraph 2).

By August 1992 the comprehensive sanctions on Serbia were beginning to bite, according to Western and Serbian experts; the incidence of sanctions violations was diminishing and Serbia no longer had easy access to oil. Social tensions were being exacerbated by the mounting economic pressure; and Radoje Kontic, a deputy prime minister in charge of the Serbian economy, declared that unless sanctions were removed 'a total collapse is inevitable'. The Serbian Academy of Arts and Sciences had written to the UN Secretary-General to say that 'the Serbian people have been brought to the edge of existence' by the sanctions and that 'children and the sick are dying'. (Some observers noted that with the focus on Serbia less attention was being paid to Croatian violations of the UN arms embargo.) In August ships flying the flag of the former Soviet Union were sailing up the Danube to Serbia in violation of UN sanctions; and Robin Cook, a frontbench spokesman for the British Labour Party, was accusing the government of allowing trade with Serbia to continue ('The trade embargo on Serbia ... appears to have been widely circumvented. British servicemen who may shortly be sent to Yugoslavia must find it extraordinary that British business still deals with Serbia'). In September senior bankers and diplomats in Cyprus and Belgrade were claiming that Serbian sanctions-busting was being organised via Cyprus with the help of the island's secretive banking laws. Serbian companies were buying essential goods (machinery, lorries, oil, consumer goods) in

Nicosia; offshore Serbian companies were buying the goods in third countries; and the goods were then despatched to countries bordering Serbia for final arrival in Serbia itself.

The 'main US effort' was in tightening economic sanctions on Serbia, represented as the principal cause of the conflict. One senior US official, claiming that sanctions had stopped about 80 per cent of Serbia's imports, announced that nine American specialists in border traffic (including members of US Customs) were to be sent to Romania and Hungary to improve the interception of Serbian imports.[97] By 1993 it seemed that the balance of forces was hugely in favour of the Serbs, whose military advantage was consolidated by the arms ban; Croatia, with its long coastline and bordering the West, had managed to circumvent the arms embargo and to build up its forces. By contrast the Bosnian Muslims were reportedly destitute and squeezed into a handful of besieged towns, helpless to resist the Serbo-Croat carve-up of Bosnia. The West was taking various desultory measures to strengthen the embargo on Serbia, but various countries (Russia, Greece and others) were enabling oil and other vital commodities to reach Serbia despite the UN blockade.

In January 1993 there was speculation that the Clinton Administration was contemplating an end to the arms embargo on Bosnia, with Britain fearing that such a concession would only aggravate the conflict. At the same time oil-carrying barges were reportedly heading up the Danube to Serbia in plain violation of the sanctions regime. Diplomats commented that a tugboat pulling a fleet of barges from the Black Sea to Serbia under the eyes of the international community was making a mockery of UN resolutions. Over a period of a few months the Sanctions Assistance Missions unit (SAM) of the European Commission had detected more than 850 sanctions-busters; but, with a mere 35 foreign customs specialists struggling to monitor a 625-mile-long border, no one doubted that the embargo was highly porous. Now the UN Security Council was expressing its concern that the Ukraine was shipping oil to Serbia via the Danube in 'flagrant violation' of UN resolutions; the Council, deploring the fact that 'some of the vessels have already reached Serbia', called on the government of the Ukraine to halt such shipments. At the same time, under a secret deal agreed in January, Russian military hardware was being flown into Serbia and Serb-controlled parts of Bosnia and Croatia – again in direct violation of the mandatory UN resolutions. In the face of such developments, Cyrus Vance and Lord Owen, struggling to keep alive their peace plan for Bosnia, threatened President Slobodan Milosevic of Serbia with tighter sanctions if he failed to discipline his Bosnian underlings. Now

Russia was objecting to a fresh UN resolution designed to tighten the sanctions embargo against Serbia. President Clinton was in no doubt that there were 'lots of things we can do to make life more uncomfortable for the Serbs', but declined to mention what he had in mind. With pressure continuing to mount for tougher sanctions it was already plain that it was the civilian population that was being hardest hit. For example, Serbian hospitals were on the brink of collapse, in part because of 'international sanctions that make few allowances for the innocent victims of the Balkan conflict'.[98]

On 17 April 1993 the UN Security Council adopted Resolution 820, designed to strengthen sanctions against the Federal Republic of Yugoslavia within nine days unless the Bosnian Serb party agreed to existing peace proposals and ceased its military attacks. This followed the adoption of Resolution 819 (16 April 1993), sponsored by Venezuela on behalf of the non-aligned members of the Council, declaring Srebrenica and its surroundings a safe area and demanding an immediate end to Bosnian Serb attacks on the town. Now Serbia's neighbours were counting the mounting cost of sanctions, with growing fears of worse to come. On 27 April the Security Council decided to tighten sanctions on Serbia still further, including a prohibition on the provision of financial and non-financial services (exempting telecommunications, postal services and some legal services). The aim was to implement Resolution 820 by appropriate enactments in the domestic law of UN member states. In one typical report, the 'defiant Serbs' were now preparing 'to reap the whirlwind' for rejecting the peace plans. As always, the international debate continued about the likely effectiveness of the toughened sanctions regime.

In early May it seemed likely that Britain would acquiesce in US moves to allow Bosnia's Muslims to arm themselves more effectively; while the Bosnian Serb leader, Radovan Karadzic, under pressure from Serbia's President Slobodan Milosevic, had agreed to sign the Vance–Owen peace plan. Washington was continuing to urge a lifting of the arms embargo against the Bosnian Muslims (Madeleine Albright, the then US ambassador to the United Nations, was reportedly urging President Clinton to table a Security Council resolution to this effect). On 23 May an Allied communiqué on Bosnia was released after talks between US Secretary of State Warren Christopher and his counterparts from Britain, Russia, France and Spain. It included the words: 'The economic sanctions imposed by the UN Security Council against Serbia and Montenegro must be rigorously enforced by all members of the UN until the necessary conditions, including the withdrawal of Bosnian Serb troops, are met.'

Economic and other sanctions remained the preferred option, despite the frequent talk of possible military action against the Serbian forces.

On 29 June 1993 the Security Council failed to adopt a resolution, nominally sponsored the non-aligned members, that would have exempted Bosnia and Herzegovina from the arms embargo imposed by Resolution 713 (1991). Six (the United States, Cape Verde, Djibouti, Morocco, Venezuela and Pakistan) voted in favour, with none voting against (the nine abstentions denied the United States its necessary majority). Now there was further evidence that the sanctions embargo was being breached in various ways. One senior customs official had commented that his team was too small to inspect all the Serbian, Macedonian and Greek registered lorries passing through the crossing points into Serbia. In July a London registered company, Epicon, was at the heart of a UN investigation over arms being smuggled into the region in violation of the sanctions regime.

The impact of sanctions remained a matter of debate but it was clear that the civilian populations were suffering. A legal judgment in London (*Regina v. H. M. Treasury and the Bank of England*, 6 September 1993) exposed the hollowness of the humanitarian exemptions in UN resolutions: '*United Nations sanctions on exports to Serbia and Montenegro are subject to exceptions, but that does not oblige a member state to apply any of the exceptions. The United Kingdom can impose an absolute freeze on funds without any exception for medical or other humanitarian supplies.*'[99] On 26 October UN Secretary-General Boutros Boutros-Ghali took the decision to suspend relief operations to central Bosnia, until the culprits responsible for the death of a UN driver were found: one judgement was that the decision could imperil the lives of 1.5 million Bosnian Muslims and Croats who relied on UN deliveries of food and medicine. It was reported also that sanctions were bearing more heavily on Serbia's urban populations than on the more self-reliant peasant communities: the black economy was 'rife with hawkers, pimps and sharks as sanctions bite deeper', according to the journalist Yigal Chazan in Belgrade. On 15 November the Bosnian government announced its intention to sue Britain in the International Court of Justice at The Hague for conspiring to genocide by opposing the lifting of the UN arms embargo. By contrast, according to the prestigious *Jane's Defence Weekly*, Serbia had completely restructured its defence industry and was now almost immune to the arms embargo.

The sanctions issue was now highly controversial: the complicated sanctions regime was affecting different parts of the region in disproportionate ways, with civilian populations suffering the most; the various embargoes were being systematically breached by companies and political factions, often with the undisguised connivance of governments; and the general debate continued about whether sanctions were simply exacerbating an already fraught situation (Milosevic: 'Sanctions imposed against Serbia ... represent a constant impetus for the Bosnian authorities to go on with the war'). In April 1994 the United States was offering the Serbian leaders an end to sanctions in exchange for progress in peace talks (signalling that it was in the gift of Washington to shape UN policy). Alternatively, efforts would be made to strengthen the sanctions regime if the Serbs refused to negotiate in good faith: on 11 August the Clinton Administration gave the Serbs until 15 October to accept a peace settlement, with the threat that otherwise the arms embargo on Bosnia's Muslim-led government would be lifted.

On 23 September 1994 the UN Security Council adopted Resolution 942, imposing new economic sanctions on the Serb-controlled areas of Bosnia and Herzegovina for refusing to accept territorial proposals; and Resolution 943, suspending some economic sanctions against the Federal Republic of Yugoslavia (Serbia and Montenegro) for an initial 100 days if the border between Serbia and Bosnia were closed (943 suspended restrictions on civilian air travel; the impoundment of vessels, freight vehicles and aircraft; maritime traffic; sporting events; and cultural exchanges). The 943 'reward' for Belgrade's breaking of ties with the Bosnian Serbs would be rescinded if Belgrade were seen to default. Now the pressure was again mounting for a lifting of the arms embargo on Bosnia. On 9 November Muhamed Sacirbey, the Bosnian representative, declared to the Security Council that the embargo had not brought peace to the region. He stated that, faced with a choice of a lifting of the embargo and the continuation of UNPROFOR, the Bosnian government would prefer to have the embargo lifted: 'The entire Balkan region was on the brink of war; if victims were not allowed to defend themselves, that danger could increase.'[100]

On 12 November 1994 the United States – in flagrant violation of UN resolutions unilaterally abandoned the arms embargo against the Muslim-led government of Bosnia. Douglas Hurd, the British Foreign Secretary, noted that this rupture in NATO policy raised 'a worrying problem' for the Atlantic alliance: 'I hope very much it can be worked out by the American and their allies in a way that keeps us together.' Alain Juppé, the French foreign minister, declared that this was 'the first time that a country like the United States has unilaterally exonerated itself from a United Nations Security Council resolution that it has voted for' (*Sunday Times*, 13 November 1994). By 1995 it was clear that the Bosnians were being covertly armed with the connivance of the United States, Turkey and other NATO powers.[101] But circumstances had conspired to alter the thrust of US foreign policy. Clinton's earlier enthusiasm for an abandonment of the embargo seemed to have shifted, and now he found himself ranged against majority opinion in the US Congress. On 1 August 1995 the House of Representatives voted 298 to 128 (8 more than the two-thirds of the House needed to override a presidential veto) to end participation in the UN arms embargo against Bosnia – an unambiguous *de jure* violation of the UN Charter and the relevant resolutions.

It now appeared that the Federal Republic of Yugoslavia was honouring its pledge to break its ties with the Bosnian Serbs. On 15 September 1995 the Security Council unanimously adopted Resolution 1015 extending the suspension of certain sanctions against Serbia. This did little to mitigate the affects of sanctions on the civilian population. For example, Vladislav Johanovic, the Yugoslavian chargé d'affaires to the United Nations, presented a report (3 November 1995) detailing the affects of sanctions in the humanitarian field (in such areas as refugees, health care, social issues and social security provisions). It is enough to cite the increases in mortality rate in various categories: senility (568 per cent), hypertensive cardiac disease (334), ischaemic cardiac disease (212), diabetes (52), chronic bronchitis (35), intercerebral haemorrhage (34) and suicide (20): 'the sanctions have hit the health sector hard'.[102]

On 29 November 1995 the Security Council resolved to terminate the arms embargo on the former Yugoslavia in phases, as soon as the Secretary-General reported that Bosnia, Croatia and Serbia had formally signed the peace agreement framed in Dayton, Ohio, United States. The decision, enshrined in Resolution 1021, was adopted by 14 votes to 0 (with the Russian Federation abstaining). The phased sequence would end after 180 days, subject to a report from the Secretary-General, when all the embargo provisions would be terminated (unless the Council had reason to decide otherwise). On 18 June 1996 the arms embargo was lifted, preparing the way for the American-led rearmament of Bosnia. Now there was scope for the 'equalising' of the opposing forces in Bosnia with arms supplied from the United States, the Middle East and elsewhere – a manifest arms race. On 1 October 1996 the Security Council adopted Resolution 1074, terminating the sanctions of the Federal Republic of Yugoslavia (Serbia and Montenegro) and the Bosnian Serbs. The Secretary-General, reporting on UNTAES (the UN Transitional Administration for Eastern Slavonia, Baranja and Western Sirmium), noted the progress in relations between Croatia and Serbia and emphasised the challenges facing the region. In November the United States authorised the delivery of more than £60 million worth of arms equipment to the Bosnian army.

The conflict was not over. By June 1997 the United States and other countries were convinced that the Dayton peace accord (November 1995) was failing; and that the sanctions option would have to be revisited. Thus US Secretary of State Madeleine Albright was again suggesting that a further round of sanctions would be introduced if the presidents of Serbia and Croatia did not do more to implement the Dayton terms. In March 1998 Russia joined the United States, Britain and three other Western countries in backing a new arms embargo against Yugoslavia – mainly to punish President Milosevic for his oppression of ethnic Albanians in the Serbian province of Kosovo. Britain threatened that Serbian assets would be frozen if the repression did not end. On 31 March the Security Council again voted for an arms embargo on Belgrade, with little prospect that the other residual sanctions would soon be lifted (industry had been stifled and the country was in chaos). The scene was set for a further escalation of conflict, another cycle of UN sanctions, and a further spate of human suffering.

Haiti and 'Democracy' (1990–4)

The traditional US affection for Haiti has been signalled in many ways, not least by the eight American invasions of the supposedly independent republic between 1867 and 1900; and by recent comprehensive economic sanctions that succeeded for a time in killing several thousand infants every month. The US policy in the post-Soviet world of the 1990s merely continued the persistent imperial intervention in the Caribbean that Washington had been happy to practise for more than a century.

On 30 October 1990 nominally democratic elections brought Jean-Bertrand Aristide to power in Haiti; a Catholic priest, aged 40, he had won 67 per cent of the popular vote, but in September 1991 Father Aristide was deposed in a military *coup d'état* led by Raoul Cedras. The country was immediately plunged into chaos and by 1993 there were reportedly 100,000 Haitian refugees ready to sail for the United States when President-elect Clinton took office on 20 January. The Bush Administration had been hostile to refugees, causing the UN High Commissioner for Refugees to declare that the US Coast Guards were acting illegally by infringing Article 33(1) of the 1967 UN Protocol on the Status of Refugees, signed by the US in 1968. Legal experts had argued that it was illegal to arrest people in international waters and to destroy their boats – the prevailing American deterrent to Haitians trying to reach the United States. Bill Clinton, during the presidential election campaign, had repeatedly condemned the Bush policy of forcing Haitians to return home; but now that he was about to become president it was a different matter.

On 16 June 1993 the Security Council, under American pressure over the refugee problem, adopted Resolution 841. The aim was to impose an oil and arms embargo on Haiti, one of the world's most desperately poor countries; to freeze foreign assets; and to establish a Security Council sanctions committee. On 27 June the United Nations began talks with the aim of restoring democracy to the beleaguered country. By early July Aristide and General Cedras were close to accepting a UN plan for the restoration of democracy. The scheme, presented by special envoy Dante Caputo, called for the return to power of Aristide by 30 October and the resignation of General Cedras from all positions of political power; as a concession to the military those involved in the *coup* would be granted an amnesty. As a further encouragement, Clinton was offering $36 million to help reform the Haitian military and to restore the devastated economy. On 14 July representatives of the parties in the Haitian parliament began discussions following the signing of the agreement. The aims were a political truce, a social pact for the peaceful transition of power, an agreement on parliamentary procedures, and an agreement on the adoption of essential laws.

The UN Secretary-General, in a report (12 July) on democracy and human rights in Haiti, was now recommending that the sanctions imposed by Resolution 841 be suspended as soon as the parliament ratified the appointment of the Prime Minister and he took office. In the event the embargo was suspended on 27 August 1993 by Security Council Resolution 861; and then, following the failure of the Cedras regime to honour the terms of the agreement, reimposed on 18 October by Resolution 873 (13 October 1993). In early October it was announced that President Clinton might be sending 700 American troops under the UN flag to ensure the peaceful transition to democracy; and that some 500 French and Canadian police would also be sent as part of the UN force. The situation remained unclear, with some observers suggesting that the death squads would still remain active whatever the new constitutional arrangements. What was the purpose of a fresh foreign occupation of Haiti? Perhaps no more than to stem the threatened flood of Haitian refugees and to protect American business interests. On 15 October Clinton sent six US naval destroyers to enforce the freshly imposed sanctions, now including an embargo on oil sales (Clinton: 'The military authorities in Haiti simply must understand that they cannot indefinitely defy the desires of their own people as well as the will of the world community'). Now it was reported that Britain, France, the Netherlands and Argentina were each sending one ship to enforce the embargo. At the same time Resolution 875 was adopted by the Security Council, urging all member states to ensure the strict implementation of the embargo by halting and inspecting ships travelling towards Haiti.

The visas of Haitian military personnel had been revoked and Haitian assets in the United States had been frozen. The Cedras regime was isolated but it seemed unclear what would happen next. One Western diplomat commented on the likely disintegration of the military: 'Thugs prevented the greatest superpower in the world from coming ashore and they are chasing the UN out. Nobody is in charge except hoodlums run by the military.' Perhaps some comfort was taken from Clinton's assertion that he was 'dead serious' about seeing that the Haitians honoured the agreement they had signed. But the American agenda remained ambiguous. What exactly were the US objectives? How supportive was Washington of Aristide's legitimate claims? And how distant was Washington from the Haitian military? The CIA was circulating an assessment of Aristide's character, suggesting that he had various psychological problems and had been implicated in gang violence and politically motivated murder; and it emerged that the CIA had been making regular payments to senior members of the military junta (*Independent*, 2 November 1993). The embargo, part of Operation Restore Democracy, was soon found to be porous as supplies reached Haiti from the Dominican Republic. Now it was being conceded that Aristide would not be allowed to return 'on time' and that the blockade would have to be maintained for the foreseeable future.

The sanctions – as with Iraq (Chapter 5) – were continuing to exact their grim toll, in one estimate responsible for 1000 child fatalities a month. This estimate (from Harvard University) emphasised the fact that a desperately poor population was being plunged into appalling hardship. Food shortages were causing malnutrition, encouraging disease, and dramatically increasing the mortality rates among the young and the old. A worker for CARE, a US aid organisation, noted that people were starving: they were unable to travel to the feeding centres, and because of the UN oil blockade the aid workers were unable to deliver food to the villagers.

By mid-1994 several thousand children were in effect starving to death every month, with the child mortality rate continuing to soar through the year. By now infant mortality was around 11 per cent, with kwashiorkor and other nutritional deficiency diseases increasingly widespread (*Guardian*, 4 July 1994). The UN Security Council, under American pressure, had exacerbated the situation by the adoption of Resolution 917 (6 May 1994), designed to block Haitian access to all commodities and products (with the nominal but unrealistic exception of foodstuffs and medical supplies); on 21 May the expanded embargo had gone into effect. As always, the sanctions were continuing to strike at ordinary civilians: the 'privileged few' were still able to 'smile at sanctions', with 'delicacies' still to be found 'on the tables of the defiant rich'.[103] One in four Haitians was now reportedly dependent on the totally inadequate food-aid provisions ('Haiti starvation crisis deepens ...' – *Guardian*, 4 July 1994).[104]

On 31 July 1994 the Security Council adopted Resolution 940, authorising a multinational force to use 'all necessary means' to remove the Haitian military leadership; and stating that a UN Mission in Haiti (UNMIH) would then assume administrative control. Now the United States was free to invade Haiti whenever it wished. As with Korea, Iraq and Libya, the Security Council had provided the legal authorisation for an American imperial initiative; and then obediently vacated the scene. The superpower invasion of a tiny crippled state would be controlled by Pentagon military planners, and by them alone.

The subsequent 'peaceful' US invasion of Haiti, following talks between General Cedras and Jimmy Carter, was advertised as a great success for American foreign policy. No attention was given to the extent of civilian suffering under the US-inspired sanctions; to CIA involvement in the original Cedras *coup* that had toppled Aristide (*Time*, 17 October 1994); or to the fact that Aristide, now dependent on the US military, would have no choice but to accede to IMF/World Bank plans for the exploitation of Haiti in the interest of American capitalism. The United States, having contrived UN authorisation for punitive sanctions and military invasion, was now confident enough to ignore the United Nations totally. This led to the resignation of UN special envoy Dante Caputo: 'The total absence of consultations, and even information, from the government of the United States of America, makes me believe that this country, in fact, has taken the decision to act unilaterally in the Haitian process.'

On 26 September 1994 President Clinton, having secured a military occupation, lifted the sanctions against Haiti and declared that he was offering the 6.4 million inhabitants of the country a symbolic 'chance of freedom'. On 29 September the UN Security Council, under US instruction, adopted Resolution 944, specifying the termination on 16 October 1994 of the sanctions measures set out in Resolutions 841, 873 and 917. Father Jean-Bertrand Aristide, his populist instincts now thwarted by American power, was duly returned to nominal and ineffectual office. His ambition to improve the miserable lot of the Haitian poor had come to nothing. General Cedras, *coup* leader and friend of the Haitian death squads, would reportedly be paid £2000 a month by the US government in rent from his two Haitian houses.[105] Washington was satisfied. A radical reformer had been tamed; the baleful influence of the Haitian military remained ubiquitous; and a largely impotent United Nations had yet again been pressured into providing Washington with a flag of convenience for its strategic policies.

Other Cases

In some instances of UN intervention the focus was almost entirely on providing authorisation for military involvement, though the results would included the economic dislocation of a country or a region. Thus, with *Somalia*, the UN Security Council voted on 26 March 1993 to transfer the US-led 'peacekeeping' operation to the United Nations. Resolution 751 (24 April 1992) had established the original UN Operation in Somalia (UNOSOM); and Resolution 794 (3 December 1992) had given authorisation for the subsequent US-led Unified Task Force (for Operation Restore Hope). Now a new resolution (814, 26 March 1993) was authorising troops, under UN command, to maintain the peace, to protect the relief effort, to clear mines, to create a police force, to support economic growth, and to encourage the development of a democratic national government. Few independent observers thought that much of this ambitious programme, estimated to cost around £1 billion, would be accomplished. It was abundantly clear that Washington, by shifting nominal responsibility to the United Nations, would be able to escape blame in the event of failure. The Italian daily newspaper *Il Giorno* commented that the United Nations was 'a little dog on the American lead'.[106]

In December 1989 a civil war began in *Liberia* when Charles Taylor's National Patriotic Front invaded the country from the Ivory Coast. President Samuel Doe was killed, West African countries despatched Nigerian-led peacekeepers, and civilians died in their tens of thousands (40,000 from starvation during Taylor's siege of Monrovia). The West African states agreed to impose economic sanctions against the warring factions in the civil conflict unless an early ceasefire was reached. On 19 November 1992 the UN Security Council adopted Resolution 788, imposing an arms embargo; Resolution 950 (21 October 1994) extended the mandate of the UN Observer Mission in Liberia (UNOMIL); and Resolution 985 (13 April 1995) established a sanctions committee in an attempt to strengthen the arms embargo. A report of the UN Secretary-General had made it plain that Resolution 788 had done little to stop the flow of arms into the theatre of war: 'Factions continue to acquire arms and ammunition across the borders and from sources within Liberia.'[107] A supplementary resolution (972, 13 January 1995), reminding member states of their obligation to observe the embargo, had done little to bolster 788. Here the Security Council had no appetite for the imposition of comprehensive economic sanctions.

Elsewhere in Africa many poverty-stricken states remained in turmoil because of the legacy of colonialism and the continuing intervention of powerful states. Thus *Angola*, like Mozambique, moved directly from more than a decade of bitter revolutionary war against Portuguese colonialism to US-fomented civil conflict that, from its outbreak in 1975, has lasted ever since. The MPLA (*Movimento Popular de Libertação de Angola*) managed to form a government in the early days of independence, despite American aid to the Portuguese struggling to crush the indigenous uprisings. (John Marcum, an American scholar, had drawn attention to 'napalm bomb casings from which the Portuguese had not removed the labels marked "Property U.S. Air Force"'.[108]) Then Washington moved quickly to support its anti-MPLA clients: the FNLA (*Frente Nacional de Libertação de Angola*) and UNITA (*União Nacional para a Independencia Total de Angola*). A subsequent US Congessional committee admitted Washington's key role in stimulating the war: the infusion of US military aid, 'unprecedented and massive in the underdeveloped colony, may have panicked the Soviets into arming their MPLA clients'.[109]

The enduring conflict (linked also to the turmoil in Mozambique and Namibia) had resisted any attempts in the United Nations to involve the Security Council. The United States, in supporting Jonas Savimbi's UNITA, would have vetoed any firm UN effort to end the war on terms favourable to the popular MPLA. The Security Council sent observers to monitor the eventual ceasefire and elections; and Resolution 785 (30 October 1992) acknowledged that the elections – which the MPLA had won – were free and fair. But Washington refused to recognise the democratically elected government; and when Savimbi again launched military attacks to destabilise the new regime, any possible response from the Security Council was blocked by the threat of an American veto. Eventually the horrors of the new

US-backed turmoil could not be ignored. A joint resolution of the US Senate and House of Representatives condemned Savimbi and noted that the (Savimbi-provoked) conflict had caused '20,000 deaths, more than 1 million persons displaced, and 3 million persons threatened by hunger, disease, and land-mines'. It then emerged that in 1987 the apartheid regime of South Africa had considered dropping an atomic bomb on the Angolan capital, Luanda.[110] On 19 May 1993, after long years of US-supported carnage, the Clinton Administration formally recognised the legitimate MPLA government. Perhaps now the Security Council would be allowed to act against Savimbi's sabotage of peace agreements and democratic elections.

Now the UNITA rebels were launching a high-level diplomatic campaign in Europe and Africa in an attempt to deflect any action by the Security Council, but seemingly in vain. On 15 September 1993 the Council unanimously adopted Resolution 864, imposing an oil and arms embargo on UNITA and creating a sanctions committee to administer and monitor the new arrangements. The embargo was set to become effective within ten days unless a ceasefire was agreed; if there was no ceasefire by 1 November 1993 then the Council might consider various trade and travel sanctions. The resolution was also used to extend the mandate of the UN Angola Verification Mission (UNAVEM II) until 15 December 1993. However, the delays incorporated in 864 served to irritate the ruling MPLA and to signal an apparent retreat from the position agreed earlier by Portugal, Russia and the United States (the 'troika' of countries that had sponsored the May 1991 peace accord). The MPLA's *Journal de Angola* described the breathing space granted to Savimbi as an attempt to 'save a ship without salvation'. Soon there were further signs of Council procrastination, an obvious sign of American attempts to protect Savimbi.

On 16 March 1994 the Security Council unanimously adopted Resolution 903, designed to block the imposition of further sanctions on UNITA – a position that would be reviewed in the light of subsequent MPLA–UNITA talks; 903 was used also to extend the UNAVEM II mandate until 31 May 1994. On 30 July the Council's unanimous adoption of Resolution 932, imposing additional measures against UNITA, seemed to show that the American protection of Savimbi had finally ended; but on 12 August the Council issued a statement temporarily deferring the additional sanctions specified in 932. Then, yet again, there was more vacillation by the Security Council. On 28 August the Council adopted Resolution 1127, designed to impose diplomatic sanctions on UNITA and to indicate that further measures (for example, financial and trade restrictions) would be imposed if UNITA failed to comply with earlier agreements and resolutions. The new sanctions would take effect on 30 September unless the UN Secretary-General informed the Council that UNITA had taken 'concrete and irreversible' steps to comply with its obligations. Then yet another Council U-turn. On 29 September the adoption of Resolution 1130 postponed the imposition of sanctions specified in 1127 – a decision to be reversed yet again by Resolution 1135 (29 October 1997), affirming the sanctions conditions stipulated in Resolutions 1127 and 1130.

Through 1998 the turmoil in Angola continued. Negotiated ceasefires proved to be insecure, and the repeated UN vacillations had done nothing to contribute to a long-term solution. In June the Security Council adopted Resolution 1173, condemning UNITA for failing to honour its obligations; and, yet again, imposing a range of sanctions. And the inevitable procrastination was built into the new resolution: 1173 would come into force on 25 June unless the Secretary-General reported that UNITA had fulfilled all its obligations by 23 June. UNITA funds would be frozen by UN member states; contacts with the UNITA leadership would be prohibited; and the receipt of Angolan diamonds from areas not under government administration would be banned. In addition, UNITA would not be allowed to acquire mining equipment and motorised vehicles. Nonetheless, it remained doubtful, bearing in mind the past record of the Security Council, whether the measures would be enforced; and, even if they were, what their affects would be. By August 1998 Savimbi's rebels had reportedly captured at least 68 towns and regions from the legitimate government and more than 200,000 refugees were fleeing from their homes to escape the war.

In *Rwanda*, where Belgian colonialism after the First World War exacerbated the tensions in what had been part of German East Africa (Ruanda-Urundi, later Burundi and Rwanda), ethnic turmoil was fomenting conflict to the level of genocide. In 1973 Juvenal Habyarimana seized power from Gregoire Kayibanda, Rwanda's first president (installed by the Hutu majority in opposition to the Tutsis). Exiled Tutsis in Uganda formed the Rwandan Patriotic Front (RPF), which invaded Rwanda in 1990 to fuel the mounting civil war. On 6 April 1994 Habyarimana and Burundi's President Cyprien Ntaryamira were both killed when their plane was shot down. Now the region collapsed into further chaos.

The 2500 UN peacekeeping troops in Rwanda seemed increasingly impotent in the face of the mounting violence. Mobs of soldiers and civilians were killing Belgian UN peacekeepers, the toll of Hutu and Tutsi dead was mounting, and the international community was well aware of what was happening; but the Security Council was doing nothing to address the escalating crisis. The UN personnel in the region were 'no more than spectators to the savagery which aid workers say has seen the massacre of 15,000 people – mainly from the traditionally dominant Tutsi minority'.[111] As UN peacekeepers struggled to escape from the turmoil the Security Council adopted Resolution 912 (21 April 1994) which expressed shock and deep concern but proposed no practical measures. The carnage was escalating (one estimate suggested that 100,000 people had been slaughtered over two weeks), yet the Security Council seemed to be paralysed. By May some 230,000 people, many of them mutilated by machetes, were fleeing to escape the slaughter; and a UNHCR statement cited reports suggesting that up to 50 Tutsis a night were being taken from a group of 5000 prisoners, to be killed. Secretary-General Boutros Boutros-Ghali urged the Security Council to consider the use of force to stop the slaughter, but his appeals were ignored.

On 17 May 1994 the Security Council stirred itself enough to adopt Resolution 918 – imposing an arms embargo and establishing a sanctions committee. The Council was now (according to 918) 'deeply concerned that the situation in Rwanda, which has resulted in the death of many thousands of innocent civilians, including women and children, the internal displacement of a significant percentage of the Rwandan population, and the massive exodus of refugees to neighbouring countries, constitutes a humanitarian crisis of enormous proportions'. The resolution also nominally expanded the UNAMIR (UN Assistance Mission for Rwanda) force up to 5500 troops, and recognised that UNAMIR 'may be required to take action in self-defence ...'. All this hardly amounted to the radical response that many observers were demanding. On 9 June the Council adopted Resolution 997, making minor adjustments to the role of UNAMIR and reinforcing the terms of Resolution 918. A subsequent resolution (1005, 17 July 1995) introduced what may have been a significant arms loophole: Rwanda would be allowed to obtain explosives 'intended exclusively for use in established humanitarian demining programmes'.

On 16 August 1995, via Resolution 1011, the Security Council suspended until 1 September 1996 the embargo on arms and related material, though the Rwandan government was required to inform the Sanctions Committee of all its arms imports; countries exporting arms to Rwanda were also required to notify the Committee. On 1 September the supply and sale of arms and related material to Rwanda were finally terminated. At the same time the provision of arms to *non*-governmental forces for use in Rwanda remained prohibited.

The tragedy of Rwanda (and Burundi) had indicated yet again the impotence of the United Nations when matters of human suffering, rather than the interests of powerful states, were the issue. The Security Council had acted, but tardily and to little affect.

In *Sierra Leone* a junta staged a successful *coup d'état* in May 1997 against the elected president, Ahmad Tejan Kabbah. On 8 October the Security Council adopted Resolution 1132, imposing an oil and arms embargo and restricting the travel of the junta members. A Sanctions Committee, established by 1132, was authorised to approve applications on a case-by-case basis by the democratically elected government for the importation of oil and oil products for humanitarian purposes. The resolution also authorised the Military Observer Group of ECOWAS (Economic Community of West African States) to ensure strict implementation of the embargo, which would involve the inspection of incoming ships where necessary (to be reported by ECOWAS every 30 days to the Committee).

The British government, which had long championed the cause of the ousted President Kabbah, then became embroiled in the 'Arms to Africa' affair when it was found that an English mercenary company had helped to stage a counter-*coup* against the junta. Had British ministers known about the shipping by Sandline International of arms from Bulgaria to West Africa – a manifest violation of Resolution 1132? If the British Foreign Office *had* remained ignorant of such events was this not a sign of gross incompetence, a deplorable failure in communications between British officials? British ministers were helped by a subsequent UN ruling that nothing illegal had been done; and by the findings of an independent inquiry headed by Sir Thomas Legg, one-time permanent secretary in the Lord Chancellor's department. A plainly unambiguous arms embargo, enshrined in a Security Council resolution, had been violated. No one was to be held guilty for a breach of international law – if only because the interests of a powerful member of the Security Council had been served. This episode provided another useful insight into the adaptability of UN resolutions.

3

The US Role

The American influence in the UN Security Council is plain: resolutions are blocked or adopted, largely according to how Washington judges their likely impact on US foreign policy. The United States, like the other Permanent Members of the Council, has the power of veto which means that American approval is essential for any resolution to stand.[1] The nominal equality of the five Permanent Members (United States, Russian Federation, Britain, France and China), according to Article 27 of the UN Charter, is a fiction (if only because of the dominant US military-financial role in such bodies as NATO, G7, the IMF, the World Bank, the WTO, and so on). This means that, despite Article 2(1) of the UN Charter, the United States enjoys totally disproportionate power within the United Nations organisation. In particular, in the context of the present book, Washington exploits its power to shape UN-mandated economic (and other) sanctions in ways that are highly congenial to American strategic policy.

However, there are important limits to US sway in the Security Council: resolutions that Washington would welcome are not always adopted. The United States would have liked a UN-mandated embargo against Libyan oil, but was blocked by the energy appetites of the European powers; Washington would have liked tough UN sanctions against North Korea (see below) in the early 1990s, but was blocked by the threat of a Chinese veto in the Security Council.[2] In such circumstances the US resorts to the option of imposing *unilateral sanctions*, following the exercise of defined presidential powers or according to new domestic legislation (examples below). In short, Washington will exploit its unrivalled influence in international bodies where it can; when blocked, it will take independent action – which in turn may irritate other influential states and groups in the international community.

The Superpower Perquisite

One of the advantages of unassailable political power is that the bothersome constraints of morality and good manners can be largely ignored. It is easy to demonstrate how Washington has bribed and bullied other states into acquiescence with the American political agenda (see Chapter 5). Washington bullied the Security Council into adopting resolutions on Libya (Chapter 2), to the point that the international lawyer Marc Weller (Cambridge University, UK) proposed that such a dereliction should be referred to the World Court; ignored UN resolutions on Indonesia, Israel, Turkey and South Africa; contrived an unjust UN 'tilt' in favour of its proxies in Angola and El Salvador; treats the World Court with contempt when (as with Nicaragua and Libya) it rules against Washington; uses the IMF and the World Bank for political bribery throughout the international community; fails to pay its UN dues, while exhorting other states to observe the Charter; exploits ungathered intelligence for its own strategic purposes (causing UN Secretary-General Perez de Cuellar to issue a rebuke); and often frustrates the humanitarian efforts on UN bodies (UNICEF, WFP, FAO, WHO and others) by pursuing a self-serving American agenda.

The American abuse of power is sometimes acknowledged in unexpected places. Thus *Time* asks whether the United States is 'in danger of becoming a global bully?'; and in the same issue (4 August 1997) James Walsh, in a Special Report headed 'AMERICA THE BRAZEN', records the 'mounting umbrage at American "arrogance" abroad' (to the point that world leaders at the Denver summit were subjected 'to humiliation and braggadocio in equal measure'). Commentators have commented on the features of the 'American Caesar', supported by a prodigiously funded military technology and huge armies that can be conveyed over oceanic distances.[3] It is not surprising in such circumstances that the seductive 'imperial temptation' should prove to be irresistible.[4] One inevitable consequence was that dissent could not be tolerated: 'All we, as people, are allowed to do is listen to the statements, then believe, agree and obey. Anyone who disagrees or disobeys will be shunned, treated with suspicion, condemned, and punished accordingly.'[5]

The military power of the United States sustains the exercise of power in other ways. In 1992 it emerged that the Pentagon was planning to target selected Third World countries, the 'pariah' or 'rogue' states, with nuclear missiles. The likely targets included Libya, Iraq, Pakistan, India, Iran, Syria and China; and even Israel, long an American proxy, might not be immune from a nuclear strike.[6] The secret Pentagon report included the presidential option of an automated 'dial a nuke' facility to hit a preselected target anywhere in the world. In August 1997 it transpired (via reports of the 300-

page *Stockpile Stewardship and Management Plan* compiled by the US Energy Department) that the United States was developing a new range of nuclear weapons, a breach of the spirit of the Test Ban Treaty. In 1996 even Newt Gingrich was admitting that the United States was in danger of looking 'like an isolated bully using very sophisticated weapons'.[7] Martin Walker, a journalist writing in August 1996, summarised the situation: 'International law is now in danger of becoming whatever Washington says it should be ... the US has not been shy of legislating on behalf of others. The difference now is that it has the untrammelled power to enforce its will.'[8] In September 1997 some five hundred US paratroopers dropped into the former Soviet Republic of Kazakhstan in the heart of Central Asia as part of a multinational military exercise involving personnel from Kazakhstan, Uzbekistan, Kyrgyzstan and the United States. The 19-hour flight of the US troops required three in-flight refuellings. General John Sheehan, US Marine Corps, explained one of the main purposes of the operation: 'I would like to leave the message that there is no nation on the face of the Earth that we cannot get to.'[9]

The United States makes no secret of its aim to develop a global hegemony (in May 1997 President Clinton reaffirmed the American intention 'to lead the world'). To this end, Washington becomes involved in countless 'peace processes' around the globe; shapes the culture of world finance; develops a framework of domestic and international law to aid US objectives; assumes the right to brand other states as 'rogue', 'pariah' or 'terrorist'; and takes steps to punish recalcitrant countries that refuse to accept Washington's self-assumed role of organising the world's affairs. The 'indispensable' United States, unpoliced by external authority and militarily unassailable, judges what punitive measures to apply to this or that member of the international community. Among such measures the imposition of economic sanctions plays an important part.

The Sanctions Options

The complexities of the modern social/industrial/financial world give much scope for punitive sanctions. A military onslaught has been depicted as a *violent* sanctions and the most punitive of all, at least in the short term; it is obvious that military actions can be of many types. *Non-violent* sanctions are equally varied. In one 'typology of non-violent sanctions', four broad categories are identified:

1. *Diplomatic and political measures*
   a) Protest, censure, condemnation.
   b) Postponement/cancellation of official visits, meetings and negotiations for treaties and agreements.
   c) Reduction of scale of diplomatic representation.
   d) Severance of diplomatic relations.
   e) Non-recognition of new governments, new states.

2. *Cultural and communications measures*
   a) Reduction/cancellation of cultural exchanges, scientific co-operation, educational links, sporting links, entertainment.
   b) Ban on tourism to/from target country.
   c) Withdrawal of visas.
   d) Restriction/cancellation of telephone, cable, postal links.
   e) Restriction/cancellation of landing, overflight privileges.
   f) Restriction/cancellation of water transit, port privileges.
   g) Restriction/cancellation of land transit privileges.

3. *Economic Measures*
   Two broad types: Financial; and Commercial and technical (see below).

4. *Measures relating to status in international organisations*
   Membership and participation
   a) Vote against admission (eg veto).
   b) Vote against acceptance of credentials.
   c) Vote for suspension.
   d) Vote for expulsion.

   Benefits
   a) Vote against loans, grants, technical aid, other benefits.
   b) Vote for removal of headquarters, regional office.[10]

Economic sanctions clearly fall within the scope of 3 ('Economic Measures', above), though most of the other (violent and non-violent) options have obvious economic relevance; and the measures under 4 (Benefits (a)) are unambiguously economic in character. It is useful to consider the 'Economic Measures' in more detail.[11] As with the other categories of non-violent sanctions these can be of various types.

Financial economic measures can involve the reduction, suspension or cancellation of aid in various fields (military, food, medical, development, technical, and so on). This is clearly the converse of using financial aid as an inducement (that is, a bribe). If a country has become dependent upon financial aid any adverse affect on this provision can have devastating consequences – which is why the donation of aid to countries desperate for assistance can represent the purchase of immense political power. Even the *threat* of aid withdrawal can coerce a national government into behaviour that is congenial to the donor. The same considerations can apply to the availability of credit facilities, particularly where these are provided at market or concessionary rates. The reduction, suspension or cancellation of such provisions can have a devastating affect on a national economy.

It is possible also to freeze or confiscate the bank assets and other assets of the target government; to ban interest payments and other transfer payments; to refuse to refinance or reschedule debt repayments (interest and principal); and to control or block capital movements. All such measures can put a national government under immense pressure; and may coerce it into adopting particular defined policies.

In the same way a range of *commercial and technical* measures may be applied to punish a targeted state or to force it into a preferred mode of behaviour. Thus imports and exports may be reduced or completely blocked (by means of quota specifications, licensing mechanisms and other means). A discriminatory tariff policy may be applied to discipline a recalcitrant state (for example, the assignment of 'most favoured nation' status may be withdrawn or blocked), despite the demands of free trade enshrined in the World Trade Organization (WTO) and other international bodies and agreements. Fishing rights may be restricted or withdrawn; joint projects and collaborative industrial ventures may be suspended or cancelled; trade agreements may be abandoned; particular individuals and firms trading with the target country may be blacklisted; the provision of insurance facilities may be banned; and the provision of technology and technical assistance may be reduced, suspended or cancelled.

The United States (by virtue of its unparalleled influence in such international bodies as G7, the IMF, the World Bank, the WTO, and so on) is in a unique position to secure the imposition of *economic measures* against targeted states. Similarly, as a leading dispenser of aid, technology and technical assistance the US is well placed to exert a wide range of economic and other pressures to countries whose behaviour is judged unhelpful to American foreign policy. The United States works hard to suborn the United Nations where it can; where it cannot it acts alone. The result is that today many countries are being subjected to sanctions either mandated by a US-managed UN Security Council or by Washington acting alone. Before attention is given to a few specific cases it is helpful to note the extent to which the United States, acting alone, has used and continues to use economic measures against targeted states.

The Sanctions Ubiquity

The United States – like many other countries, groups and alliances – has long used economic sanctions as a strategic tool against other states: sometimes as a unilateral policy (Table 3.1), sometimes as an architect of decisions in the UN Security Council (Chapter 2), and sometimes in concert with allies or other states (as with the UK against Mexico, 1938–47; with the UK against Iran, 1951–3; with the UK and France against Egypt, 1956; with Canada against South Korea, 1975–6; with Japan and West Germany against Burma, 1988–; and so on).

The development of the sanctions option by the United States involves a wide range of presidential and other powers. Thus laws that can be used by the President for this purpose can involve imposing limits on: US government programmes (such as foreign aid, landing rights, and so on), US exports, US imports, private financial transactions, and the activities of international financial institutions.[12] Presidential powers vary greatly from one option to another: he has considerable discretion with exports and bilateral government programmes, much less with imports and international financial transactions. Congress may choose to curtail the scale of foreign assistance proposed by the President and so to exercise its own sanctions discretion; and specific laws (such as the Export Administration Amendments Act, 1985) may act as a brake on presidential largesse. But a resourceful Administration will exploit legislative loopholes to avoid significant constraints.

The imposition of a sanctions regime by the United States may involve any of the *economic measures* indicated above. These may be cited to threaten UN Security Council members in order to secure compliance with US-supported resolutions (often drafted by a proxy United Kingdom or other state). Aid supplied to a country (the 'carrot') may be withdrawn (the 'stick'), so focusing the collective government minds in dependent nations. The threatened (or actual) withdrawal of food aid can be most effective: the prospect of a starving civilian population is a persuasive pressure for most

Table 3.1 Some states targeted by US (acting alone) for sanctions

Country	Year imposed	Issue	Country	Year imposed	Issue
Japan	1917	Containment	Uruguay	1976	Human rights
Japan	1940	Withdrawal from	Taiwan	1976	Nuclear
		South-east Asia	Ethiopia	1976	Expropriation
Argentina	1944	Remove Peron	Paraguay	1977	Human rights
Netherlands	1948	Indonesian			
		Federation	Guatemala	1977	Human rights
Israel	1956	Borders	Argentina	1977	Human rights
UK and			Nicaragua	1977	Somoza
France	1956	Suez	El Salvador	1977	Human rights
Laos	1956	Communism	Brazil	1977	Human rights
Dominican			Libya	1978	Gaddafi
Republic	1960	Trujillo	Brazil	1978	Nuclear
Cuba	1960	Castro	Argentina	1978	Nuclear
Ceylon	1961	Expropriation	India	1978	Nuclear
Brazil	1962	Goulart	USSR	1978	Dissidents
United Arab	1963	Yemen and	Iran	1979	Hostages
Republic		Congo	Pakistan	1979	Nuclear
Indonesia	1963	Containment	Bolivia	1979	Human rights
South Vietnam	1963	Diem	USSR	1980	Afghanistan
Chile	1965	Copper price	Iraq	1980	Terrorism
India	1965	Agriculture	Nicaragua	1981	Communism
Arab League	1965	Anti-boycott	Poland	1981	Martial law
Peru	1968	French jets	Argentina	1982	Falklands
Peru	1968	Expropriation	USSR	1982	Poland
Chile	1970	Allende	USSR	1983	Korean Air
India and					Lines Flight 007
Pakistan	1971	Bangladesh	Zimbabwe	1993	UN voting record
Various			Iran	1984	Terrorism; war
countries	1972	Terrorism	South Africa	1985	Apartheid
Various			Syria	1996	Terrorism
countries	1973	Human rights	Angola	1986	Cuban troops
South Korea	1973	Human rights	Panama	1987	Noriega
Chile	1973	Human rights	Haiti	1987	Democracy
Turkey	1974	Cyprus	El Salvador	1987	Amnesty
USSR	1975	Emigration	Sudan	1989	Human rights
Eastern Europe	1975	Emigration	Iran	1992	Terrorism
Vietnam	1975	Communism	Sudan	1997	Terrorism
South Africa	1975	Nuclear	Iran	1998	Terrorism
Kampuchea	1975	Post-war	Libya	1998	Terrorism

Source: (largely) G. C. Hufbauer *et al.*, *Economic Sanctions Reconsidered*, Volumes I and II, Institute for International Economics, Washington D.C., 1990.

governments. The President is authorised to block any state's access to Commodity Credit Corporation (CCC) export credit guarantees for agricultural products, so denying a country famine relief (or, having agreed such aid, withdrawing it). Thus Reagan froze Food for Peace aid to Nicaragua in 1981 and blocked a $9.6 million wheat sale to that country. Washington is well prepared to starve a civilian population as perhaps the most drastic form of economic sanctions (see Cuba, below; 'The Case of Iraq', Chapter 5). In the same way, the United States, using 'its alliances with other countries and ... informal persuasion',[13] can exploit its overwhelming influence in such bodies as the IMF and the World Bank to deny target states essential financial support. US powers in international bodies do not derive solely (or even mainly) from publicly accessible statutes, protocols, regulations and rules of procedure. Instead the power that derives from cynical *realpolitik* means that written rules can be ignored, 'corridor threats' can be made to effective purpose, and national legislation and international treaties can be treated with contempt.

In this context Washington is well able to protect its friends from the possibility of international sanctions; and to arrange for the imposition of severe economic measures against states unwilling to acquiesce in America's energetic pursuit of its foreign-policy objectives. Thus in January 1993, with Israel once again in violation of a Security Council resolution (this time Resolution 799), there were suggestions within the United Nations that sanctions should be applied to ensure compliance. The Arabs and others waited in vain: Israel, with support, ignored Resolution 799 and so reinforced an observation made by UN Secretary-General Boutros Boutros-Ghali: '... by not pressing for Israeli compliance, [the Security Council] does not attach equal importance to the implementation of all of its decisions'. By contrast, a US Senate Committee urged in early 1995 that economic sanctions be imposed on Colombia to coerce the regime into action against the drug cartels; there were suggestions that sanctions might be imposed on China if it continued talking to Iran about the supply of civilian nuclear technology (Clinton: 'I am convinced that instituting a trade embargo with Iran is the most effective way our nation can help curb Iran's drive to acquire devastating weapons and support for terrorist activities'); on 16 May 1995 Washington announced plans for $6 billion worth of economic sanctions against Japan unless it opened up its car market to American products; and some US factions were encouraging the imposition of harsh sanctions on Nigeria (in addition to the arms ban introduced in 1993) as a means of toppling the military regime. In November 1997 Washington tightened its economic sanctions on a destitute Sudan because of what

Madeleine Albright charged was the country's involvement in international terror and its 'abysmal record' on human rights.

In July 1998 one estimate suggested that *two-thirds of the world's population was subject to some sort of US sanctions.*[14] It was suggested that this 'sanctions overload' was seriously affecting the conduct of US foreign policy, with US companies 'alarmed about the threat to their global ambitions'. More than half of the sanctions imposed by the United States had been imposed over the last four years, with the current Congress giving attention to 26 sanctions measures against 10 nations (China, Russia, Vietnam, Azerbaijan, Syria, Mexico, Croatia, Yugoslavia, Nigeria and Sudan).[15] With the collapse of the Soviet Union and the much diminished reduction in the constraints on American action, many US Congressmen came to regard sanctions as a low-cost and pain-free way of achieving US foreign-policy aims. It is plain that particular American lobbying groups have been influential in pushing for sanctions in their own areas of concern. Thus the Cuban-American community in Florida offered financial encouragement to Jesse Helms, chairman of the Senate Foreign Relations Committee, to promote intensified sanctions against Cuba (see below); just as the American-Israeli lobby has been influential in encouraging tighter sanctions against Iran and Libya. The campaign of the religious right to punish countries for alleged religious persecution could have sanctions consequences for as many as 80 states.

Again there is debate about the effectiveness of the sanctions option. For example, this approach may damage US interests more than the targeted countries. Thus in one survey the Institute for International Economics discovered that American exports to 26 targeted countries were $15–16 billion lower than they would have been in the absence of sanctions.[16] Said Institute researcher Jeffrey Schott: 'Sanctions are blunt policy tools that are easily circumvented. Targeted regimes often adapt to sanctions, even if their people suffer. Meanwhile ongoing sanctions become increasingly burdensome to US firms and workers.'[17] Sanctions also have the effects of damaging confidence in the United States as a trading partner, since economic and other sanctions may be abruptly introduced for political reasons; and of causing deep resentment among nominal US allies, so hampering US strategic policy. It has even been suggested, by US Under-Secretary of State for Economic Policy, Stuart Eizenstat, that proposed new sanctions would put at risk such US initiatives as trade liberalisation, nuclear non-proliferation and counter-terrorism campaigns. Doubts were reportedly emerging in Congress: against the former enthusiasm for sanctions was the growing realisation that such punitive measures could damage export prospects, with elements in the business community resolving to withhold funds from the 'sanctions hawks' in Congress. Senator Trent Lott was now appointing an 18-member bipartisan taskforce to recommend ways of reforming the American policy on sanctions; and there were suggestions that any existing sanctions regime should automatically end unless reauthorised by Congress.[18]

The American enthusiasm for economic sanctions, as a way of furthering strategic policy without risk to US lives, may have been tempered by the manifest survival of such US-unfriendly leaders as Gaddafi, Castro and Saddam Hussein. Nonetheless, the ubiquity of American-imposed sanctions remains a fact in the modern world. It is useful to profile a few specific cases.

Cuba

The Birth of Sanctions

On 1 January 1959 the popular Cuban revolutionary forces led by Fidel Castro overthrew the US-sponsored military dictatorship of General Fulgencio Batista – so setting the scene for one of the longest and most severe sanctions regimes of the twentieth century. Within weeks Washington was taking measures to restrict American exports to Cuba (Figure 3.1).[19] On 5 June Senator George Smathers, a Florida Democrat, proposed legislation for a drastic reduction in the Cuban sugar quota purchased by the United States; and early in 1960, after planes flying from American territory had dropped bombs on Havana and sugar cane fields in Camagiley and Oriente, the Eisenhower Administration began moves to block all imports of Cuban sugar. On 3 July a Sugar Act was passed by Congress to allow the President to cancel all Cuban imports; three days later, Eisenhower cancelled the entire sugar quota, including the 700,000 tons in the formerly agreed 1960 quota, and declared that other measures ('economic, diplomatic and strategic') against Cuba must now be considered. Throughout 1960 the sanctions regime was strengthened, a policy later described by Vice-President Richard Nixon as an 'all-out "quarantine" economically, politically and diplomatically – of the Castro regime'. John F. Kennedy, the Democratic presidential candidate, was now urging that a freeze be imposed on all Cuban assets held in the United States; and that concerted international action be taken against Cuba. Fidel Castro commented:

This action ... is an attack on the people, an attempt to keep us from having more schools, teachers, roads, houses and universities ... Now they're planning something else, thinking that, if they cause economic difficulties, they'll get the people's support. That's how they think the people will react to their tactic of 'I make you go hungry and have a hard time ... I'm not content with having exploited you for 50 years ... even though I've done all that to you and I don't want you to make any progress, I can count on you now; I'm going to make you grow hungry so I can count on you'.[20]

In October 1960 Washington moved to implement the Kennedy proposal of internationalising the economic isolation of Cuba; other sovereign states were now coming under heavy American pressure to reduce their trade with the island. US officials were discussing with their Canadian counterparts how US exports could be prevented from reaching Cuba via Canada; and in December Eisenhower set the 1961 sugar quota at zero, pushing the Castro regime into increased dependence on Socialist-bloc sugar imports. On 31 March the new US president, John F. Kennedy, confirmed that the zero-quota for Cuban sugar imports would remain; and three weeks later (on 22 April) discussed with the National Security Council the possibility of imposing a total embargo on US trade with Cuba. The United States

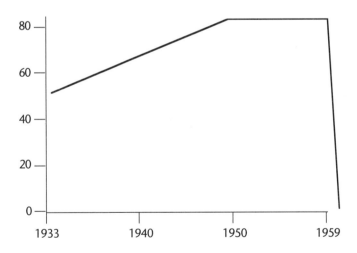

Figure 3.1   Percentage of Cuban imports supplied by the US

Source: *Guardian*, 6 September 1994.

(today's population 240 million) was beginning its campaign – now four decades long – to overthrow the Castro regime in Cuba (population 11 million), deemed a threat to the most powerful nation the world had known.

On 3 February 1962 President Kennedy signed Decree no. 3447 to impose a total trade embargo (effective on 7 February), excepting some foodstuffs and medical supplies; on 23 March the embargo was extended to imports of all goods containing any Cuban materials, even if manufactured in other countries. Now it was plain that Washington was striving to impose policies with extraterritorial reach, pressurising sovereign states into support for America's anti-Cuba posture. On 8 September the United States secured a pledge from other NATO members that they would block all financial credits to Cuba; and on 6 February 1963 Kennedy ruled that foreign vessels that had docked at a Cuban port on or after 1 January of that year would not be allowed to transport US government-funded shipments. American ports were now closed to any country allowing its ships to transport arms to Cuba; any ship that docked at a Cuban port was not allowed to dock at a US port during the voyage; any country allowing ships or planes to carry materials to Cuba would not be eligible for US aid; and no US ships would be allowed to support trade with the island.

The US Treasury Department then (8 July) used the wartime Trading with the Enemy Act (1917), later exploited in the Cuban Democracy Act of 1992 (below), to supplant the Cuban Import Regulations with the tougher Cuban Assets Control Regulations, designed to strengthen the embargo. Now US citizens were prohibited from all unlicensed commercial and financial transactions with Cuba, and from all importing of or dealing abroad in Cuban products; US citizens would not be allowed to use US currency for such transactions as expenditure in Cuba and the purchase of Cuban airline tickets.

On 10 January 1964 Dean Rusk, Secretary of State in the Johnson Administration, increased the pressure on other states to join the US anti-Cuban campaign, saying that those countries trading with Cuba were 'prejudicing the efforts ... to reduce the threat from Cuba'; on 13 March he explained to the Senate Foreign Relations Committee the purposes of the embargo (to reduce Castro's ability to export 'subversion and violence'; to demonstrate to the Cuban people that the regime could not serve their interests; to demonstrate that communism had no future in the Western Hemisphere; and to place extra burdens on the Soviet Union), and declared again that Washington's allies could be more helpful ('We are disturbed when other free world countries supply products that cannot help but increase Cuba's capacity for mischief'). The following day Washington announced that foodstuffs and medical supplies would no longer be exempted from the embargo. The Western media, to their credit, denounced this move.[21]

The embargo was held in place over subsequent years, making Cuba increasingly dependent on aid and trade support from the Socialist bloc. The regime had withstood a continuous campaign of CIA-orchestrated terrorism, military invasion, industrial sabotage, agricultural arson, assassination, threat of assassination, the manipulation of regional bodies, the pressures of the 'missile crisis' (which involved a high-seas embargo within the continuous trade blockade), intimidation of domestic and foreign companies, threats to trading nations, and all the many burdens of the broad economic war being waged by a superpower against a relatively small Caribbean island. Despite everything, Castro appeared to remain positive and optimistic: on 26 July 1974 he declared that 'the isolation of Cuba is slowly withering away' (and, relishing the current Watergate scandal, observed that the CIA and its trained subversives had been 'much more effective' in destroying the US presidency than in overthrowing the Cuban Revolution). On 29 July the OAS voted (16 to 3, with 2 abstentions) to end the US-instigated collective sanctions against diplomatic relations with Cuba (with OAS countries now 'free to normalise or carry on relations' with Cuba 'at the level and in the form that each state deems convenient'). On 21 August the Ford Administration terminated the prohibition of exports to Cuba by foreign subsidiaries of US companies. President Carter, in turn, removed a number of petty restrictions; but it was plain that the broad sanctions regime would remain in place – as would the US-inspired terrorist attacks against the island.[22]

On 16 June 1977 the Senate Foreign Relations Committee blocked moves to end the embargo; with Carter himself currently opposing even a relaxation of the embargo on foodstuffs and medical supplies. Nonetheless, Castro was forced to acknowledge a 'lessening of tension' during the period of the Carter Administration (noting such developments as the halting of spy-plane surveillance, though spy satellites were now in use; US–Cuban agreement on fishing and maritime boundaries; the easing of travel restrictions; and various diplomatic moves). On 19 June 1979 Ted Weiss, a New York Democrat, introduced legislation to end the embargo and to re-establish diplomatic relations with Havana, but this initiative came to nought. Soon a new Republican president would be in the White

House: the sanctions, for a while under threat, would soon be toughened.

In June 1984 the Reverend Jesse Jackson briefed members of Congress about his recent trip to Cuba and Central America, and commented that talks about migration would begin soon. President Ronald Reagan, predictably hostile to any rapprochement with Cuba, responded (in a 2 July recording for the Fourth of July) by questioning the legality of such missions to Cuba; a few days later, Reagan admitted that he had gone 'astray' in raising the matter of legality. But now the scene was set for tougher sanctions. On 22 August 1986 the US Treasury Department introduced new measures: 'crackdowns' on trade with Cuban front companies located in other countries; and greater control of organisations promoting travel to Cuba; new limits were imposed on the cash and gifts that Cuban Americans were allowed to send to their relatives in Cuba; tighter controls were imposed on organisations shipping humanitarian goods to the island; and politicians were discouraged from seeking any easing of the sanctions regime. It was now clear that the Reagan Administration was intent on increasing the pressure on the Cuban people.

The Cuban Democracy Act (1992)

In early 1990 the US State Department's Bureau of Public Affairs took further steps to reinforce the economic embargo on Cuba, claiming that US property had been illicitly confiscated and confirming the ban on exporting to and importing from Cuba. On 28 February Senator Connie Mack announced his intention to enlist the new governments in Eastern Europe in the US anti-Castro crusade; and in April Dante B. Fascell, Chairman of the House Committee on International Relations, introduced a bill to prevent US foreign subsidiaries from trading with Cuba; and to block the supply of US aid to countries buying Cuban sugar. In addition, US ports would be closed to all ships that had conveyed goods to Cuba in the previous six months. Now, with Cuba no longer able to rely on the Socialist bloc, observers predicted that the economic sanctions would begin to bite. On 26 October 1990 the US Congress passed legislation that included the Mack Amendment, designed to stop US companies abroad from trading with Cuba. But US opposition to the embargo was growing: it violated provisions of the US constitution; and foreign governments were becoming increasingly alarmed at American attempts to abolish their sovereign trading rights. The American Civil Liberties Committee (ACLC) lodged a suit against the government because the embargo included works of art, so violating both the Constitutional right of freedom of expression and a 1988 enactment that exempted such items from the blockade; in June a group of political, religious and union organisations in Puerto Rico condemned the mounting US campaign of 'harassment and pressure' against the Cuban people; and even the *Miami Herald* (25 September 1990) was forced to consider the problems faced by the US Congress keen to pass laws that would conflict with legislation in other countries. In Canada and elsewhere there was growing hostility to the possibility of American domestic legislation intended to restrict aspects of international trade. Thus Joe Clark, Canada's Minister for External Affairs, condemned the Mack Amendment as 'clearly unacceptable'; while Denis Laliberte, a Foreign Ministry spokesman, emphasised that the laws governing Canadian exports were a matter for Canada. And it was now plain that Canada was not alone: few countries were prepared to concede that the United States had the right to legislate for the control of commercial activities outside its borders. In the event President Bush procrastinated over signing the bill, and it fell; but now, with growing support among the American Right for the Mack Amendment, or some equivalent, new legislation along these lines would not be long delayed.

It soon emerged that the new torch-bearer for fresh anti-Cuba legislation would be Robert Torricelli, a New Jersey Democrat who in November 1988 had been impressed by the absence of destitution in Havana ('living standards are not high, but the homelessness, hunger and disease that is witnessed in much of Latin America does not appear evident'). On 5 February 1992, sharing a press conference with Jorge Mas Canosa, a Bay of Pigs veteran and now president of the anti-Castro Cuban-American National Foundation, Torricelli introduced the proposed Cuban Democracy Act of 1992. (*Time* magazine, 20 October 1992, revealed that the Foundation had spent more than a million dollars to buy influence in Congress; $57,000 had been donated to the George Bush election campaign, and $26,000 had gone to Robert Torricelli himself.)

The Torricelli bill was intended (like the Mack Amendment) to end the US corporate subsidiary trade with Cuba (most of which was in foodstuffs and medical supplies); to encourage presidential pressure on Western allies; to apply sanctions on Latin American countries trading with Cuba; to deny ships trading with Cuba any US port facilities for the following six months; and to provide US government funds and supplies for anti-Castro groups (that is, terrorists) both within and outside Cuba. One report suggested that Torricelli's main financial backer was the 'Free Cuba' Political Action Committee, including terrorists and linked to the Foundation.[23] Bush had already signed a decree banning foreign ships from US ports if they visited Cuba; and now, sensitive to the views of the American Right, he was ready to support the Torricelli bill. Torricelli was then ready to boast that the government had 'accepted the inevitability of the embargo being strengthened', but he soon faced a problem. When the House Foreign Affairs Committee voted on the bill (21 May), a Ted Weiss amendment was passed (11 to 10) exempting medicines and medical supplies. A horrified Torricelli responded by tagging on a mandate (that Cuba would be sure to reject, as would any country) that a US official must be allowed to accompany any medical sale to oversee distribution); a further Weiss amendment to exempt foodstuffs also failed. The Act was then passed, including a *de facto* ban on food and medical exports from the United States and subsidiary companies to Cuba. In due course the entire bill was appended to the Defense Appropriations Act, already approved by the House.

The new legislation aroused substantial domestic and foreign opposition. Thus Victor Sidel (of the American Public Health Association (APHA)), after praising Cuba's 'exemplary national health system', commented that surely the United States could devise a policy 'that does not cause suffering among an entire population in order to accomplish our national policy objectives'. In the same spirit, Ricardo Valero, head of the Foreign Relations Commission in the Mexican Chamber of Deputies, declared that the new measures 'confirm the United States as the leading violator of international law'. Canadian politicians continued to denounce the new legislation; and even the normally supine Britain found the Torricelli law too much to swallow (Trade Secretary Peter Lilley: it was 'for the British government, not the US Congress, to determine the UK's policy on trade with Cuba'). On 4 June the US Senate Foreign Relations Committee approved the Torricelli bill, now widely perceived as a fresh attempt to cripple the Cuban economy.

Washington was now committed to a comprehensive sabotage of Cuba's industrial and social programmes. Domestic legislation could be used; or direct communication (letters or telephone calls) may be employed to coerce American and foreign firms into subservience to US strategic policy. In his address to the UN General Assembly in November 1991 (before the enactment of the Cuban Democracy Act), Richard Alarjon, Cuba's UN ambassador, cited 27 cases of trade contracts sabotaged by US intimidation of foreign companies. Dozens of companies have been affected in this way: for example, Royal Dutch Shell, Clyde Petroleum (according to *Petroleum Economist*, September 1992), Tate & Lyle, British Cable & Wireless, the Monterrey Group, Eli Lilly Canada, Cargill SACI, Continental SACINF and many others. Now the Clinton Administration was making it plain that the economic blockade of Cuba would continue, despite the plight of a civilian population 'trembling on the brink of famine and chaos';[24] and despite the damage caused to the trade of US allies.[25] All this was not enough: on 15 February 1995 Jesse Helms suggested that it was time to introduce further legislation to tighten the noose around Cuba.

Cuban Liberty and Democratic Solidarity (Libertad) Act (1996)

The prospect of fresh US legislation to implement the Libertad Act was soon creating tensions with America's closest allies and others. The new law would, among other things, punish European-based subsidiaries of US corporations for dealings with Cuba, ban European sugar companies from doing business in the United States if they import Cuban sugar, and deny US visas to executives of companies trading with Cuba. Here was the prospect of draconian legislation with deliberate extraterritorial reach, designed to further cripple the Cuban economy by attacking foreign companies prepared to trade with the island. The European Union was now warning that the new legislation before Congress would breach international trade laws and damage already strained transatlantic relations. Thus in April 1995 Sir Leon Brittan, vice-president of the European Commission, wrote to the US Secretary of State Warren Christopher to say that the new measures would violate the rules of the General Agreement on Tariffs and Trade (GATT) and could cause 'legal chaos' – without encouraging a 'peaceful and orderly' transition to democracy in Cuba.

On 18 April 1995 Senator Jesse Helms (with Representative Dan Burton one of the two principal sponsors of the Libertad Act), talking to Cuban-American exiles, called for a total blockade of Cuba and attacked British companies that continued to trade with the island. One purpose of the Helms–Burton law would be to threaten legal action against any firm 'trafficking' in property confiscated by the Castro government (Helms: 'Let this be the year Cubans say farewell to Fidel. I don't care whether Fidel leaves horizontally or vertically, but he's leaving').

There were signs that President Clinton, well aware of European alarm at the prospect of the Helms–Burton (Libertad) law, was reluctant to agree the new legislation. But then, on 24 February 1996, Cuban MiG fighters shot down two Miami-based private light aircraft flying in Cuban airspace off Havana. The resulting turmoil in the Miami anti-Castro community, horrified at the killing of four Cuban-American exiles, made it increasingly difficult for Clinton to resist Helms–Burton. In early March the US Senate overwhelmingly approved the bill, which meant that the Helms–Burton initiative had now secured substantial congressional approval. On 12 March President Clinton, standing with the families of the four men killed, signed into law the Cuban Liberty and Democratic Solidarity Act (and so performed a massive U-turn). Said Clinton: 'In their memory I will continue to do everything I can to help the tide of democracy that has swept our entire hemisphere finally reach the shores of Cuba.'

The passing of new anti-Cuba sanctions legislation, designed to have extraterritorial reach, provoked an immediate international response. The Canadian Prime Minister Jean Chrétien telephoned Clinton to denounce the improper US interference in trade outside the United States and denounced Helms–Burton as contrary to the spirit and the letter of the North American Free Trade Agreement (NAFTA). The European Union (EU) declared that it would not accept unilateral decisions prejudicing other countries, unless such decisions had passed before a multinational court. Spain noted that the new legislation was in violation of international law and contrary to agreements made by international bodies such as the WTO. Few doubted the powerful extraterritorial scope of the new law (Figure 3.2), designed to bend international trade into support for US policy.

The Act, a massive and unambiguous attempt to interfere in the affairs not only of Cuba but of many other sovereign trading nations with the aim of toppling the internationally recognised Cuban government (seat in the UN, and so on) and of securing a pro-Washington puppet regime in Havana, includes the words (Section 201(2)):

> The policy of the United States is ... to recognise that the self-determination of the Cuban people is a sovereign and national right of the citizens of Cuba which must be exercised free of interference by the government of any other country.

This risible self-contradiction may be judged an apt metaphor on all US claims to ethical commitment while pursuing a cynically untrammelled self-interest.

The Cuban regime was taking heart at the widespread international condemnation of Helms–Burton and the likelihood that the new legislation would be ignored. Thus Carlos Amat, Cuba's Justice Minister, commented after a five-day official visit to Britain, that Lord Mackay (the Lord Chancellor) and Sir Nicholas Bonsor (Minister of State at the Foreign Office), amongst others, informed him that no attention was being paid to the legislation (Amat: 'I was assured ...

that our current economic relations were set to improve'). Senior officials from Canada and Mexico (well aware that Helms–Burton was in conflict with NAFTA) continued to object to the new law; and further objections were expressed in France, Belgium, Brazil, Peru, Costa Rica, Paraguay, Uruguay, Panama, Nicaragua, Vietnam, Haiti, Bolivia, North Korea, Venezuela, Russia, Chile, the Middle East and the European Union (this latter declaring that it was heading for a serious confrontation with Washington).

It was now being reported that under the new US sanctions legislation the chief executives of 26 British companies (including Body Shop, Tate & Lyle and Cable & Wireless) faced possible arrest at American airports, banishment from the United States and multi-million-pound fines for trading with Cuba. At the end of May 1996 the UK Foreign Secretary Malcolm Rifkind flew to Washington to protest at the new sanctions legislation. One observer noted that the colonnaded British embassy in Havana could be classed under Helms–Burton as 'stolen property', nominally belonging to a family that emigrated to Miami in the 1980s. Could the British Foreign Office be sued in the US courts? (When a British official dismissed the possibility he was dubbed 'callous' by a spokesman for the Cuban – American National Foundation.)

On 10 July 1996 a group of Canadian executives were told that they would be barred from the United States under the requirements of Helms–Burton; visas would be denied to nine senior employees and shareholders in the Sherritt International nickel mining corporation. At the same time more than 20 leading British companies (including BAT, ED & F Man, Tate & Lyle, Fisons and Glaxo) were concerned that they could soon be facing charges in American courts. On 11 July the Mexican government formally protested that the Helms–Burton Act violated the principles of the United Nations, the World Trade Organization and NAFTA. Now there were signs that Clinton was beginning to bend under the mounting international pressure; that he might exercise his right to waive the most controversial Helms–Burton provisions for six months. One observer noted that the Act was the most blatant example of extraterritoriality since the Arabs imposed third-party sanctions against countries which traded with Israel following the 1972 Yom Kippur War.[26] In September the Canadian government introduced a bill, amending the Foreign Extraterritorial Measures Act, to counter Helms–Burton; and in October the United States moved to block an EU initiative for WTO scrutiny of Helms–Burton.

On 6 November 1996 Jorge Perez-Otermin, the Uruguay ambassador to the United Nations, made available to the Secretary-General

SEC. 102 ENFORCEMENT OF THE ECONOMIC EMBARGO OF CUBA
(a) Policy
(1) Restrictions by other countries. – The Congress hereby reaffirms section 1704(a) of the Cuban Democracy Act of 1992, which states that the President should encourage foreign countries to restrict trade and credit relations with Cuba in a manner consistent with the purposes of that Act.

(2) Sanctions on other countries – The Congress further urges the President to take immediate steps to apply the sanctions described in section 1704(b)(1) of that Act against countries assisting Cuba.

(b) Diplomatic Efforts. – The Secretary of State should ensure that United States diplomatic personnel abroad understand and, in their contacts with foreign officials. are communicating the reasons for the United States economic embargo of Cuba, and are urging foreign governments to cooperate more effectively with the embargo.
[...]
SEC. 103 PROHIBITION AGAINST INDIRECT FINANCING OF CUBA

(a) Prohibition. – Notwithstanding any other provision of law, no loan, credit, or other financing may be extended knowingly by a United States national, a permanent resident alien, or a United States agency to any person for the purpose of financing transactions involving any confiscated property the claim to which is owned by a United States national as of the date of the enactment of this Act, except for financing by the United States national owning such claim for a transaction permitted under United States law.

SEC. 104 UNITED STATES OPPOSITION TO CUBAN MEMBERSHIP IN INTERNATIONAL FINANCIAL INSTITUTIONS
[...]
(a) Continued Opposition to Cuban Membership in International Financial Institutions. –
(1) In General – Except as provided in paragraph (2), the Secretary of the Treasury shall instruct the United States executive director of each international financial institution to use the voice and vote of the United States to oppose the admission of Cuba as a member of such institution until the President submits a determination under section 203(c)(3) that a democratically elected government in Cuba is in power.
[...]
(b) Reduction in United States Payments to International Financial Institutions. – If any international financial institution approves a loan or other assistance to the Cuban Government over the opposition of the United States, then ... the Secretary of the Treasury shall withhold from payment to such institution an amount equal to the amount of the loan or other assistance, with respect to either of the following types of payment:
(1) The paid-in portion of the increase in capital stock of the institution.
(2) The callable portion of the increase in capital stock of the institution.

(c) Definition. – For purposes of this section, the term 'international financial institution' means the International Monetary Fund, the International Bank for Reconstruction and Development, the International Development Association, the International Finance Corporation, the Multilateral Investment Guaranty Agency, and the Inter-American Development Bank.

[...]

SEC. 105 UNITED STATES OPPOSITION TO TERMINATION OF THE SUSPENSION OF THE CUBAN GOVERNMENT FROM PARTICIPATION IN THE ORGANIZATION OF AMERICAN STATES

The President should instruct the United States Permanent Representative to the Organization of American States to oppose and vote against any termination of the suspension of the Cuban Government from participation in the Organization until the President determines under section 203(c)(3) that a democratically elected government in Cuba is in power.

SEC. 106 ASSISTANCE BY THE INDEPENDENT STATES OF THE FORMER SOVIET UNION FOR THE CUBAN GOVERNMENT

(a) Reporting Requirement. – Not later than 90 days after the date of the enactment of this Act, the President shall submit to the appropriate congressional committees a report detailing progress toward the withdrawal of personnel of any independent state of the former Soviet Union (within the meaning of section 3 of the FREEDOM Support Act (22 U.S.C. 5801)), including advisers, technicians, and military personnel, from the Cienfuegos nuclear facility in Cuba.

[...]

SEC. 401 EXCLUSION FROM THE UNITED STATES OF ALIENS WHO HAVE CONFISCATED PROPERTY OF UNITED STATES NATIONALS OR WHO TRAFFIC IN SUCH PROPERTY

(a) Grounds For Exclusion. – The Secretary of State shall deny a visa to, and the Attorney General shall exclude from the United States, any alien who the Secretary of State determines is a person who, after the date of the enactment of this Act –

(1) has confiscated, or has directed or overseen the confiscation of, property a claim to which is owned by a United States national, or converts or has converted for personal gain confiscated property, a claim to which is owned by a United States national;

[...]

(2) traffics in confiscated property, a claim to which is owned by a United States national;

(3) is a corporate officer, principal, or shareholder with a controlling interest of an entity which has been involved in the confiscation of property or trafficking in confiscated property, a claim to which is owned by a United States national; or

(4) is a spouse, minor child, or agent of a person excludable under paragraph (1), (2), or (3).

Figure 3.2   Helms–Burton Act, 1996 – Extracts

'Decision 377', adopted at the 12th regular meeting of the Latin American Council (Montevideo, 23–25 October 1996). Decision 377 included the words:

> *The Latin American Council ... Decides...*

> Article 1: *To reaffirm* its strongest rejection of the 'Helms–Burton Act' ... because it disregards the fundamental principles of respect for sovereignty; contravenes the rules governing co-existence among States; imposes unilateral and extraterritorial sanctions; and constitutes a flagrant violation of international law and the principles and rules of international trade;

> Article 2: *To reiterate* its position in favour of the immediate lifting of the economic, commercial and financial embargo imposed by the United States ... against Cuba and to call on the Government of the United States ... to repeal the 'Helms–Burton Act';

> Article 3: *To promote* among member States an official exchange of information and experience in elaborating and applying 'antidote' or 'mirror' laws against the 'Helms–Burton Act' ... .

The pressure against Helms–Burton continued to mount. On 16 December 1996 Jacques Santer, EC president, meeting Bill Clinton in Washington, urged a lifting of the sanctions threats against European firms. On 18 February 1997 Sir Leon Brittan, a European trade commissioner, described Helms–Burton as unacceptable, unjustified and unproductive ('Fidel Castro must be laughing all the way to the bank'). And even the 82-year-old David Rockefeller, speaking in October 1997, said that he felt a sense of horror when President Clinton signed the unjustified Helms–Burton Act. On 23 January 1998 the Pope, visiting Camaquey during his time in Cuba, took pains to condemn America's 'deplorable' blockade of Cuba – a statement that induced Clinton to make some minor adjustments to the sanctions regime.

The international attitude to the American economic blockade of Cuba has become unambiguous, as signalled not least by the annual votes in the UN General Assembly (Table 3.2). The bishops at the Americas Synod, inaugurated by the Pope in late 1997 (in session until 12 December) demanded the lifting of all economic blockades in particular the sanctions regime maintained by Washington against Cuba. At a press conference Monsignor Oscar Rodriguez Maradiaga, president of the Latin American Bishops Conference (CELAM), noted the conviction of the church in that region that economic sanctions are unjust because they increase the suffering of the poorest sectors of society (embargoes should be imposed 'on the sale of weapons, which create more conflicts and constitute immoral trade').

Table 3.2   General Assembly votes against US blockade of Cuba

Year	Against US	For US	Abstentions
1992	59	3	71
1993	88	4	58
1994	101	2	49
1995	117	3	39
1996	137	3	25
1997	143	3	17
1998	157	2	12

In March 1998 Cuban-American organisations opposed to the sanctions regime were mounting a campaign in support of a bill authorising the sale of food and medicines to the Cuban people. In a joint statement issued in Miami, support for the bill was expressed by the Antonio Maceo Brigade, the Cuban Community Workers Alliance, the African-Cuban Cultural Rescue and the Coalition against the Blockade. The bill was being sponsored by representatives Esteban Torres and Charles Rangel and by Senator Christopher Dodd; with support offered by David Rockefeller, Craig Fuller (Presidential Secretary under Bush), Lyon M. Bentsen (Treasury Secretary in Clinton's first term), Frank Carlucci (Pentagon head under Reagan) and others. It seemed unlikely that the proposed bill would succeed. Secretary of State Madeleine Albright was indicating that some economic measures against Cuba would be removed but that the main features of the blockade would remain. Castro had no doubt that Cuba had won the argument: on 1 May 1998, at a ceremony held to decorate the year's National Heroes of Labour, he pronounced the blockade 'morally crushed, morally defeated' – the almost unanimous opinion of governments throughout the world.[27] In June the Brazilian judge José Mario Peixoto da Costa presented before the International Court of Justice at The Hague a lawsuit denouncing the continuing American blockade against Cuba. In interview with *Granma International* (21 June 1998) he commented:

> My motivation is known to all: for almost 40 years, the world's greatest economic power has unscrupulously been supporting assassination attempts and trying to destroy 11 million people.

Genocide is considered a crime by the laws of every country and for this reason the United States should be prosecuted ...

I know all about the Nuremberg trial and I have come to the conclusion that the crimes committed by the United States are similar to those carried out by the Nazis. Without issuing a declaration of war, the US has maintained the blockade against such a small neighbour. And if that wasn't enough ... it has tightened this blockade with the Torricelli and Helms–Burton Acts.

José Mario declared also that he would try to demonstrate by means of the Compensation Law that the United States owed Cuba more than $50 billion. The US demanded compensation for the properties confiscated by the Revolution: 'Cuba has every right to demand compensation for the damage caused by the blockade ... .' In July the Cuban Foreign Minister Roberto Robaina, speaking at the Rome headquarters of the UN Food and Agriculture Organization, denounced the blockade as a crime against humanity. At the same time US scientists and social scientists were condemning the blockade as immoral, illegal and inhumane.[28] World opinion was plain, but as late as September 1998 it was doing little to erode Washington's determination to exterminate the Cuban people.

Genocide I

The years-long US attempt to deny Cuba access to food, medicine and drinkable water represents a clear case of genocide. The UN Genocide Convention[29] defines as genocide any of various acts intend to destroy 'in whole or in part, a national, ethnical, racial or religious group'. These acts include: killing members of the group, causing them serious bodily or mental harm, and deliberately inflicting on the group conditions of life calculated to bring about its physical destruction in whole or in part. Genocide itself is punishable, as are the conspiracy, incitement or attempt to commit genocide, and complicity in genocide. Persons who may be punished include 'constitutionally responsible rulers, public officials or private individuals'.

The American blockade has had incalculable consequences for the health and general well-being of the Cuban people. With a *de facto* and *de jure* embargo on Cuban access to food and medicine, the incidence of disease and malnutrition has soared; with no sign of relief for a civilian population posing no conceivable strategic threat to the United States. As a few examples (apart from the broad trading prohibition): the US Treasury refused to license Medix (Argentina) to sell Cuba spare parts for medical equipment; the Ayerst Laboratories (Canada) has been blocked from supplying colyrum (for the treatment of gas and chemical damage to the eyes) to the Cuban health service; CGR Thompson (France) has been denied a US licence to sell Cuba spare parts for medical X-ray equipment; Siemens (Germany) has been blocked from selling Gamma Cameras, an ultra-sound system and a Magnetic Nuclear Resonance system – all intended for use in the Cuban health service; Toshiba (Japan) has been denied licences to sell medical equipment to Cuba; and Alfa-Laval (Sweden) has been blocked from supplying filtration cartridges to the Cuban health service.[30] Maria del Carmen, aged 27 (in July 1996), had been suffering seriously worsening sight for months and was unable to obtain glasses because of the blockade. Francisco Rodriquez, a journalist, commented: 'Most people are affected by this blockade in terms of medicine, food, transport, water, electricity, all those basic needs. Living under this continual lack has made Cuban people very stressed, very nervous.' Silvana Mayoral, a teacher, directed her anger at Washington: 'They are crazy sometimes, the Americans. What gives them the right?'

A press release (30 November 1996) for the prestigious British medical journal the *Lancet* indicated the scale of the US embargo against the supply of medical supplies to Cuba. Dr Anthony F. Kirkpatrick (Tampa, Florida) was cataloguing firms (Johnson & Johnson, Merck, International Murex and others) that had been prevented from exporting medical equipment to Cuba. He has noted that the Inter-American Commission on Human Rights of the Organization of American States has denounced the Cuban embargo on food and medicines as a violation of international law. In early 1997 journalists were continuing to report the affects of the US embargo on the civilian population: 'The shortages of food and medicine meant that the kids became a bit more asthmatic and the adults got skinnier than ever ... Today, Fidel's market reforms are gradually solving the food problem. But the kids are still sick.'[31] In March 1997 the American Association for World Health – the US Committee for the World Health Organization (WHO) and the Pan American Health Organization (PAHO) – issued a report on the consequences of the embargo on Cuban health: 'The outright ban on the sale of American foodstuffs has contributed to serious nutritional deficits, particularly among pregnant women, leading to an increase in low birth-weight babies ... food shortages were linked to a devastating outbreak of neuropathy numbering in the tens of thousands ... The embargo ... has led to serious cutbacks in supplies of safe drinking water ... a factor in the rising incidence of morbidity and mortality rates ... Due to the direct or indirect effects of the embargo, the most routine medical supplies are in short supply or entirely absent from some Cuban clinics.'[32] Media coverage of the report in the West was minimal. The *Guardian* (7 March 1997), under the heading 'Children die in agony as US trade ban stifles Cuba', gave various details:

> Child cancer sufferers are some of the most distressing victims of the embargo, which bans Cuba from buying nearly half of the world-class drugs in a market dominated by US manufacturers.
>
> This team visited a paediatric ward which had been without the nausea preventing drug, metclopramide HCl, for 22 days. It found that 22 children undergoing chemotherapy were vomiting on average 28 to 30 times a day.
>
> Another girl, aged five, in a cancer ward lacking Implantofix for chemotherapy, was being treated through her jugular vein because all her other veins had collapsed. She was in excruciating pain.

The American Association for World Health (AAWH) noted that few other embargoes had banned food and denied life-saving medicines to ordinary citizens: *'Such an embargo appears to violate the most basic international charters and conventions governing human rights, including the United Nations charter, the charter of the Organization of American States, and the Articles of the Geneva Convention governing the treatment of civilians in wartime.'*[33]

North Korea

When the UN sanctions imposed on North Korea at the start of the Korean War (1950) were relaxed after the war, the United States continued to maintain a sanctions regime against the communist state; the bulk of this regime has been maintained to the present day – sustained, according to Washington, because of North Korean recalcitrance, its support for terrorism and its nuclear ambitions. On 18 November 1991 – at the beginning of a new phase of US rhetoric about the need to strengthen sanctions – Richard Cheney, US Defense Secretary, and General Colin Powell, the Chairman of the Joint Chiefs, voiced alarm at what they perceived as the growing nuclear threat from North Korea. No mention was made of North Korean anxiety about a possible nuclear threat from the South: the United States was allegedly storing some 60 nuclear bombs and 40 nuclear-tipped artillery shells at the Kunsan Air Base near Seoul. (On 21 November it was reported that South Korea's President Roh Tae Woo would announce in January that the US nuclear weapons had been withdrawn, but the issue remained controversial: for example, would Seoul allow North Korean nuclear inspectors to crawl over the South?; and the United States, with its air-launched and sea-borne missile capability, still represented a local nuclear threat. In such circumstances observers may have thought it unremarkable that the North would be encouraged to develop its own nuclear potential.)

There was another matter. North Korea was also upsetting the United States by shipping Scud-C ballistic missiles to the Middle East. In early March 1992 a North Korean cargo ship carrying missiles for Iran and perhaps Syria avoided US Navy ships and entered an Iranian port. A Pentagon spokesman, Pete Williams, commented: 'We were certainly looking for it. I don't know why we never found it.' In one commentary, even if the Americans had found Scuds aboard the ship, the *Dae Hung Ho*, the vessel would have been allowed to proceed – if only because Iran, Syria and North Korea are not signatories to the Missile Technology Control Regime. The United States had no legal authority to stop ships on the high seas, but this was regarded as a minor irrelevance in the area of *realpolitik* calculation.

The nuclear issue remained primary. In May 1992 Hans Blix, the IAEA Director-General, with senior advisors, visited North Korea and inspected several nuclear installations. The North Korean authorities declared that IAEA personnel would be allowed to visit any site, irrespective of whether it appeared in an initial report submitted to the Agency. But the atmosphere of apparent accord was not set to last. In February 1993 North Korea rejected an IAEA request for further inspections, whereupon Hans Blix convened a meeting of the Agency's governors to consider the deteriorating situation. In March the United States and Britain were pressing for a Security Council resolution to impose sanctions on North Korea, but were forced to reckon with the likelihood of a Chinese veto.[34] It seemed clear that, denied the opportunity of UN sanctions, Washington would intensify its unilateral embargo on North Korea.

Commentators were quick to urge intensified economic sanctions and other measures. Thus Zalmay M. Khalilzad, director of strategy at the Rand Corporation (and one-time Assistant Under-Secretary of Defense in the Bush Administration), declared that North Korea was playing a frightening game of cat and mouse: 'Other countries, and particularly the United States, should not let the North Koreans get away with it. We should threaten them with economic sanctions, and soon.' Here there is focus on UN-mandated sanctions, but with the option of unilateral American action: Washington 'should increase US military action in the region, and South Korea's. This would help discourage North Korean adventurism and signal to Pyongyang that it is on a dangerous course. *It would also enforce a blockade, if need be*' (my italics).[35] On 12 March 1993 North Korea announced that it was withdrawing from the Nuclear Non-Proliferation Treaty (1968), a decision it was fully entitled to take under Article X(1) of the treaty. The announcement drew immediate condemnation from the United States, South Korea and Japan (Pyongyang declared its withdrawal a 'well-justified self-defensive measure against the nuclear war manoeuvres of the secretariat of the IAEA' and condemned the US 'nuclear threats against North Korea'). By 1994 it was clear that Washington, thwarted by the prospect of a Chinese veto in the Security Council, would be unable to secure a UN sanctions resolution.

Now, in a cynical change of strategic tack, the United States began offering North Korea trade deals, aid and diplomatic recognition to persuade Pyongyang to allow IAEA inspectors to visit suspect nuclear sites. The US unilateral economic sanctions were increasingly recognised as ineffectual: the North Korea economy was already in disarray, with widespread human suffering, but there were already so few outside trading contracts that there was little scope for further external economic pressure. There were suggestions also that any attempt to impose even tougher sanctions might provoke a desperate North into war with the South, a conflict that the United States and its allies would inevitably win but only after likely devastation of Seoul and much of the South.

In early 1995 a radical South Korean newspaper, *Hankyoreh*, reported that America was planning to ease the current trade embargo on North Korea as a means of opening up the country to outside scrutiny. Washington was reportedly about to give permission to US companies to sell in North Korea and to send investment study teams to the Communist country. One suggestion was that a direct telephone link would be set up between North Korea and the United States, the first development of its kind since the Korean War. Now Pyongyang was declaring that it would lift its restrictions on the import of US goods and end the ban on the entry of American merchant shipping. Agreement had already been reached (in October) on the lowering of certain trade and investment barriers ('within three months of the date of the agreement'). At the same time, as an element in its emerging 'carrot and stick' policy, Washington continued to threaten the possibility of UN sanctions (in the hope that bribes to China would prevent a Security Council veto).

On 13 January 1995 the South Korean government announced that its citizens may now send up to $5000 a year to help their beleaguered relatives in the North. It was not thought that the move would make much difference to the North's economic plight but symbolised the perception that North Korea might be less dangerous if its international isolation were to be gradually eroded. Former prohibitions had not stopped many South Koreans sending cash to their relatives across the border, and now the volume of such transfers was expected to increase. There were other signs of a growing rapprochement: for example, for four years southern businesses had been quietly buying minerals and labour from the North; and since October 1994 Seoul had allowed its companies to invest in tourism and factories in North Korea. On 20 January 1995 the US State Department announced a partial lifting of economic sanctions: American telecommunications firms would be allowed to do business in North Korea, and US citizens would be allowed to engage in credit-card transactions there. In addition, North Korea would be allowed to use the American banking system for certain transactions; and to export to the US magnesite, a material used in the steel industry. Such measures – a consequence of the October (1994) deal signalled a new phase in US–North Korean relations, one based on Pyongyang's pledge to dispose of its nuclear reactors. Now US firms would be allowed to participate in a proposed $4 billion deal under which the existing reactors in North Korea would be replaced by modern, light-water reactors (thought to pose less of a military threat).

Tensions were again mounting in February. Questions were being raised about who would pay for the new reactors (no one doubted the parlous state of the northern economy); and Washington and South Korea, keen to exploit the North's predicament, were tying food aid to the degree of North Korean flexibility in new negotiations. Desultory talks continued for months, during which time the northern economy continued to deteriorate and millions of North Korean children were reportedly on the brink of starvation. On 24 April 1997 North Korea demanded diplomatic recognition, large-scale food aid and a further easing of trade sanctions before it would join in new peace talks with the United States, South Korea and China. The wrangles continued with no real progress, but now there was no talk of an intensification of unilateral US sanctions or a US-inspired sanctions resolution being presented to the UN Security Council.

On 9 June 1998 President Clinton suggested that the international (non-UN) sanctions that continued to isolate North Korea might be withdrawn: 'the necessary steps to ease sanctions' would be taken if Pyongyang provided plausible guarantees that it would not develop nuclear weapons. This followed a comment by the South Korean president Kim Dae-jung that the best way to avoid military confrontation might be to loosen the punitive sanctions and to prepare the way for trade and dialogue ('It is time to take a bolder approach. It would be desirable for the United States to ease its economic sanctions ...'). Washington remained cautious: nothing had been settled, and now there were signs that Pyongyang was preparing to restart its nuclear programme. There were plans to unseal, for 'maintenance', the main nuclear reactor at the Yongbyon research centre; and the North Koreans were refusing to finish transferring the spent fuel rods into safe canisters – a clear breach of the 1994 US–North Korean agreement. The United States was failing to honour its pledges under the Agreed Framework by not delivering the specified heavy fuel oil (as compensation for freezing the Yongbyon reactor); and the supply of the light-water reactors was a year behind schedule.[36]

Some observers were suggesting that North Korean ambitions were being stimulated by nuclear developments in India and Pakistan, castigated by a seemingly impotent United States (see below). In any event little had been done to reduce the tensions in the Korean peninsula. Despite Washington's failure, over a seven-year period, to secure sanctions resolutions through the UN Security Council, a substantial array of US-led international sanctions against North Korea would remain. The country's economy would continue to deteriorate, millions of civilians would suffer, and the continuing tensions in the region would be fed.

Vietnam

With the ending of the Vietnam War in 1975 it was widely assumed that the Vietnamese would be able to begin rebuilding their devastated land. Nothing was farther from the truth: the United States was not about to forgive Vietnam for the defeat and humiliation that had been inflicted on the most powerful country in the world. Vietnam would continue to be punished, but by lower-profile means; namely, by means of harsh economic sanctions. The new phase, set to last into the 1990s began with an international trade embargo, the blocking of access to global finance, the vetoing of international aid programmes, and other measures designed to block any Vietnamese attempt at national reconstruction. In a secret protocol to the 1973

Peace Agreement, confirmed by President Richard Nixon in a letter (1 February 1973) to Vietnamese premier Pham Van Dong, Washington was pledged to contribute $4.5 billion to aid the reconstruction of Vietnam. The United States now reneged on this agreement: everything would be done to block all Vietnamese attempts to rebuild its ruined society.

The economic sanctions imposed on North Vietnam in 1963 were extended to the whole of Vietnam in 1975; $150 million of Vietnamese assets were frozen; and a Congressional amendment to the Foreign Assistance Appropriation Act of 1976 explicitly prohibited any aid whatsoever for Vietnam, Cambodia and Laos. The US policy achieved its intended results: the economic crisis in Vietnam intensified and throughout Indochina the regional tensions mounted. Throughout the 1980s American policy remained largely unchanged, ensuring that the bulk of the Vietnamese population continued to live in penury. In the early 1990s Washington was continuing to block Vietnamese access to world finance from third parties (such as Japan), the World Bank, the IMF and the Asian Development Bank; French efforts, at the 1991 IMF/World Bank conference, to settle Vietnam's debts, were sabotaged by the United States. It was now clear that US policy was exacerbating the problem of the 'boat people' and other Vietnamese crises.

In mid-May 1991 the situation began to improve. The US business community, noting the commercial opportunities in the Vietnamese commercial environment, was now pressing for change.[37] In November 1992 Japan issued a large commodity loan for Vietnam, marking an end to a 14-year ban and suggesting that the crippling American embargo would soon be over. Through 1992 some 43 American trade missions, sensitive to the trade possibilities, had visited Vietnam; and leading US companies were now expressing their commercial interests. In July 1993 President Clinton announced that Washington would no longer oppose Vietnam's interest in securing IMF help; and in September partially lifted the embargo. On 28 January 1994 the US Senate voted (68 to 32) for the removal of the US trade embargo on Vietnam; on 6 August Warren Christopher opened Washington's first embassy in Vietnam for 20 years, and at once urged the Vietnamese regime to introduce market reforms.

Libya, Iran and the D'Amato Act

The United States introduced unilateral sanctions on Libya in 1978, long before the Lockerbie outrage and long before Washington's successful efforts to suborn the United Nations into adopting anti-Libya sanctions resolutions (Chapter 2). In 1978 the US banned military equipment sales to Libya in retaliation for alleged Libyan support for terrorist groups (on 2 March 1979 the US State Department gave approval for the sale of three Boeing 747s and two 727s, after Libyan assurances that these planes would only be used for the national airline). On 29 September 1979 the State Department, acting in accordance with an amendment on terrorism added to the Revised Export Administration Act, named Libya, Syria, Iraq and South Yemen as terrorist states banned from receiving certain US exports (the export of some other goods is made contingent upon Congressional approval). On 28 October 1981 the United States imposed controls on exports of small aircraft, helicopters, aircraft spares and avionics to Libya to 'limit Libyan capacity to support military adventures in neighbouring countries'. In November the Exxon Corporation abandoned its Libyan operations.

The Reagan Administration was quick to allege further evidence of terrorist acts supported by the Libyan regime. On 11 December 1981 Washington urged Americans residing in Libya (mainly 1500 technicians) to leave 'as soon as possible' because of 'the danger' posed to them by the Libyan regime. At the same time US oil firms agreed to withdraw American personnel but declared that they would be replaced by other foreign technicians. On 10 March 1982 Reagan prohibited the import of crude oil from Libya, invoking Section 232 of the Trade Expansion Act (1962). A Presidential Proclamation (49072) noted that Libyan actions supported by oil revenues were 'inimical to United States national security'. In addition, the export to Libya of sophisticated oil and gas equipment was banned.

Throughout the 1980s the Reagan Administration continued to press for further sanctions on Libya. In December 1983 the State Department proposed to block the export of any US-made product that would aid the development of the Libyan economy; the proposed policy would have prohibited the supply of 'almost all major exports to Libya'. It was soon obvious that Washington was not relying solely on economic sanctions against the Gaddafi regime: the *Washington Post* (3 November 1985) reported that Reagan had authorised terrorist operations to undermine the Libyan regime, following a CIA assessment that only Gaddafi's 'fall will bring any significant and enduring change in Libyan policies'. Washington then moved to ban the import of refined petroleum products from Libya.

On 7 January 1986 President Reagan invoked the International Emergency Economic Powers Act to toughen the sanctions regime against Libya. A ban was now imposed against most exports to Libya, imports of goods, technology, services (except where humanitarian), all loans and credits to the Libyan government, and transactions 'relating to travel by a United States citizen ...'. Then Reagan, sensitive to the lack of support for his policies among allied countries, urged the leaders of other states 'not to undercut US sanctions against Libya ... '. Reagan officials were prepared to admit that they had not consulted with their allies before taking action (*New York Times*, 8 January 1986). Now Reagan was freezing the comprehensive Libyan assets in the United States and despatching Deputy Secretary of State John C. Whitehead to NATO countries to garner support for the US sanctions policy.

In February the United States relaxed the sanctions regime to prevent Libya from gaining a 'substantial economic windfall' that would accrue from the abandonment of contracts and concessions. At the same time American companies were urged to dispose of their Libyan holdings 'as soon as practical on fair and appropriate terms' (*New York Times*, 8 February 1986). In May, after the US bombing of Libya (15 April, see Chapter 2), Washington announced that the special exemptions for US oil companies would end on 30 June. On 13 May the Libyan Arab Foreign Bank filed suit in London seeking payment of funds under the terms of the US freeze on Libyan assets.

On 25 January 1990, a year after the Lockerbie outrage and long before Washington had thought of suborning the UN Security Council against Libya, President George Bush extended the unilateral US sanctions for another year, stating that Libya continued to pose an 'unusual and extraordinary threat' to US national security (*Journal of Commerce*, 26 January 1990). The unilateral US sanctions had failed to topple the Gaddafi regime, as did the UN sanctions imposed by a suborned Security Council. Washington then moved to another phase of extraterritorial legislation; namely the Iran and Libya Sanctions Act of 1996 (the so-called D'Amato Act, introduced by Senator Alfonse D'Amato). Before considering this legislation it is necessary to note the prior US sanctions against Iran.

On 16 January 1979 Shah Reza Mohammad Pahlavi, an American client leader, was evicted from Iran by the revolution inspired by the Ayatollah Ruhollah Khomeini. After Khomeini's return to Tehran (1 February), the US embassy was attacked and about 100 hostages were taken but released a few hours later under pressure from Khomeini supporters. On 9 March the large American oil companies, urged by the US government, announced that they would boycott Iranian oil on the world markets. On 4 November the US embassy was again overrun and 100 hostages, about 60 of them American, were taken. Khomeini refused to meet American envoys, whereupon

(8 November) the United States blocked the shipment of military spare parts to Iran. On 12 November, invoking Section 232 of the Trade Expansion Act of 1962, President Carter embargoed oil imports from Iran; Tehran immediately responded with an oil export embargo against the United States. Then, invoking the International Emergency Economic Powers Act, Carter froze all Iranian assets in US banks and their foreign subsidiaries.

The United States then proposed to the UN Security Council that economic sanctions be imposed on Iran if attempts at mediation failed. On 12 January the Council vote was delayed to allow consideration of Iranian proposals, including a demand that the United Nations investigate the 'crimes' of the Shah and that the Shah's assets be returned to Iran. The following day, with little heed paid to the Iranian appeal, the Council resolution for sanctions was blocked by a Soviet veto. The United States reiterated its determination to apply a unilateral economic embargo and immediately sought allied support. On 7 February the US State Department threatened further economic sanctions but agreed to hold them in abeyance pending UN negotiations. On 7 April President Carter toughened the sanctions regime, broke diplomatic relations with Tehran, imposed an export embargo (excluding food and medicine), ordered $8 billion in frozen assets to be used to settle US financial claims against Iran, cancelled all Iranian entry visas, closed the Iranian embassy and five consulates, and ordered the departure of 35 remaining diplomats and 209 military students. Ten days later, Carter announced further economic measures, prohibiting all financial transactions between US citizens and those of Iran, imposed an import embargo, banned travel to Iran (exempting journalists), released (for US purchase) impounded military equipment intended for use in Iran, and asked Congress to pass legislation to allow the use of frozen assets for claims and reparations.

On 19 January 1981 an escrow account was established in the Bank of England for the transfer of frozen Iranian assets; an agreement was reached for the settlement of claims; the bulk of sanctions were revoked (following agreement on the release of hostages); the transfer of the Shah's wealth was blocked, with the government of Iran given access to US courts to sue for its return; and the hostages and their families were prohibited from making legal claims against Iran for seizure of the embassy. On 20 January the inauguration of Ronald Reagan as the new US president was accompanied by the release of the American hostages in Tehran in exchange for a partial transfer of Iranian assets and other agreed relaxations of the sanctions measures. In August, in accordance with the agreements, the Iranian funds were transferred to an escrow account in The Hague. In April 1983 the situation, soon to deteriorate yet again, was more or less normalised: 'Business contacts and commercial agreements between the United States and Iran, interrupted four years ago when Ayatollah Ruhollah Khomeini came to power, are slowly, haltingly, resuming' (*Washington Post*, 10 April 1983). In one judgement the economic sanctions, 'in particular, the financial controls' had made 'a modest contribution' to the safe return of the hostages. There had been a 'very high economic and political cost'.[38]

In October 1983 more than 200 US Marines were killed in Beirut when a barracks was bombed. On 23 January 1984 the United States alleged Iranian involvement in the outrage, branded Iran a terrorist state, and imposed a range of export controls. In September President Reagan introduced a policy to deny licence applications for export to Iran of aircraft, helicopters, spares and avionics: Iran was now blocked from obtaining most of the items on the US national security export control list. The State Department remained opposed to a total trade ban, favoured by the Defense Department, because it would have violated the 1981 agreement under which the American hostages were released.

On 26 October 1987, following the passage of bills in both houses of Congress, Reagan invoked Section 505 of the International Security and Development Co-operation Act (1985) to embargo all imports from Iran and to prohibit exports of 14 types of potentially useful military goods (including inboard and outboard motors, mobile communications equipment, electrical generators and hydrofoil vessels). In June 1989, after the death of Khomeini, President Bush improved US relatious with Iran with the new government in Tehran agreeing to 'renunciation of terror' efforts in order to 'facilitate' the release of US hostages in Lebanon. By the end of the 1980s substantial Iranian assets remained frozen and the United States was admitting that military spare parts that Iran had paid for were being withheld. It was plain that Washington still regarded Iran as a terrorist state, with little prospect of a full normalisation of relations between the two countries.

In March 1992 the United States declared its intention to intercept and search a North Korean cargo ship thought to be transporting Scud missiles to Iran and Syria. Now there was growing American concern that Iran may be developing a military potential that could threaten Israel and other US interests in the region: one worry was that Iran may have been diverting credits and aid in order to purchase arms. Said one senior US official: 'This is a guns and butter issue. They want credits to buy butter and then they use their oil money to buy guns.'

Here was a case for further financial restrictions on the Tehran regime. In November Washington launched a campaign to block Western exports to Iran of all high-technology equipment with potential military uses. It was essential, declared the American strategists, to prevent Iran from producing conventional arms, ballistic missiles, nuclear weapons and germ warfare technology. The campaign was not well received by other trading nations, increasingly resentful of American efforts to dictate the patterns of global commerce. In May 1993 the Clinton Administration was reportedly planning a new effort to persuade Britain and other countries to cut off loans, investment and arms sales to the Tehran regime. At the same time there were hints that Washington regarded sanctions as ineffective and counterproductive.

Nonetheless the United States continued to discourage trade with Iran and to put in place a progressive sanctions regime. On 6 March 1995 Secretary of State Warren Christopher attacked a deal negotiated between the US company Conoco for the development of two huge offshore oil fields in Iran (Christopher: the transaction would put money into 'the evil hand of Iran'). The Conoco deal was legal, but 'also complicated in its consequences'.[39] At the same time Washington was drawing up a new sanctions regime, including a ban on the purchase of Iranian oil by US companies. Efforts had been made, without success, to prevent Russia selling Iran $1 billion worth of peaceful nuclear technology, including two light-water nuclear reactors – and so now the White House had resolved to apply mounting economic pressure on the regime. Now there were reports that Senator Alfonse D'Amato, the Republic banking committee chairman, was introducing a bill that would severely restrict trade with Iran and other countries. On 30 April President Clinton announced that he was cutting of all trade with and all investment in Iran by US firms, including oil purchases: 'I am convinced that instituting a trade embargo with Iran is the most effective way our nation can help curb Iran's drive to acquire devastating weapons and support for terrorist activities.' Doubts were expressed by America's allies, and there were immediate adverse affects on the world oil markets. Again, as with many sanctions regimes, commentators were pointing out that the US-imposed embargo would be porous.[40]

Now increased attention was being given – both within the United States and internationally – to the implications of the proposed D'Amato legislation, a framework of measures with deliberate *extraterritorial reach*. In early 1996 Britain was reportedly waging a 'desperate diplomatic campaign' to persuade the US Congress to drop the legislative plans for sanctions against foreign companies trading with Libya and Iran. The legislation, later to emerge as the *Iran and Libya Sanctions Act of 1996*, was designed to penalise non-US companies trading with Iran or Libya by denying them loans, by prohibiting their exports to the United States, and by excluding them from US government contracts. In particular, the D'Amato bill was directed against the large operators, intended to impose sanctions on any (US or non-US) company that invested more than $40 million in prohibited oil and gas sectors. One Western analyst in Tehran commented that the D'Amato bill had already affected some 12 major energy projects costing $7 billion, projects that would have boosted Iran's revenue by a quarter.

On 5 August 1996 President Clinton signed the Iran and Libya Sanctions Act into law, so setting the scene for a new confrontation with America's allies and trading partners. A Foreign Office spokesman in London declared: 'We cannot accept US pressure on its allies to impose sanctions under the threat of mandatory penalties'; and now there was the prospect of the European Commission considering the imposition of retaliatory sanctions against Washington. Minutes after the White House ceremony launching the new legislation, Clinton gave an address at George Washington University: terrorism was, he declared, 'the enemy of our generation', and Iran and Libya were the 'most dangerous sponsors of terrorism' in the world; 'before long' the European countries would have to make up their minds whether 'they can do business by day with people who turn around and fuel attacks on their innocent civilians by night'. The scope of the new legislation was comprehensive and open-ended (Figure 3.3). In addition to the specific sanctions, the President is authorised to imposed additional sanctions 'as appropriate, to restrict imports with respect to a sanctioned person' (according to Section 6(6); note that a 'person', in the Act is 'a natural person; a corporation, business association, partnership, society, trust ...'). The scope of the legislation – in particular, its extraterritorial reach – had promoted outrage throughout the commercial world. By what right did Washington presume to dictate the trade practices of other countries?

The D'Amato Act was soon perceived as an embarrassment to Washington rather than an effective mechanism for taming the Iranian regime. Europe was incensed; Russia was continuing to sell nuclear technology to Tehran; Turkey was developing a $20 billion gas development project with Iran; the French oil giant Total was agreeing a $2 billion natural gas deal with Tehran; the European Commission was complaining about D'Amato to the World Trade Organization; and a growing number of states were declaring that they would pay little heed to US sanctions policy on Iran, Libya and

SEC. 6 DESCRIPTION OF SANCTIONS.

The sanctions to be imposed on a sanctioned person under section 5 are as follows:

(1) EXPORT-IMPORT BANK ASSISTANCE FOR EXPORTS TO SANCTIONED PERSONS.— The President may direct the Export-Import Bank of the United States not to give approval to the issuance of any guarantee, insurance, extension of credit, or participation in the extension of credit in connection with the export of any goods or services to any sanctioned person.

(2) EXPORT SANCTION.—The President may order the United States Government not to issue any specific license and not to grant any other specific permission or authority to export any goods or technology to a sanctioned person under

(i) the Export Administration Act of 1979;

(ii) the Arms Export Control Act

(iii) the Atomic Energy Act of 1954; or

(iv) any other statute that requires the prior review and approval of the United States Government as a condition for the export or reexport of goods or services.

(3) LOANS FROM UNITED STATES FINANCIAL INSTITUTIONS.—The United States Government may prohibit any United States financial institution from making loans or providing credits to any sanctioned person totalling more than $10,000,000 in any 12-month period unless such person is engaged in activities to relieve human suffering and the loans or credits are provided for such activities.

(4) PROHIBITIONS ON FINANCIAL INSTITUTIONS.—The following prohibitions may be imposed against a sanctioned person that is a financial institution:

(A) PROHIBITION ON DESIGNATION AS PRIMARY DEALER.—Neither the Board of Governors of the Federal Reserve System nor the Federal Reserve Bank of New York may designate, or permit the continuation of any prior designation of, such financial institution as a primary dealer in United States Government debt instruments.

(B) PROHIBITION ON SERVICE AS A REPOSITORY OF GOVERNMENT FUNDS.— Such financial institution may not serve as agent of the United States Government or serve as repository for United States Government funds. The imposition of either sanction under subparagraph (A) or (B) shall be treated as 1 sanction for purposes of section 5 and the Imposition of both such sanctions shall be treated as 2 sanctions for purposes of section 5.

(5) PROCUREMENT SANCTION.—The United States Government may not procure, or enter into any contract for the procurement of, any goods or services from a sanctioned person.

(6) ADDITIONAL SANCTIONS.—The President may impose sanctions, as appropriate, to restrict imports with respect to a sanctioned person, in accordance with the International Emergency Economic Powers Act (50 U.S.C. 1701 and following).

Figure 3.3   Iran and Libya Sanctions Act of 1996 – Extract

Cuba. Such events were forcing President Clinton to reconsider the implications of the new legislation, with suggestions that Washington may waive sanctions on foreign companies if their governments put pressure on Iran to end its terrorism and its quest for nuclear weapons.

By 1998 the 'more moderate' Iranian regime of President Mohammed Khatami was making an unprecedented proposal for dialogue with the United States (with the 'great American people'). Sandy Berger, Clinton's National Security Advisor, responded by declaring Iran 'a principal sponsor of terrorism'; with commentators suggesting that the Khatami olive branch should be set against satellite reconnaisance that had revealed engine tests for a new generation of Iranian ballistic missiles (tests detected on 15 December 1997 were the sixth or eighth in the year, according to rival intelligence interpretations). Clinton, noting Khatami's suggestion for a 'thoughtful dialogue', declared himself 'encouraged': 'In the meantime, we think it's important to maintain the current policy of military pressure, economic pressure and opposition to their acquisition of weapons of mass destruction.'

The US sanctions regime on Iran would remain, but tensions were building between Europe and Washington. The British Foreign Secretary Robin Cook was talking of a 'wedge' being driven between Europe and the United States; while Russia was continuing with its plans to build a nuclear power plant in Iran. In May 1998 European officials were expressing confidence that EU companies would be exempted from the sanctions specified in the Helms–Burton and D'Amato legislation. At a mid-May US–EU summit in Brussels a senior American official commented: 'Officials will continue to work on the issue through the weekend but ... this has to be a political decision at the very highest level. The negotiators have done all they can.' It was now plain that Clinton favoured waivers in the application of the legislation; and in response the EU had agreed to abandon its appeal to the World Trade Organization: 'France, with strong backing from Spain, led the demand for what amounts to a US climbdown.' Washington had signalled that it would give Total a waiver, but France now seemed determined to block once and for all the American attempt to give US domestic legislation an extraterritorial impact. On 18 May 1998 a deal was agreed whereby EU countries would be exempted from American trade sanctions against companies investing in Cuba, Iran and Libya. A month later (23 June), President Clinton vetoed legislation designed to impose sanctions on firms that sell missile technology to Iran: calling the measure 'inflexible and indiscriminate', Clinton commented that it would require the imposition of sanctions 'based on an unworkably low standard of evidence'.

In a remarkable observation (mid-June 1998) President Clinton declared that the United States had become 'sanction-happy'. It was clear that US sanctions policies were not working: failing to damage recalcitrant regimes but often causing immense suffering among civilian populations. Moreover, the American approach to economic and other sanctions was becoming increasingly isolated, a circumstance that represented a significant constraint on US global ambitions. It seemed obvious that the posture of a 'sanction-happy' Washington was becoming increasingly counterproductive.

India and Pakistan

On 11 May 1998 India exploded three nuclear devices in the Rajasthan desert; two days later, two more nuclear tests were conducted. Pakistan, in long-running dispute with India over Kashmir and other issues, immediately called for international sanctions against India, and vowed that it would make itself impregnable to the possibility of Indian aggression. The United States, judging (in violation of UN protection of national sovereignties – Article 2(1)) that only certain US-approved nations are allowed to possess nuclear weapons, declared that it was 'deeply disappointed' with India, and threatened to impose sanctions: the Indian tests did 'not contribute to building a safe 21st century. This action not only threatens the stability of the region but goes against the international consensus to stop the proliferation of nuclear weapons.' It was reported that top US officials were scouring the fine print of the Nuclear Proliferation Prevention Act, a hitherto unused federal law which mandates the US president to impose penalties on certain countries (effectively those disapproved of by Washington) which develop nuclear capabilities and who then test or sell their weapons.

The federal law in question effectively obligated the United States to block billions of dollars of aid to India, to prohibit American banks from making loans to India, and to prohibit any US firm from exporting products to India which could be used in the manufacture of military goods. In addition, Washington would oppose any plans of the World Bank or the International Monetary Fund to extend loans to India. Already India had $40 billion in loans and was expecting a further loan of $3 billion in 1998; over the same period, US loans to India amounted to around $100 million. A World Bank official commented that cutting off loans to India 'would have serious implications for their budget, serious detrimental effects'. It was also significant that the United States was India's largest trading partner ($9 billion worth of business in 1995, the last year for available figures).

On 13 May 1998 the United States – joined by Japan, Canada, Sweden, Denmark and Germany – imposed harsh economic sanctions on India. Pakistan, keen to conduct its own tests in response to the Indian action, was urged by Clinton 'to resist the temptation to respond to an irresponsible act in kind'. Japan suspended its grant aid to India and also cancelled a World Bank meeting in Tokyo of India's aid donors. Canada moved to ban military exports to India. Russia, France and the European Union (Britain currently holding the rotating presidency) decided to take no immediate action. The Indian Finance Minister Yashwant Sinha declared that India had nothing to fear from sanctions. Overseas aid, amounting to only 1 per cent of gross domestic product (GDP), was making little contribution to economic growth. Said one senior official: 'Choking off aid will not have any significant impact.' The rupee dropped sharply to a record low of 40–55 to the dollar, but the share market recovered considerably as a feeling of national pride spread through the country.

The United States was soon moving to block Indian access to sources of world finance. On 26 May Washington asked the World Bank to postpone consideration of more than $800 million in development loans to India. Four projects were to have been considered: a $130 million package to support India's renewable energy plans; a $450 million loan for the national power grid; a $275 million loan for road development in Haryana; and a $10 million loan to a private sector project. At a G8 summit the United States, Japan and Canada (opposed by Britain, France and Germany) led the call for joint sanctions against India.

On 28 May Pakistan, in retaliation for India's action, exploded five nuclear devices of its own. Surveillance satellites had confirmed that preparations for tests were under way in its western desert near the Iranian border, but warnings to Pakistan from the United States and other countries were ignored. Clinton commented in predictable terms: 'By failing to exercise restraint in responding to the Indian test, Pakistan has lost a truly priceless opportunity to strengthen its own security, to improve its political standing in the eyes of the world. I have made it clear to the leaders of Pakistan that we have no choice but to impose sanctions.' But now it was emerging that the United States was virtually alone in proposing tough sanctions on

India and Pakistan. Limited US sanctions (mainly arms) were already being imposed on Pakistan, and few states had much appetite now for the imposition of draconian measures against the two offending states. The EU had been unable to agree a comprehensive sanctions passage, and at the G8 summit Russia had been able to veto sanctions against India. It was significant also that US aid to Pakistan, as with India, represented only a small proportion of the national income (US aid: around $60 million a year). The World Bank was reporting that Pakistan had already received all the $808 million aid promised in its current fiscal year. It seemed that in reality little economic pressure could be applied to either state, with moral exhortation the only option.

In the event, despite the nominal support of various countries for sanctions, very little practical action was taken against either India or Pakistan. Washington's impotence, and that of the broader world community, was amply demonstrated. It was expected that the EU would review its preferential trade relations with Pakistan, and there were signs that a flight of investment capital from India was having an affect on economic growth: the nuclear tests had made it less likely that India would be regarded as a safe haven. Some of India's largest companies were badly hit: thus stocks of Reliance Industries, India's largest petrochemical company, fell 13 per cent; the Bank of India, the largest commercial bank, experienced a loss of 22 per cent. Observers suggested that the market would recover, but slowly. At the same time the imposition of economic sanctions had achieved little. Thus James Clad, professor of Asian studies at Georgetown University, commented: 'It is pretty clear that our policy in South Asia is in tatters. Containment of nuclear proliferation is a farce, and sanctions are doing nothing. President Clinton's foreign policy team are simply in over their heads.'

Various desultory sanctions gesture were being made (for example, the Dutch government blocked five shipments of goods to Pakistan that may have been destined for weapons programmes), but the Indian and Pakistan regimes, buoyed by popular support, were experiencing little economic pain as a result of the international response. On 22 June Russia went so far as to promise India delivery of two nuclear reactors, soon after the G8 leaders had agreed not to supply India and Pakistan with weapons technology. Delhi and Islamabad had now agreed test moratoria, and there was fresh hope of dialogue between the two countries.

On 9 July the US Senate voted to exempt agriculture credit programmes from the sanctions imposed on India and Pakistan. Said Senator Mitch McConnell: 'Sanctions are supposed to squeeze the targeted country, not the American producer. We should not sacrifice our farmers in an effort to put the nuclear genie back in the bottle.' Now the World Bank was resuming aid to India: the mild economic 'slap on the wrist' for India and Pakistan was history. Economic sanctions had done nothing to change the nuclear policies of the offending states, but Washington had been forced to rethink its sanctions policy. A spokesman for US Senator Ron Wyden, a supporter of agricultural exports, noted: 'There is a lot of scepticism about unilateral sanctions generally. In the modern global economy, unilateral sanctions are of decreasing utility and there is clearly an interest in Congress revisiting the whole issue.' The perception was growing that the US policy, in certain circumstances, of automatic unilateral sanctions was doing no more than damaging America's commercial interests.

Other Cases

The United States has traditionally imposed sanctions on other states as a result of US-contrived UN initiatives, as a result of mandatory domestic legislation (for example, the Nuclear Proliferation Prevention Act), or as a matter of unilateral decision (where concerted international action may have been preferred). One key piece of domestic legislation is known as 'Super 301', passed by Congress in 1988 to force the Bush Administration to adopt a firmer stand with America's trading partners, notably Japan. In 1989 various countries (including Japan, India and Brazil) were targeted by Super 301, and were forced to make trading concessions to the United States. In such circumstances the US aim was to intimidate targeted countries into acquiescence with American policies, without the need for Washington to move to punitive economic sanctions. Super 301 expired in 1990 but was reactivated by President Clinton in early 1994, principally as a mechanism for exerting economic (trade war) pressure on Japan.

In early 1990 the economic strains between *Japan* and the United States suggested an imminent trade war, with the likelihood of economic sanctions being imposed by both powers. In January 1992 President Bush visited Japan, taking with him some 21 chief executives from US firms, including the heads of the three large American car manufacturers – so signalling the overriding commercial purpose of the visit. A principal aim of the US delegation was to pressure Japan into opening its market to US imports. Here much of the pressure was being exerted by the car manufacturers but many other American companies had an interest in the Japanese market. Thus in June 1993 the US trade representative Mickey Kantor was threatening Japan with economic reprisals if it did not open its market to foreign (that is, American) public construction companies. Japan, declared Kantor, would have 60 days (from 23 June) to end its discriminatory practices or Washington would take action to curb Japan's access to the US market. In July an agreement was reached on a trade pact designed to reduce the huge trade imbalance that favoured Japan. But by early 1994 it was plain that little had been achieved.

On 12 February 1994, following his failure to reach a trade agreement with Prime Minister Morihiro Hosokawa, President Clinton was reportedly drawing up a list of retaliatory economic sanctions to open up the Japanese market to American manufacturers. It seemed likely that the new measures would include: Congressional legislation to give Clinton powers to retaliate against unfair trading practices; removing tax privileges enjoyed by Japanese manufacturers; imposing fresh customs control on Japanese imports; and filing anti-dumping cases against Japanese firms. Some observers were pointing out that the US plans were a violation of the GATT, but Washington was gambling that Japan would be well punished before the GATT complaints procedure was over. Now the European Commission was responding angrily to US policies. Sir Leon Brittan, the EU Trade Commissioner, commented that the Commission 'is as determined as the US to see Japan enforcing bold measures' to cut trade surpluses, 'but experience shows that any attempt to force those markets open through numerical targets risks being counter-productive as well as being incompatible with Europe and America's mutual commitment to free trade ...'.

On 31 July, after weeks of mutual recrimination, the Clinton Administration launched a range of trade sanctions against Japan for its alleged violation of fair-trading practices. In addition, Washington announced that on 30 September the United States would designate 'priority' countries for trade investigations that could lead to broad economic sanctions. Japan now had 60 days to meet US demands or to face the risk of higher tariffs on selected Japanese exports into America. Then, with minds concentrated, US–Japanese negotiators managed to reach an agreement that fended off the worst consequences of the Super 301 trade law: Japan was now willing to increase its imports of US glass, medical products, telecommunications goods and other items, and to open its market more to US insurance companies. The Clinton Administration hailed the agreement as a clear vindication of its tough stand on Japan.

Again the agreement soon seemed to be delivering less than it had promised. By 1995 tensions were again rising, with fresh US threats of economic sanctions – now in the form of substantial tariff increases on imported luxury cars: a 'car war' had now replaced the trade wars that focused on other products. The European Union was soon threatening to challenge any 'sweetheart deal' between Washington and Tokyo (such an agreement would pose an obvious threat to such European firms as BMW and Jaguar). Under Japanese and European pressure the United States agreed a deal to avert the need for punitive economic measures. Few observers thought that this was the end of the matter.

The United States ('sanction-happy' – Clinton) has also thought it appropriate to use economic pressure in the war against the illegal drug trade. Thus in March 1996 Washington cut off aid to *Colombia* as a protest against the escape of the drug baron José Santacruz Londoño from jail on 11 January. Santacruz was later shot dead, but this seemed unlikely to change the American decision. At the end of February 1997 the United States was considering whether Colombia should be 'certified' as an effective ally in the war on drugs (Colombia was 'decertified' on 1 March 1997). Decertified countries receive little or no direct aid and the United States automatically rejects their loan applications to development banks. Decertification by Washington is thus yet another powerful form of economic sanction, dubbed 'odious' by Alfonso Valdivieso, Colombia's chief prosecutor. It also seemed likely that Washington would withdraw Colombia's landing rights and increase the tariffs on Colombian imports.

Again it is useful to consider various possible US agendas in the decertification of Colombia. Left-wing rebels were known to be levying 'taxes' on the illegal cocaine trade, allowing Washington to divert aid into fighting the insurgency and so to further US strategic objectives. American aid ($37 million in 1998) was to be used in the southern half of the country where the guerrilla/drug-trafficker link was the clearest. Fabian Ramirez, a commander of the Revolutionary Army of Colombia (FARC), has commented: 'The claim that the United States is combating drugs in Colombia is a sophism. All the military and economic aid it is giving to the army is to fight the guerrillas, and most army battalions have US advisors.' In short, any American decision on aid to Colombia – highly relevant to the issue of economic sanctions – must be considered in the context of US strategic policy in the region.

The United States has also considered imposing economic sanctions on *China* for delivering missile components to Iran and Pakistan. Said White House spokesman Mike McCurry in June 1995: 'When we make a determination that there's been a transfer of missile technology in violation of guidelines our law requires the imposition of sanctions.' Tensions were increased in July when China tested surface-to-surface guided missiles just 100 miles north of Taiwan's coast. In these worsening circumstances Washington continued to threaten Beijing with economic and other consequences, to some effect: on 27 September 1995 China informed the United States that it would not proceed with a controversial deal to sell two nuclear reactors to Iran. But this gesture alone was far from sufficient to placate a Washington worried about its trade deficit with China, Beijing's strategic ambitions, human rights issues, and the likelihood that China would soon again be supplying military technology to unreliable states. In these circumstances the United States continued to block China's application to join the World Trade Organization, and to threaten the possibility of further economic measures against the Beijing regime.

By mid-October, having performed a speedy U-turn, China was again declaring its willingness to supply Iran with uranium-processing technology that could be used to aid the manufacture of nuclear weapons. Three months later, there were more complaints from American observers that Beijing had sold advanced cruise missiles to the Iranians, while the CIA was suggesting that the Chinese had provided Pakistan with uranium-enrichment equipment. On 7 March 1996 a senior US official declared that the United States was considering the imposition of economic sanctions against China. Two months later, President Clinton was reportedly about to announce $1 billion of trade sanctions against Beijing, as punishment for Chinese piracy of American videos and compact discs. At the same time Clinton and Bob Dole, his presidential rival, were quietly agreeing a bipartisan policy to expand China's trade with the United States. On 15 May the Clinton Administration announced more than $3 billion worth of economic sanctions against China, whereupon Beijing responded quickly with the threat of counter-sanctions that ranged from heavy duties on vegetable oils to telecommunications and films. A delay of 30 days in the US imposition of sanctions provided an opportunity for negotiation.

On 16 May 1996 a bemused US Congress was formally told that the Clinton Administration was seeking to extend China's Most Favoured Nation trading status, even though massive sanctions were being threatened against the Beijing regime. Said Under-Secretary of State Peter Tarnoff: 'There is no contradiction in these policies.' Washington was keen to expand trade with China, but equally determined to ensure that Beijing learned to abide by the rules of the game. On 17 June China and the United States managed to back off from a tit-for-tat trade war, with the Chinese agreeing to do more to enforce intellectual property rights (IPR) protection on the mainland. Again, it remained to be seen whether the deal would hold. What *was* clear was that the threat of economic sanctions was continuing to play a major part in the conduct of US foreign policy designed to protect perceived American commercial and strategic interests.

Washington continues to use economic pressures of many different types to further its advantage in the world. Some American sanctions campaigns – for example, those against Libya (Chapter 2) and Iraq (Chapter 5) – receive substantial publicity. Others are given less exposure in the public media. Thus little journalistic time was devoted to the backing being given by the Republican majority in the US Congress in September 1997 for legislation (the proposed Freedom From Religious Persecution Act) that would impose mandatory sanctions against countries that suppress minority religious groups; though significant media discussion focused on American threats to boycott Swiss banks over the issue of restitution of funds to Holocaust survivors.

In November 1998 the United States, ignoring legal recourse, was threatening a trade war against the European Union (EU). Since 1993 Washington had bitterly resented the EU rules on banana imports which favour former British and French colonies in Africa, the Caribbean and the Pacific. On 10 November Washington published a list of goods that would be subject to 100 per cent import duties from February 1999 unless the EU agreed to rewrite its banana trade rules in favour of American corporate profits. Why, reasoned Washington, should some of the world's poorest countries be helped at the expense of vast American multinationals? The legality of the matter was of no interest to the United States. But many observers were quick to point out that if the United States had a complaint it should apply to the World Trade Organisation, not (in the words of Leon Brittan, EU trade commissioner) 'set itself above the law'.

The American resort to economic sanctions in the furtherance of US foreign and commercial interests is multifaceted, shameless and ubiquitous. It is important to consider its implications – in ethics and in law.

4

Law and Natural Justice

The imposition of economic sanctions – whether done unilaterally or by various governments acting in concert – raises many ethical and legal questions. At one level this is unremarkable: actions of governments, often uniquely powerful, have diverse consequences and implications. At another level the imposition of economic sanctions – like war-making and the state funding of terrorism – can impact with graphic significance on the lives of ordinary people in society. It is usually claimed that sanctions are directed at regimes, not at civilian populations; but it is invariably innocent men, women and children who suffer.

The Key Question

We have seen that the world of economic sanctions is immense and multifaceted, ranging from the simple domestic household to the international collaboration of sovereign states. *International* economic sanctions, a principal theme of the present book, are often confused in ethics and law because of (1) the competing ethical claims of the states concerned, and (2) the untidiness and uncertain legal status of explicit international treaties, agreements, Statements, Declarations and Covenants. If economic sanctions are imposed by a government or by a group of collaborating states (for example, via the mechanism of consensus within the European Union or in observance of a UN Security Council resolution), what are the proper ethical and legal constraints on the operation of such sanctions? There are clues, at least in one instance, in the UN Charter: Article 103 stipulates that the obligations of UN members 'under any other international agreement' shall be regarded as less binding than obligations under the Charter. Such a provision has limited scope and leaves many questions unanswered. For example, UN resolutions, although adopted with due observance of constitutional procedure, may be surrounded with a host of improper blandishments, threats and other pressures (see 'The Relevance of Coercion', below). Such circumstances have immense ethical significance (with ethics *a priori*

162

superior to law: it is logically possible to have an unjust law), though it is impossible to control such pressures within a juridical framework.

Much of the problem derives from the contentious character of international law: the very phrase 'international law' appears to be weighty and coherent, and yet it is surrounded by confusion and uncertainty. The Harvard academic Michael Walzer describes well a principal element of the difficulty:

> international society as it exists today is a radically imperfect structure ... that society might be likened to a defective building, founded on rights; its superstructure raised, like that of the state itself, through political conflict, cooperative activity, and commercial exchange; the whole thing shaky and unstable because it lacks the rivets of authority. It is like domestic society in that men and women live in peace within it (sometimes) ... It is unlike domestic society in that every conflict threatens the structure as a whole with collapse. Aggression challenges it directly and is much more dangerous than domestic crime, because there are no policemen .... The rights of the member states must be vindicated, for it is only by virtue of these rights that there is a society at all. If they cannot be upheld ... international society collapses into a state of war or is transformed into a universal tyranny ... .[1]

In this context it is often difficult to judge the ethical and legal status of obligations that bear on sovereign nations. This is true in the area of economic sanctions as it is true elsewhere. Thus it is essential to address the key question:

How, if at all, are the inevitable consequences of comprehensive economic sanctions to be reconciled with the many authoritative international Declarations and Covenants that demand an entirely different obligation?

If no reconciliation is possible, then either comprehensive economic sanctions are demonstrably flawed as an element of national and supranational policy or a substantial volume of consistent humanitarian principles has to be abandoned.

Are Food Embargoes Legitimate?

A principle feature of comprehensive economic sanctions in the modern world is a *de facto* or *de jure* food embargo (see Cuba, Chapter

3; Iraq, Chapter 5). To a large extent this follows ancient practice: the destruction of enemy food supplies was a standard procedure in warfare. Thus: 'The Palatinate was wasted [in the Thirty Years War] in order that the imperial armies should be denied the military produce of the country; Marlborough destroyed the farms and crops of Bavaria for a similar purpose [in the War of the Spanish Succession] ... .'[2] In the American Civil War Sherman burned the farms in Georgia to starve the Confederate army; in more modern times the US forces in Vietnam used chemical weapons, napalm and other methods in an attempt to destroy the food supplies of their Vietnamese enemies. In such a context it is often impossible to distinguish between civilian and military targets – making it possible to argue that an attack on military resources sometimes has 'unfortunate' and 'regrettable' consequences for innocent men, women and children. By contrast, it is inevitable that the imposition of a regime of comprehensive economic sanctions will unambiguously target the civilian population: there can be no excuse that the primary target is a military one.

The United Nations, in direct recognition of the invidious character of a food embargo that targets civilian populations, has directly and indirectly articulated many explicit prohibitions (see, for example, those listed in Figure 4.1). Even the text of GATT, little concerned with inconvenient humanitarian matters that might impede the initiatives of entrepreneurial capitalism, acknowledges to some small extent the importance of human well-being. Thus Article XX includes the words: '... nothing in this Agreement shall be construed to prevent the adoption or enforcement by any contracting party of measures ... *necessary to protect human, animal or plant life or health'* (my italics).

In the same spirit the Protocol 1 Addition to the Geneva Convention, 1977, includes (as Article 54) provisions for the 'Protection of Objects Indispensable to the Survival of the Civilian Population':

1. Starvation of civilians as a method of warfare is prohibited.
2. It is prohibited to attack, destroy, remove or render useless objects indispensable to the survival of the civilian population, such as foodstuffs, agricultural areas for the productions of foodstuffs, crops, livestock, drinking water installations and supplies and irrigation works, for the specific purpose of denying them for their sustenance value to the civilian population or to the adverse Party, whatever the motive, whether in order to starve out civilians, to cause them to move away, or for any other motive ... .[3]

The theme is a common one in international Covenants and Declarations. Thus, for example, the International Covenant on Economic, Social and Cultural Rights, notes (Annex, Part 1, Article 1(2)): 'In no case may a people be deprived of its own means of subsistence.' This Covenant, an Annex to the General Assembly resolution adopted on 16 December 1966, enshrines many of the

'Everyone has the right to a standard of living adequate for the health and well being of himself and his family, including food, clothing, housing and medical care and necessary social services, and the right to security in the event of unemployment, sickness, disability, widowhood, old age, or other lack of livelihood in circumstances beyond his control.' **Universal Declaration of Human Rights, 1948**

'The enjoyment of the highest standard of health is one of the fundamental rights of every human being without distinction of race, religion, political belief, economic, or social condition.' **Constitution of World Health Organization, 1946**

'Calls upon the developed countries to refrain from exercising political coercion through the application of economic instruments with the purpose of inducing changes in the economic or social systems, as well as in the domestic or foreign policies, of other countries;
  Reaffirms that developed countries should refrain from threatening or applying trade and financial restrictions, blockades, embargoes, and other economic sanctions, incompatible with the provisions of the Charter of the United Nations ...' **UN General Assembly Resolution 44/215 (22 December 1989). Economic measures as a means of political and economic coercion against developing countries**.

'We recognise that access to nutritionally adequate and safe food is a right of each individual. We affirm ... that food must not be used as a tool for political pressure.' **International Conference on Nutrition, World Declaration on Nutrition, United Nations FAO/WHO 1992**

'Food should not be used as an instrument for political and economic pressure. We reaffirm ... the necessity of refraining from unilateral measures, not in accordance with the international law and the Charter of the United Nations and that endanger food security.' **Rome Declaration on World Food Security adopted by the World Food Summit, 13 November 1996**

Figure 4.1 UN declarations prohibiting food embargoes

principles that are today taken as basic to any comprehensive framework of human rights. One of the most fundamental of these rights is that civilian populations should not be deliberately denied access to food, medical supplies and drinkable water. This consideration bears directly on the imposition of any comprehensive regime of economic sanctions.

The Relevance of Coercion

The imposition of economic sanctions, however contrived and accomplished, is an overt attempt at coercion. The inevitable coercive element says nothing about whether the particular sanctions regime is moral or legal: it is easy to imagine circumstances where a resort to coercion in international affairs would be right in ethics and law. But it is important to appreciate also *illegitimate* coercion can play a significant role in the establishment of a sanctions regime.

The use of illegitimate coercion has been particularly apparent in the United States manipulation of the UN Security Council in its adoption of specific sanctions resolutions. Thus Marc Weller, then a Research Fellow in International Law at St Catharine's College, Cambridge (UK), noted that in efforts to secure sanctions resolutions against Libya (see Chapter 2) the claimant states (that is, mainly Washington) 'had to expend considerable political capital and goodwill in the Security Council, *bullying fellow members to obtain the necessary votes, and enraging many non-members of the Council who keenly observed this spectacle*' (my italics).[4] Weller judged that Washington and London, in behaving in such a fashion, 'may well have contributed to, or brought about, an abuse of rights by the Security Council'; and that it may now be necessary for the World Court to seek a judicial review of Council decisions 'if the constitutional system of the UN Charter is to recover from the blow it has suffered in this episode'.[5]

The United States resorted to the same tactics of intimidation in securing the sanctions resolutions and so-called 'use of force' Resolution (678) against Iraq following the 1990 invasion of Kuwait.[6] In addition, in order to secure Resolution 678, other forms of coercion in terms of bribery and 'debt forgiveness' were comprehensively employed.[7]

The American use of coercion to secure UN sanctions resolutions has important implications. What is the status of resolutions secured in such a fashion? It is obvious that the resolutions are formally legal (apart from the illegal Russian occupation of the former Soviet seat on the Security Council), though votes cast following intimidation may be regarded as invalid. If such a conclusion were to be reached then all the sanctions resolutions against (for example) Libya and Iraq would be invalid and those two countries would be (ethically) owed billions of dollars in compensation for the massive years-long damage to their economies. In fact there is at least one treaty which, though not applicable to the sanctions resolutions, provides a nice metaphor on how coercion can invalidate a country's commitment to international law.

The Vienna Convention on the Law of Treaties (an outcome of the work of the International Law Commission and sessions of the UN Conference on the Law of Treaties) stipulates (Section 2, Invalidity of Treaties) in Article 51: 'The expression of a State's consent to be bound by a treaty which has been procured by the coercion of its representative through acts or threats ... shall be without any legal effect'; and in Article 52: 'A treaty is void if its conclusion has been procured by the threat or use of force in violation of the principles of international law embodied in the Charter of the United Nations.' In short, a coerced state has no legal obligation to a treaty to which it is a nominal signatory. If any of the states who voted for the sanctions resolutions in the UN Security Council were coerced to do so in any fashion it is reasonable to argue *mutatis mutandis* that the resolutions have no legal (or ethical) weight.

The United States and Food Denial

The US attempts to block Cuban, Libyan and Iraqi access to food are not only a violation of many international Declarations and Conventions, but also significant violations of important affirmations of the United States itself. Thus Washington

> *Condemns* [via its signing of Security Council Resolution 787 of 16 November 1992 on Bosnia and Herzegovina] *all violations of humanitarian law, including ... the deliberate impeding of the delivery of food and medical supplies to the civilian population* ... . (Paragraph 7)

> Defines 'international terrorism' as '*acts dangerous to human life ... that appear intended to coerce a civilian population or to influence the policy of a government by intimidation or coercion*' (Title 18, 2331, US Legal Code).

Thus the United States stands condemned – not only by its violation of the internationally recognised right of civilians to food but also by copious documents (including the US Legal Code). In response to such considerations, Ramsey Clark, a former US Attorney-General, has issued a *'Criminal Complaint Against the United States of America ... for Causing the Deaths of More Than 1,500,000 People including 750,000 Children Under Five ... By Genocidal Sanctions'*. This particular case – that of Iraq – deserves a separate chapter.

5

The Case of Iraq

The imposition of sanctions on Iraq following the invasion of Kuwait in August 1990 is a unique case – not only in the trivial sense that *all* cases are unique but because here we continue to witness (in late 1998) the imposition of economic sanctions *in extremis*. The sanctions war being waged against Iraq has now been maintained for well over eight years, as I write. The United States works hard to spare nothing of this nation. By denying Iraq the capacity to conduct effective trade at any level, an entire society – all life – becomes a target: human beings (however young, old or sick), livestock and plants: even the animals in Baghdad's famous zoo were long since condemned to oblivion.[1] The metaphors have accumulated with the suffering: the whole of Iraq, once vigorous and thriving (and boasting the best national health service in the Middle East), has been reduced to a *vast refugee camp*, a *concentration camp*, a *nightmare*. We have mentioned (Chapter 1) the ancient cities under siege – a dire form of economic warfare. In harrowing testimony before a UN Commission, Warren A. J. Hamerman of the International Progress Organization likened Iraq to *a medieval city under siege*: 'cut off from outside assistance; its population, deprived of adequate food, water, medical care and the means to produce for its subsistence, is condemned to perish. It is only a matter of time.'[2]

Background

The forces of Saddam Hussein invaded Kuwait on 2 August 1990, following explicit British advice (albeit of some time ago). In 1930 the British High Commissioner in Baghdad declared *'that Britain should encourage the gradual absorption of Kuwait into Iraq'*, with representatives of the British government observing *'that Kuwait was a small and expendable state which could be sacrificed without too much concern if the power struggles ... demanded it'*.[3] Saddam could not have put it better himself. More recently – in the period from April to the end of July 1990 – various American spokesmen and one celebrated spokeswoman (April Glaspie, Ambassador to Baghdad) gave Saddam

Hussein an unambiguous 'green light' for his invasion of Kuwait.[4] US businessmen, well aware of the nature of the Iraqi regime, were paying compliments to Saddam Hussein; Secretary of State James Baker was blocking attempts to add Iraq to the US list of terrorist states; Assistant Secretary of State John Kelly was emphasising to the House of Representatives that the United States had no defence treaties with any Gulf country (including Kuwait); and Ambassador April Glaspie, face-to-face with Saddam Hussein, was declaring: 'I admire your extraordinary efforts to rebuild your country. I know you need funds. We understand that, and our opinion is that you should have the opportunity to rebuild your country. *But we have no opinion on Arab–Arab conflicts like your border disagreement with Kuwait*'[5] (my italics). The subsequent Iraqi invasion of Kuwait, encouraged historically by Britain and in 1990 by the United States, led immediately to a severe sanctions regime without parallel in modern times.[6] The most drastic consequence was that the Iraqi civilian population now found themselves caged within the bars of a genocidal situation, forced to confront a *de facto* denial of access to food, medicine and drinkable water. It was not long before the morbidity and mortality statistics were soaring.

The Sanctions Regime

The economic sanctions on Iraq were imposed almost immediately after the invasion of Kuwait on 2 August 1990 (not at the end of the 1991 Gulf War, as some commentators continue to suggest): the impact of sanctions was already being felt before the start of the war on 16 January 1991. On 2 August, immediately after the invasion, the UN Security Council adopted Resolution 660, demanding an unconditional Iraqi withdrawal from Kuwait. Washington at once imposed economic sanctions: President Bush signed executive orders freezing all Iraqi government assets and Kuwaiti assets now under the control of Baghdad. On 6 August the Council imposed sanctions on Iraq by adopting Resolution 661 (13 votes to 0, with Yemen and Cuba abstaining):

> The Security Council ... Decides that all States shall prevent:
>   (a) The import into their territories of all commodities and products originating in Iraq or Kuwait ...
>   (b) Any activities ... which would promote ... the export or transshipment of any commodities or products from Iraq or Kuwait;

and any dealings in ... any commodities or products originating in Iraq or Kuwait ... including in particular any transfer of funds to Iraq or Kuwait ...

(c) The sale or supply ... of any commodities or products ... to any person or body in Kuwait ...

(d) Decides that all States shall not make available to the Government of Iraq ... any funds or any other financial or economic resources ...

The scene was set for the most draconian sanctions regime in the history of the United Nations. The 1991 war was predictably won by the superpower United States with (largely) spurious allied support. The American fatalities were 137 (many of theme from so-called 'friendly fire'), with Iraqi casualties – dead, wounded, ill, traumatised, and so on – numbered in the millions. Now a merciless sanctions regime was in place, guaranteed to cause millions more Iraqi casualties, the bulk of them children.

On 3 April 1991 the UN Security Council adopted Resolution 687, the 'ceasefire' resolution designed to reinforce Resolution 661 pending the satisfying of various conditions, primarily the destruction of Iraq's 'weapons of mass destruction'. The new resolution included a statement (Paragraph 22) to the effect that once various stipulated conditions had been met 'the prohibitions against the import of commodities and products originating in Iraq and the prohibitions against financial transactions related thereto contained in resolution 661(1990) shall have no further force or effect ...'. Iraq thus found itself in an anomalous position. The Saddam regime still ruled a nominally sovereign state, a UN member with sovereignty protected by Article 2(1) of the Charter; but was forced to endure a massively intrusive foreign presence set to last for years. In due course a group of 'weapons inspectors' (UNSCOM staff and others), many associated with a United States committed to the overthrow of the Iraqi regime, would gradually gain access to buildings and institutions at the heart of the Iraqi security apparatus. This the Iraqis, a proud Arab nation, were expected to endure over a period of years while the civilian population was reduced to penury, disease and starvation.[7]

A complex and rigorous international system had been constructed to block the flow of goods to Iraq. The nominal exemption of humanitarian supplies was largely meaningless: Iraq was systematically denied the means to purchase food and medical supplies in adequate quantities; and all purchases had to be authorised through a deliberately cumbersome and procrastinatory licensing bureaucracy. The much-hyped 'oil for food' resolution (986) was a farce, doing nothing to improve the miserable lot of the Iraqi civilian population but promptly feeding Iraqi oil revenues to US-friendly claimants in the United States, Kuwait and elsewhere (according to the terms of 986, Paragraph 8). The sanctions system has evolved as a genocidal tool administered jointly by the US-directed official bureaucracies in individual countries and the UN Iraq Sanctions Committee.

Anyone wanting to send goods (purchases or gifts) to Iraq must first apply to the appropriate government department for a licence: without a licence you cannot send a knitted gift for a baby! In Britain applications are made to the Sanctions Unit, run by the DTI Export Control Organisation, whereupon they may wait in a queue for several weeks; if an application is incomplete it is returned to the sender for correction, then resubmitted at the end of the queue. When, after often a lengthy period, the Sanctions Unit is satisfied, the application is fed into the queue at the UN Iraq Sanctions Committee in New York, which continuously receives many applications from various countries. Any member on the Sanctions Committee, a reflection of the UN Security Council, can veto an application or ask for more details. Meetings of the Sanctions Committee are held intermittently and decisions cannot be openly debated or questioned. The private Committee discussions often focus on whether a particular application is humanitarian or not. The whole procedure is a recipe for massive delay and procrastination.[8]

The United States dominates the Sanctions Committee, just as it dominates the UN Security Council – which often causes Committee debate to proceed at the level of 'Why should ping-pong balls be allowed? We don't believe that this is an essential need.'[9] Figure 5.1 describes a few of the thousands of items vetoed by the Western powers and Japan.[10]

The attitudes in the US-dominated Sanctions Committee have continued to cause delays in the delivery of humanitarian goods to Iraq over an eight-year period. Thus items delayed or prohibited have included: baby food, clothes, leather for shoes, shoe laces, shroud material, school books, glue for textbooks, notebooks, paper, pencils, pencil sharpeners, erasers, blankets, nail polish, sanitary towels, soap, deodorants, tissues, toothpaste, toilet paper, shampoo, medical syringes, incubators, bandages, catheters for babies, surgical gloves, surgical instruments, stethoscopes, acrylic yarn, dialysis equipment, drugs for angina, and so on. It is not obvious to many observers why denying the Iraqis access to such items (and countless more of the same type) should make Saddam Hussein less of a threat to his neighbours. What *is* obvious is that the activities of the Sanctions

---

6 February 1992 A consignment of ping-pong balls from Vietnam vetoed by United States, Britain, France and Japan.
3 April 1993 A consignment of tennis balls, children's clothes, adult clothes, pencils, sharpeners, erasers and school notebooks from Pakistan vetoed by United States, Britain, France and Japan.
4 August 1992 A consignment of children's bicycles vetoed by United States and Britain.
17 September 1993 Shroud material vetoed by United States and Britain; later released from UK; then export licence revoked under new UK DTI regulations; whole process of applications had to begin again.
26 April 1992 Water purification chemicals vetoed by United States and Britain.
24 July 1993 Cotton for medical use (swabs, gauze, etc.) vetoed by Britain.
1 June 1992 Application from Spanish consortium to help rebuild medical syringe factory (bombed in war) vetoed by Britain and France.
14 August 1993 Application from Japan to supply communication links for hospital use (i.e. pagers, hospital–ambulance links) vetoed by United States and Britain.
12 December 1991 A consignment of paper for hospital doctors vetoed by United States.
29 October 1992 Boxes of nail polish and lipsticks vetoed by Britain.

Figure 5.1   Some items for Iraq vetoed in Sanctions Committee

Committee and the parallel activities of the national financial institutions in blocking Iraqi transactions are continuing to ensure that Iraq remains in an impoverished and deteriorating condition. We should remember what this means for the civilian population of a nation under comprehensive siege.

The Sanctions Impact

The (mainly) US war against Iraq involved the dropping of some 88,000 tons of bombs from the 16 January to 27 February 1991. This meant that Iraq was subjected to the equivalent of one Hiroshima-size atomic bomb a week (seven in all) over the period of the war, a scale of destruction that has no parallels in the history of warfare. Few objective observers could doubt that this was a totally dispro-portionate policy of destruction in view of the declared UN aim of expelling the Iraqi forces from Kuwait. The consequences were a devastated land, a ruined society, massive human casualties, and a traumatised survivor population struggling to comprehend the apocalypse that had befallen it. Now the United States insisted on imposing a fresh sanctions-based onslaught on the Iraqi people – denied any means to rebuild a shattered society, denied sewage-free drinking water, denied medical facilities, and denied food in adequate supply. In these terms the American policy represented one of the most comprehensive campaigns of *biological warfare* in modern times – denying essential humanitarian relief to an increasingly diseased and starving people.

At the end of the war the likely consequences of the sanctions regime were soon obvious to informed observers. Thus Martti Ahtisaari, UN Under-Secretary-General for Administration and Management, led a mission (10–17 March 1991) to Iraq and subsequently published a report on the findings: '... nothing that we had seen or read had quite prepared us for the particular form of devastation which has now befallen the country. The recent conflict has wrought near apocalyptic results ... the flow of food through the private sector has been reduced to a trickle ... Many food prices are already beyond the purchasing reach of most Iraqi families ... widespread starvation conditions are a real possibility.' A Harvard study team was reporting that 'at least 170,000 young children under five years of age will die in the coming year' as a result of the war and the sanctions. The many witnesses were unanimous:

A German Doctor Tells How Iraq's Children Are Being Killed[11]

Children condemned to a lingering death[12]

Child victims of the sanctions syndrome[13]

Sanctions that should shame the UN
('Denying Iraqi babies medicines amounts to cold-blooded murder')[14]

In March 1991 Dr Margit Fakhoury, a German paediatrician, visited hospitals in Iraq and observed the unprecedented incidence of 'malnourished babies and toddlers ... with kwashiorkor, severe deficiencies of vitamins, or dying of a simple flu or diarrhoea'. Four months later, the situation had worsened: now Fakhoury witnessed the growing number of babies being fed on nothing more than water with added sugar, an unprecedented generation of bloated Iraqi 'sugar babies'. In all Iraqi hospitals the doctors, being denied access to virtually all medical supplies in adequate quantity, were seeing 'increasing numbers of cases of cholera and typhoid fever'.[15] In July 1993 the UN Food and Agriculture Organization (FAO) reported that the sanctions had paralysed the whole Iraqi economy land generated persistent deprivation, chronic hunger, endemic undernutrition, massive unemployment and widespread human suffering'; a 'grave human tragedy' was unfolding, with a large and growing number of Iraqis having lower food intakes 'than those of the populations in the disaster stricken African countries'.[16] The situation was set to deteriorate further as the sanctions regime was maintained through the whole of the 1990s.

In September 1995 the UN World Food Programme (WFP) reported that '70 per cent of the population has little or no access to food ... Nearly everyone seems to be emaciated'; in December Sarah Zaidi and Mary Fawzi commented in the prestigious medical journal the *Lancet* that since August 1990 some 567,000 children in Iraq had been killed by 'an international community intent on maintaining sanctions'; in 1996 the WHO reported that the health conditions in Iraq were deteriorating 'at an alarming rate' because of sanctions: 'the vast majority of Iraqis continue to survive on a semi-starvation diet'; and in May 1997 conservative estimates suggested that some 5600 children under five were dying every month as a direct result of the sanctions regime, with the number still rising.[17] The situation has long been obvious, a direct consequence of deliberate American policy.

The United States has worked to delay or block food and medical shipments that are nominally allowed under the term of Resolution 986.[18] Washington has prevented US corporations from supplying free medicines to Iraqi hospitals; and worked to intimidate American aid workers active in trying to supply medicines and toys to dying Iraqi children. Thus David H. Harmon (Acting Supervisor, Office of Foreign Assets Control in the US Department of the Treasury) wrote on 22 January 1996 to Kathy Kelly (of the aid charity Voices in the Wilderness) to threaten charity aid workers with imprisonment and fines:

This office has learned that you and other members of Voices in the Wilderness recently announced your intention to collect medical relief supplies for the people of Iraq at various locations in the United States and to personally transport the supplies to Iraq ... you and members of Voices in the Wilderness are hereby warned to refrain from engaging in any unauthorised exportation of medical supplies and travel to Iraq. Criminal penalties for violating the Regulations range from up to 12 years in prison and $1 million in fines.

In April 1997 the Iraqi Ministry of Health published a UNICEF-acknowledged total of 750,000 children under five suffering from malnutrition; a UNICEF–Iraqi meeting (20 July 1997) revealed that charitable donations to Iraq had diminished because of the false expectations regarding the impact of 'oil for food' Resolution 986. In August 1997 UNICEF–Iraqi statistics suggested that the sanctions regime had so far killed some 878,856 Iraqi children (Table 5.1). At the same time the UN Commission on Human Rights (Economic and Social Council), via the mechanism of the Sub-Commission on Prevention of Discrimination and Protection of Minorities, was adopting a resolution that noted the *Adverse Consequences of* Economic Sanctions on the Enjoyment of Human Rights: sanctions 'most seriously affect the innocent population, in particular the weak and the poor, especially women and children'.[19] An FAO/WFP report (3 October 1997) noted that the situation for most of the Iraqi people had become 'deplorable', with a growing number of children in hospital wards seen to be suffering from 'severe wasting, (especially visible in the ribs, limbs and head'). A detailed Iraqi/UNICEF report (November 1997) report concluded that there was no evidence that the nutritional status of Iraqi children had improved since the adoption of Resolution 986 (and the supplementary Resolution 1111);[20] Philippe Heffinck, the UNICEF Representative in Baghdad, agreed that there was no sign of improvement, and added that it was the Iraqi children who were suffering most because of the sanctions regime.[21] A report in the prestigious London-based *British Medical Journal* (29 November 1997) noted the virtual collapse of the Iraqi health system.

On 22 May 1998 Eric Falt, the Spokesman for the UN Humanitarian Co-ordinator in Iraq, reported that the nutritional status of Iraqi children (more than a quarter of whom were malnourished) had failed to improve over the last year: 27 per cent of children under five were suffering from chronic malnutrition; 9 per cent were suffering from acute malnutrition; and 24 per cent were underweight. The survey on which these figures were based showed that a substantial improvement in the Iraqi population's nutritional status could only come with improvements in other areas, such as sanitation and water quality.[22] It was now plain that Resolution 986, advertised as a means of relieving the suffering of the Iraqi civilian population, was little more than a cynical ploy designed to transfer Iraqi oil revenues to US-friendly claimants. Iraq had frequently complained

Table 5.1   Total number of Iraqi child deaths due to sanctions

Periods	Age Group Under (5)	Over (5)	Total
1990	8,903	23,561	32,464
1991	27,473	58,469	85,942
1992	46,933	76,530	123,463
1993	49,762	78,261	128,023
1994	52,905	80,776	133,681
1995	55,823	82,961	138,784
1996	56,997	83,284	140,281
1997 JAN.–AUG.	39,353	56,865	96,218
GRAND TOTAL	338,149	540,707	878,856

Source: Iraqi Ministry of Health with UNICEF support.

that it was allowed no mechanism to challenge the claims, many of which were spurious, but to no avail. Thus Tariq Aziz, the Iraqi Deputy Prime Minister, commented:

> The truth of the matter is that the Government of Iraq has no role, however small, which allows it to respond to the allegations contained in claims ... It is unable to give its legal and objective opinion on claims, even when those are exaggerated ... The [Compensation] Commission ... decides which claims should be settled, who is authorised to submit a claim, what should be considered direct losses, and what constitutes sufficient proof ... *These measures create a legal screen which conceals the systematic subjugation of the Iraqi people. There are no reasonable grounds for this collective punishment of the Iraqi people* ... If this is not done [the verification and scrutiny of claims in accordance 'with international law and the rules of justice and equity'] *the compensation process will become simply an organised operation to strip the Iraqi people of their property*, which they desperately need in order to rebuild their society and economy ... .[23] (my italics)

The United States continued to work to buttress the sanctions regime, while doing what it could to transfer Iraqi oil revenues to Kuwait, the United States and elsewhere. Richard Butler, the Executive Chairman of UNSCOM – by dint of a bogus 'road map' (of disarmament actions to be completed by Iraq), pointless and proliferating questions ('Had the tyres of your vehicle been punctured?', 'Who handed over the pump?', 'When did you ask to be given one pump?', and so on) – laboured to prolong indefinitely the time when sanctions might be lifted. At the same time the condition of the Iraqi people continued to deteriorate, with Washington seemingly unaffected by the mounting international opposition to the callousness of American policy.

In June 1998 a UN document based on Iraqi government figures indicated that cancer rates had increased sixfold in parts of southern Iraq after the 1991 war.[24] And now the Iraqi health authorities were being deliberately denied the means to treat the growing incidence of disease (of all types). The periodic UNSCOM–Iraqi talks in Baghdad were increasingly perceived as a cynical fraud, designed mainly to preserve a sanctions regime that had lost all international support and credibility: '*The ritual in Baghdad is being played out at the expense of Iraq's ordinary citizens, as many as two million of whom have been brought to the edge of starvation by sanctions.*'[25] In early August a fresh phase of talks broke down, with Tariq Aziz accusing Butler of playing 'games and tricks' as a deliberate ploy to prolong sanctions.

The sanctions regime continued to exact its terrible toll on the people of Iraq through 1998, with some commentators choosing to highlight a UNICEF survey (March) indicating that 58 per cent of Iraqi children under five were now suffering from malnutrition.[26] Again the facts are well known. Habib Rejeb, the head of the World Health Organization in Baghdad, has commented: 'Acute malnutrition here is about the same as in Haiti. Everything is breaking down. People have to drink polluted water ... so they become too sick to benefit from food.'[27] The minimal extra supplies of food and medicine that arrive after all the obstructive hurdles have been negotiated have not reduced the number of Iraqi starving and dying – because the total social and industrial infrastructure is collapsing, so making it impossible to pump sewage and water. Power cuts last for 20 hours a day in the country, and even for up to eight hours in Baghdad which is given priority attention. Pools of raw sewage continue to accumulate in the streets of the major cities: as one example, many of the people living next to sewage covered in green scum in Saddam City, a neighbourhood of Baghdad, are on the brink of starvation. In July 1998 Denis Halliday, the UN Humanitarian Co-ordinator for Iraq, resigned in desperation.

A New Holocaust

The United States, today almost totally isolated among the nations of the world, is the knowing architect of the Iraqi apocalypse. With conscious and cynical resolve an army of American officials work hard to withhold relief from a sick and starving people. And, in moments of breathtaking candour, Washington sometimes admits the grotesque facts of the case. Thus Madeleine Albright, now US Secretary of State, was prepared to assert in interview on CBS's *60 Minutes* (12 May 1996) that *the killing of 500,000 Iraqi children was justified to protect US interests.* It is easy to demonstrate that in this cruel and cynical context American policy on Iraq in a clear violation of the UN Genocide Convention. The US defence – that the suffering of the Iraqi people is all the fault of Saddam Hussein – has only to be stated for its absurdity to be obvious. Does Washington really expect us to take seriously the argument that a civilian population should be denied food and medical supplies in order to punish a tyrant over whom they have no control?

On 27 November 1996 the UN General Assembly adopted Resolution 51/22, designed to encourage the *Elimination of coercive economic measures as a means of political and economic compulsion.* The Resolution:

1. *Reaffirms* the inalienable right of every State to economic and social development and to choose the political, economic and social system which it deems most appropriate for the welfare of its people ...
2. *Calls for* the immediate repeal of unilateral extraterritorial laws that impose sanctions on companies and nationals of other States ...
3. *Calls upon* all States not to recognise unilateral extraterritorial coercive economic measures or legislative acts imposed by any State.

This resolution – a thinly disguised criticism of the US Helms–Burton and D'Amato legislation (Chapter 3) – signalled the growing international awareness that no individual state, even a superpower, has the right to enact domestic laws in an attempt to coerce other sovereign nations. A subsequent Iraqi comment (5 May 1997) on Resolution 51/22 noted: '*The first victims of such practices are the vulnerable sectors of the population, such as children, women and the elderly. The serious humanitarian suffering of the population of Iraq. which has been confirmed by the reports of United Nations agencies and missions, is a result of the insistence of the United States of America on subjecting the Iraqi people to the most offensive form of these coercive measures.*'

By 1998 the deliberate US-contrived starvation of the Iraqi civilian population was being widely questioned in the Western media. Thus typical headlines included: 'Iraq: who do sanctions hurt?', 'Why do we support starvation?', 'Food crisis worsening, UN warns', 'Suffer the children', and 'Sick and dying in their hospital beds, the pitiful victims ...'. Dr Juad Rashid, an Iraqi consultant paediatrician, asked: 'Why are you making war on our children?'[28] In 1995 UN Secretary-General Boutros Boutros-Ghali had said that the international community had failed to confront 'the ethical question of whether suffering inflicted on vulnerable groups in the target country is a legitimate means of exerting pressure on political leaders, whose behaviour is unlikely to be affected by the plight of their subjects'. Throughout 1998, despite the early negotiated agreement with Secretary-General Kofi Annan,[29] the Iraqi authorities came to believe that Richard Butler, head of UNSCOM, would never be prepared to present a report to the Security Council that would allow the sanctions to be lifted. In July Saddam predicted that, with the growing isolation of Washington in the world community, sanctions would gradually wither away; in August fresh UNSCOM–Iraqi talks collapsed, while Washington was reportedly planning new terrorist acts against the Iraqi regime.[30]

On 9 September Washington secured the adoption of UN Resolution 1194 to prevent any further reviews of sanctions by the Security Council. This cynical move nullified a key pledge of the Annan agreement (February) whereby the character of the genocidal sanctions regime was to be addressed. In October the UN Committee on the Rights of the Child reported its 'grave concern' about the deterioration in the health of Iraqi children because of sanctions. On 31 October President Clinton signed into law the Iraq Liberation Act authorising $97 million worth of military equipment and training for terrorists active in Iraq, a sovereign member of the United Nations. Thus by 1999 Washington had significantly extended its political and financial support for genocide and state terrorism.

The US-inspired economic sanctions against Iraq continue to represent an extreme case – the use of virtual economic siege to reduce a national population to penury, disease and starvation. No serious study of economic sanctions can ignore the dire experience of the Iraqi people, where a powerful state was able to contrive international measures of a genocidal nature for the gradual extermination of a national people in violation of UN Covenants, Statements and Declarations, the Geneva Conventions, other elements of international law, and all human decency.

Notes

Introduction

1. Francis A. Beer, *Peace Against War*, W. H. Freeman, San Francisco, 1981, pp. 281–2, quoted in M. S. Daoudi and M. S. Dajani, *Economic Sanctions: Ideals and Experience*, Routledge and Kegan Paul, London, 1983, p. 125. See also G. H. Snyder and P. Diesing, *Conflict Among Nations: Bargaining, Decision Making, and System Structure in International Crises*, Princeton University Press, Princeton, New Jersey, 1977, pp. 554–5.
2. Discussed, with other examples, in Daoudi and Dajani, *op. cit.*, pp. 123–58.
3. B. Y. Boutros-Ghali, 'The Arab League: Ten Years of Struggle', *International Conciliation*, May 1954, p. 421 ('The interpretation given by the Arab League is that the boycott will bring about the eventual economic collapse of the state of Israel and will reveal that it is not economically viable in the midst of a hostile world').
4. Gary Clyde Hufbauer, Jeffrey J. Schott and Kimberly Ann Elliott, *Economic Sanctions Reconsidered, Volume I, History and Current Policy; Volume II, Supplemental Case Histories*, Institute for International Economics, Washington D.C., 1990.
5. Nancy Dunne, 'Sanctions overload', *Financial Times*, 21 July 1998, p. 19.
6. Simon Tisdall, 'US plays down illegal Israeli missile sales', *Guardian*, 28 October 1991.
7. For example, Security Council Resolutions 242, 465, 476, 478, 672 and 673. The sanctions against Israel demanded by UN Secretary-General Boutros Boutros-Ghali in January 1993 for Israel's violation of Resolution 799 were predictably blocked by Washington ('UN chief calls for sanctions over Israeli expulsions', *Guardian*, 27 January 1993).
8. 'US backs off sanctions, seeing poor effect abroad', *New York Times*, 31 July 1998.
9. Quoted in *ibid*.
10. Quoted in *ibid*.

Chapter 1

1. M. S. Daoudi and M. S. Dajani, *Economic Sanctions: Ideals and Experience*, Routledge and Kegan Paul, London, 1983, p. 2.
2. Gerhard Von Glahn, *Law Among Nations*, Macmillan, New York, 1976, p. 502.
3. William L. Safire, *Safire's Political Dictionary*, Random House, New York, 1978, p. 548.
4. Daoudi and Dajani, *op. cit.*, p. 7.
5. William Norton Medlicott, *The Economic Blockade*, Her Majesty's Stationery Office, London, 1952–9, reprinted 1978; cited in James A. Boorman III, 'Economic Coercion in International Law: The Arab Oil Weapon and the Ensuing Judicial Issues', *Journal of International Law and Economics*, 9 (1974), p. 210.
6. Margaret P. Doxey, *International Sanctions in Contemporary Perspective*, Macmillan, London, 1987, p. 4.
7. *Ibid.*
8. Michael Walzer, *Just and Unjust Wars: A Moral Argument with Historical Illustrations*, Penguin Books, Harmondsworth, 1980, p. 160.
9. Aristophanes, *The Acharnians*, quoted in Charles Fornara, 'Plutarch and the Megarian decree', *24 Yale Classical Studies*, 1975, pp. 213–28; cited in Gary Clyde Hufbauer, Jeffrey J. Schott and Kimberly Ann Elliott, *Economic Sanctions Reconsidered: History and Current Policy*, Institute for International Economics, Washington D.C., 1990, pp. 4–5.
10. Charles Chaney Hyde, *International Law* (2nd revised edition, Boston, 1945), III, 1802.
11. The Works of Josephus, trans. Tho. Lodge, London, 1620; *The Wars of the Jews*, Book VI, Chapter XIV, p. 721; quoted by Walzer, *op. cit.*, p. 161.
12. *Ibid.*
13. *Ibid.*, p. 722.
14. Madeleine Albright, interviewed by Lesley Stahl, *60 Minutes*, CBS, 12 May 1996.
15. See, for example, Jim Bradbury, *The Medieval Siege*, The Boydell Press, Suffolk, 1992.
16. *Ibid.*, p. 15.
17. Cited, with sources, in *ibid.*, pp. 81–2.
18. Ibid., p. 83 (cited sources; 'devastate far and wide since, when the supplies of the countryside were used up, they would begin to hunger'; 'famine will fight for them').
19. *Ibid.*
20. D. T. Jack, *Studies in Economic Warfare*, London, 1940, pp. 1–42.

21. *American State Papers, Naval Affairs I*, pp. 278–79; quoted in Russell F. Weigley, *The American Way of War: A History of United States Military Strategy and Policy*, Macmillan, New York, 1973, pp. 50–1.

22. Daniel Ammen, 'Du Pont and the Port Royal Expedition', *Battles and Leaders of the Civil War*, Volume 1, Castle, New Jersey, 1887, p. 673.

23. *Ibid*, p. 674.

24. Quoted in *ibid*.

25. Quoted in *ibid.*, p. 670.

26. James M. McPherson, *Battle Cry of Freedom: The American Civil War*, Penguin, London, 1988, p. 378.

27. Richard S. West Jr, *Mr Lincoln's Navy*, New York, 1957; quoted in *ibid*.

28. Robert Carse, *Blockade: The Civil War at Sea*, New York, 1958, p. 41; quoted in McPherson, *op. cit.*, pp. 378–9.

29. McPherson, *op. cit.*, p. 379.

30. *Ibid.*, p. 380.

31. Citations in *ibid.*, p. 381.

32. Citations in *ibid.*.

33. Edmond de Goncourt, *Journal*, quoted in Alistair Horne, *The Fall of Paris: The Siege and the Commune 1870–71*, Macmillan, London, 1965, p. 176.

34. *Ibid.*, p. 177.

35. Ibid.; Victor Hugo, frustrated at one woman's refusal to dine with him, wrote:

> *Je vous aurais offert un repas sans rival:*
> *J'aurais tué Pégase et je l'aurais faire cuire.*
> *Afin de vous servir une aile de cheval.*

> (I would have offered you a meal beyond compare:
> I would have killed Pegasus and had him cooked,
> So as to serve you with a horse's wing.)

36. An American estimate (cited in *ibid.*, p. 178) suggests that through the period of the siege Parisians consumed 65,000 horses, 5000 cats, 1200 dogs and 300 rats.

37. Quoted in Horne, *op. cit.*, p. 184.

38. Quoted in Horne, *op cit.*, p. 260.

39. Edward S. Miller, *War Plan Orange: The US Strategy to Defeat Japan, 1897–1945*, US Naval Institute, Annapolis, Maryland, 1991.

40. General Board of the Navy, United States, 1906 Plan, pp. 1–3; quoted in *ibid.*, p. 162.

41. John Costello, *The Pacific War*, Pan Books, London, 1981, p. 99.

42. D. T. Jack, *Studies in Economic Warfare*, Chemical Publishing Company, New York, 1941, pp. 83–6.
43. *Ibid.*, pp. 87, 91.
44. *Ibid.*, p. 108.
45. Louis Guichard, *The Naval Blockade: 1914–1918*, D. Appleton and Company, New York, 1930, p. 39.
46. *Ibid.*, pp. 120–1.
47. At this time the legal status of *blockade, contraband, enemy goods* and *neutral goods* was defined in large part by practice in the Napoleonic Wars, the Declaration of Paris (18 April 1856) and the unratified Declaration of London (26 February 1909). See 'Legal Notes', Gary Clyde Hufbauer, Jeffrey J. Schott and Kimberly Ann Elliott, *Economic Sanctions Reconsidered: Supplemental Case Histories*, Institute for International Economics, Washington D.C., 1990, pp. 3–4.
48. Medlicott, *op. cit.*, p. 9.
49. Margaret P. Doxey, *Economic Sanctions and International Enforcement*, Macmillan, for The Royal Institute of Economic Affairs, London, 1971, p. 12.
50. D. Mitrany, *The Problem of International Sanctions*, Oxford University Press, London, 1925, p. 35.
51. Doxey (1971), *op. cit.*, p. 18.
52. B. H. Liddell Hart, *The Real War: 1914–1918,* Boston, 1964, p. 473.
53. Quoted in Llewellyn Woodward, *Great Britain and the War of 1914–1918*, Methuen, London, 1967, p. 193.
54. Quoted in H. A. L. Fisher, *A History of Europe*, Edward Arnold, London, 1949, p. 1138.
55. See, for example, Patrick Devlin, *Too Proud to Fight: Woodrow Wilson's Neutrality*, Oxford University Press, New York, 1974, pp. 200–16, 350–5, 504–19, 646–8.
56. *Ibid.*, p. 505.
57. For a profile of both these blockades, see Hufbauer *et al.* (*Supplemental Case Histories*), *op. cit.*, pp. 9–16.
58. John Bigelow, *The Principles of Strategy Illustrated Mainly from American Campaigns*, Greenwood Press, New York, 1968; reprint of 2nd edition, Lippincott, Philadelphia, 1894, p. 185.
59. Woodward, *op. cit.*, pp. 561–2.
60. Hugh Brogan, *Longman History of United States of America*, Longman Group, London, 1985, p. 500.
61. *Ibid.*
62. A. C. Bell, *A History of the Blockade of Germany*, London, 1937, pp. 213–14.
63. Walzer, *op. cit.*, p. 173.
64. Thomas S. Kuhn, *The Structure of Scientific Revolutions*, University of Chicago Press, Chicago and London, 1962, p. 10.

65. Included, with other GST statements, in Daoudi and Dajani, *op. cit.*, pp. 18–19.
66. These quotations are given (sometimes in more extensive form) with citations in *ibid.*, pp. 22–6; dissident views (especially W. Arnold Forster) are included here as a prelude to a more detailed profile of an alternative approach.
67. Quotations with citations in *ibid.*, pp. 28–30.
68. *Ibid.*, pp. 29–30.

Chapter 2

1. Bertrand Russell, *Which Way to Peace?*, Michael Joseph, London, 1936, p. 61.
2. Wilson's Fourteen Points: (i) open diplomacy, (ii) freedom of navigation on the seas, (iii) free trade, (iv) a reduction in armaments, (v) an adjustment of all colonial claims, (vi–xiii) matters of territorial adjustment of sovereignty, and (xiv) the herald of the League of Nations ('A general association of Nations must be formed ...').
3. George Scott, *The Rise and Fall of the League of Nations*, Hutchinson, London, 1973, p. 24.
4. F. S. Northedge, *The League of Nations: Its Life and Times 1920–1946*, Holmes and Meier, New York, 1986, p. 28.
5. Jan Christian Smuts, 'The League of Nations: A Practical Suggestion', quoted in *Jan Christian Smuts* by his son, J. C. Smuts, Cassell, London, 1952, pp. 214–18.
6. John Spencer Bassett, *The League of Nations*, Longman, Green Company, New York, 1930, p. 15.
7. Albert E. Hindmarsh, *Force in Peace*, Harvard University Press, Harvard, Massachusetts, 1933, p. 152.
8. David Hunter Miller, *Drafting of the Covenant*, G. P. Putnam's Sons, New York, 1928, p. 570.
9. Kim Richard Nossal, 'Economic sanctions in the League of Nations and the United Nations', in David Leyton-Brown (ed.), *The Utility of International Economic Sanctions*, Croom Helm, London, 1987, p. 14.
10. Irving Fisher, *League or War?*, Harper Brothers Publishers, New York, 1923, p. 122.
11. Helen Howell Moorehead, 'International administration of narcotic drugs, 1928–1934', *Geneva Special Studies*, Volume VI, Number 1, 27 February 1935, p. 12.
12. Ruth B. Henig (ed.), *The League of Nations*, Harper and Row, New York, 1973, p. 175.

13. Gaetano Salvemini, *Prelude to World War II*, Victor Gollancz, London, 1953, p. 124.
14. Scott, *op. cit.*, pp. 211–12.
15. Kellogg Pact (27 August 1928), initiated by US Secretary of State Frank B. Kellogg and French foreign minister Aristide Briand, declaring an end to war as an instrument of national policy. This 'Pact of Paris' was originally signed by 15 nations and subscribed to by 62. Lack of enforcement measures rendered the Pact ineffective.
16. Quoted in Scott, *op. cit.*, p. 213.
17. Gilbert Murray, *Manchester Guardian*, leader, 8 December 1931.
18. H. L. Stimson and McGeorge Bundy, *On Active Service in Peace and War*, Harper, New York, 1947, p. 220.
19. Salvemini, *op. cit.*, p. 127.
20. Henry P. Fletcher to Secretary of State, 16 January 1926, Container 12 FP, quoted in John P. Diggins, *Mussolini and Fascism: The View from America*, Princeton University Press, New Jersey, 1972, p. 266.
21. Stimson and Bundy, *op. cit.*, p. 269.
22. Quoted in Diggins, *op. cit.*, p. 276.
23. *Chicago Daily Tribune*, 4 October 1934, quoted in *ibid.*, pp. 287–8.
24. *New Republic*, LXXXIII, 7 August 1935, pp. 347–9.
25. It is worth remembering that the West was raising no protest about Italy's continuing occupation of Libya, another African state subjected to all the abuses of Western colonialism. This occupation had included vast concentration camps in the desert, and the genocide of Libyan men, women and children. Such events have helped to shape the attitudes of modern Libyan leaders – which in turn have influenced the imposition of US-orchestrated sanctions against Libya (see pp. 88–97, 145–54).
26. The Earl of Avon, *The Eden Memoirs: Facing the Dictators*, London, 1962, p. 227.
27. Gerhard von Glahn, *Law Among Nations: An Introduction to Public International Law*, 3rd edition, Macmillan, New York, 1976, p. 502.
28. John I. Knudson, *A History of the League of Nations*, Turner F. Smith, Atlanta, 1938, p. 98.
29. Thomas H. Holland, *The Mineral Sanctions as an Aid to International Security*, Oliver and Boyd, London, 1935.
30. M. S. Daoudi and M. S. Dajani, *Economic Sanctions: Ideals and Experience*, Routledge and Kegan Paul, London, 1983, p. 63.
31. Robert E, Dell, *The Geneva Racket*, Robert Hale, London, 1941, p. 117.
32. Robert A. Divine, *Roosevelt and World War II*, Penguin, Baltimore, Maryland, 1969, p. 12.
33. Quoted in Scott, *op. cit.*, p. 317.
34. Quoted in *ibid.*, p. 318.

35. *Ibid.*, p. 367.
36. Hugh Thomas, *The Spanish Civil War*, Penguin, Harmondsworth, 1965, p. 338.
37. T. R. Fehrenbach, *This Kind of Peace*, Frewin, London, 1967, p. 68.
38. Ernst B. Haas, *The Web of Interdependence: The United States and International Organisation*, New Jersey, 1970, p. 3.
39. Trygve Lie, *In the Cause of Peace*, Macmillan, New York, 1954, p. 55.
40. *Ibid.*, p. 59.
41. The capitalist interest in these developments was nicely illustrated by the gift of $8,500,000 by John D. Rockefeller Jr for the purchase of the East River property, New York, as the UN headquarters site: 'If this property can be useful to you in meeting the great responsibilities entrusted to you by the peoples of the world, it will be a source of infinite satisfaction to me and my family.'
42. Quoted in Scott, *op. cit.*, pp. 404–5.
43. Ted Morgan, *FDR: A Biography*, Grafton, London, 1986, p. 574.
44. *Ibid.*
45. W. N. Medlicott, *The Economic Blockade*, HMSO and Longmans Green, London, 1952, Hufbauer *et al.* (*Economic Sanctions Reconsidered*, Volume II, *Supplemental Case Histories*, 1990, pp. 45–52) profile in detail the character of the Allied economic warfare against Germany and Japan (1939–45).
46. Frank Owen, *The Fall of Singapore*, Pan, London, 1967, pp. 184–94.
47. Harrison E. Salisbury, *The 900 Days: The Siege of Leningrad*, Pan, London, 1971. A poignant Leningrad child's diary, that of Tanya Savicheva, records in detail the expiry of her family: 'Zhenya, died Dec. 28; Granny, died Jan. 25; Leka, died March 17; Uncle Vasya, died April 13; Uncle Lyosha, died May 10; Mummy, died May 13 at 7.30 morning 1942.' Tanya herself died of chronic dysentery in the summer of 1943.
48. The most important provision designed to prevent any powerful state from dominating military operations authorised by the Security Council is the required formation of a Military Staff Committee comprising the Chiefs of Staff of the five Permanent Members (Article 47) to control any military action: 'The Military Staff Committee shall be responsible under the Security Council for the strategic direction of any armed forces placed at the disposal of the Security Council.' In reality, since Washington prefers to control any 'UN' military initiative, no attempt is ever made to constitute a Military Staff Committee. This represents a persistent and deliberate violation of the UN Charter whenever military action is authorised.
49. David Leyton-Brown (ed.), *op. cit.*, p. 17.
50. *Ibid.*
51. *Ibid.*, p. 18.

52. Ralph Zacklin, *The United Nations and Rhodesia*, Praeger, New York, 1974, p. 45.
53. *Ibid.*
54. Citations in Daoudi and Dajani, *op. cit.*, p. 76.
55. D. F. Fleming, *The Cold War and Its Origins 1917–1960*, Allen and Unwin, London, 1961, p. 507.
56. *Ibid.*, p. 508.
57. *Ibid.*, p. 509.
58. See, for example, Andrew Gilligan, 'Berlin thanks RAF heroes who saved city', *Sunday Telegraph*, 28 June 1998.
59. The Korea Question is set against a history of Korea in Geoff Simons, *Korea: the Search for Sovereignty*, 2nd edition, Macmillan, London, 1998.
60. Roy Jenkins, *Truman*, Collins, London, 1986, p. 169. Jenkins reckoned this violation of the UN Charter 'a very minor fault and one on the right side'.
61. Margaret P. Doxey, *International Sanctions in Contemporary Perspective*, Macmillan, London, 1987, pp. 33–4.
62. Article 39 includes specific reference to Articles 41 and 42 of the UN Charter, so allowing for the options of measures 'not involving the use of armed force ... complete or partial interruption of economic relations ...'; and, if necessary, of other measures: 'demonstrations, blockade, and other operations by air, sea, or land forces of Members of the United Nations'. Thus the Security Council had scope, if it so decided, to use economic sanctions and/or military action in response to South African apartheid.
63. Mark David, 'United States–South African Relations – 1962–67', in Sidney Weintraub (ed.), *Economic Coercion and American Foreign Policy: Implications of Case Studies from the Johnson Administration*, Westview Press, Boulder, Colorado, 1982, p. 217.
64. The General Assembly Resolution (2145, XXI, 21 October 1966) was subsequently upheld by Security Council Resolutions (276, 30 January 1970; 284, 29 July 1970).
65. Margaret Garritsen de Vries, *The International Monetary Fund 1966–71*, Volume 2, 1976, Washington D.C., pp. 409–16.
66. John A. Marcum, 'Africa: A Continent Adrift', *68 Foreign Affairs*, 1988–9, p. 161.
67. Martin Bailey, 'Thatcher sanctions policy under renewed attack', *Observer*, 15 April 1990.
68. Tony Barber, Tim Kelsey, Chris McGreal, Adrian Bridge and Leonard Doyle, 'Germany crashes the sanctions barrier', *Independent on Sunday*, 30 December 1990; Phillip van Niekerk, 'South Africa arms trade torpedoed by scandal', *Observer*, 9 October 1994.
69. Ben Lawrence, 'Investment is up but South Africa still hit by capital outflow', *Guardian*, 5 April 1994.

70. Allister Sparks, 'How sanctions fuelled a crisis', *Observer*, 26 September 1993.
71. Hufbauer *et al.* (Volume II, 1990), *op. cit.*, p. 236.
72. Chapter XI, *Declaration Regarding Non-Self-Governing Territories*, Articles 73 and 74 (dealing mainly with progress towards self-government and the need to take into account the interests and well-being of the rest of the world).
73. The Portuguese position is presented in Franco Nogueira, *The United Nations and Portugal: A Study of Anti-Colonialism*, Sidgwick and Jackson, London, 1963.
74. Doxey, *op. cit.*, p. 34.
75. Zdenek Cervenka, *The Unfinished Quest for Unity: Africa and the OAU*, Africana Publishing Company, New York, 1977, p. 135.
76. Peter Wallensteen, 'Economic sanctions: ten modern cases and three important lessons', in Miroslav Nincic and Peter Wallensteen (eds), *Dilemmas of Economic Coercion: Sanctions in World Politics*, Praeger, New York, 1983, p. 94.
77. Martin Bailey, *Oilgate: The Sanctions Scandal*, Coronet, London, 1979.
78. Doxey, *op. cit.*, p. 37.
79. *Ibid.*
80. Bailey, *op. cit.*.
81. Donald L. Losman, *International Economic Sanctions: The Cases of Cuba, Israel and Rhodesia*, University of New Mexico Press, Albuquerque, 1979, pp. 94–5.
82. Robert Lillich and Frank C. Newman, *International Human Rights: Problems of Law and Policy*, Little, Brown, New York, 1979, p. 402.
83. Doxey, *op. cit.*, p. 41.
84. *Ibid.*, p. 46.
85. Hufbauer *et al.* (Volume II, 1990), *op. cit.*, p. 292.
86. If this US terrorist act gave the Libyans a motive for reprisal then attention should be given also to the action of the USS *Vincennes*. On 3 July 1988 this guided-missile cruiser, illegally in Iranian territorial waters, shot down an Iranian airliner, killing all 286 people on board.
87. George Wilson, 'Colonel "was the target"', *Guardian*, 19 April 1986.
88. Leonard Doyle, 'Ghali finds merit in Tripoli shift', *Independent*, 5 March 1992.
89. *Convention for the Suppression of Unlawful Acts against the Safety of Civil Aviation* (Montreal, 23 September 1971).
90. As one commentator among many, Professor Francis A. Boyle, Professor of International Law at the University of Illinois, prepared a Memorandum of Law on the US–Libyan dispute. It is enough to quote briefly from the detailed document:

Libya has fully discharged its obligations ... there is no obligation whatever for Libya to extradite its two nationals to either the United States or the United Kingdom ... .

both the United States and the United Kingdom have effectively violated most of the provisions of the Montreal Convention.

the United States government has admitted that it will pay no attention whatever to its obligations mandating the peaceful resolution of international disputes as required by UN Charter articles 2(3) and 33 ... .

The United States government has purposely and illegally made it impossible for there to be a pacific settlement of the dispute ... .

91. The idea that Washington might consider the use of starvation against the Libyan people will surprise no one who has considered the systematic US attempts to use starvation as a political weapon against Cuba (Chapter 3) and Iraq (Chapter 5).
92. Ian Black, 'Politics make sanctions against Libya lack bite', *Guardian*, 1 December 1993.
93. See, for example, Geoff Simons, *Libya: The Struggle for Survival*, 2nd edition, Macmillan, London, 1996, pp. 30–88.
94. 'UK plane parts break Libya sanctions', *Sunday Times*, 21 April 1996.
95. Ian Black, 'New move to force trial of Lockerbie bomb suspects'; 'Lockerbie: the West takes a gamble', *Guardian*, 21 July 1998.
96. Robert Fisk, '"Cleansing" Bosnia at a camp called Jasenovac', *Independent*, 15 August 1992.
97. David Binder, 'US sending specialists to Balkans in effort to strengthen sanctions', *International Herald Tribune*, 18 September 1992.
98. Yigal Chazan, 'No medicine for Serbian children', *Guardian*, 21 April 1993.
99. 'Freeze on Serbian cash for medicines allowed', Law Report, *Guardian*, 11 October 1993.
100. Security Council, United Nations, 3454th Meeting, SC/5934, 9 November 1994.
101. Julian Borger, 'Bosnians "are being covertly armed"', *Guardian*, 25 February 1995; Richard Dowden, 'Nato angers UN in Bosnia arms mystery', *Independent*, 27 February 1995; 'Turks accused of secret flights to arm Bosnia', *Sunday Times*, 5 March 1995. In July 1995 Malaysia and other Muslim states were offering military assistance to Bosnia.
102. Annex on affects of sanctions, submitted to UN Secretary-General by Vladislav Johanovic, Yugoslavian chargé d'affaires to UN,

A/50/710, 3 November 1995; another report (A/C.2/50/6, 3 November 1995) detailed the many adverse affects of sanctions on the Yugoslavia environment.

103. Kenneth Freed, 'Privileged few smile at sanctions', *Guardian*, 29 June 1994.

104. Maggie O'Kane, 'A land starved of its "saviour"' ('Haiti's poor are living out a nightmare, even by the standards of their tortured history'), *Guardian*, 6 August 1994.

105. Maurice Weaver and Andrew Downie, 'Haiti faces long, hard road, says Clinton', *Daily Telegraph*, 15 October 1994.

106. In the event the US-led involvement in Somalia was a disaster – involving the torture and massacre of innocent Somalis, economic and social disruption, and yet another discrediting of the United Nations (see *Observer*, 28 November 1994; *The Militant*, New York, 28 November 1994; *Observer*, 22 March 1998).

107. Eighth progress report of the Secretary-General on the UN Observer Mission in Liberia, S/1995/9, 6 January 1975, Paragraph 23.

108. John A. Marcum, *The Angolan Revolution, Volume I: 1950–1962*, MIT Press, Cambridge, Massachusetts, 1969, pp. 229–30.

109. Hearings before the House Select Committee on Intelligence (the Pike Committee) published in *CIA: the Pike Report*, Nottingham, 1977, p. 199.

110. John Carlin, 'Pretoria came close to dropping nuclear bomb on Luanda', *Independent*, 30 March 1993.

111. Mark Huband, 'UN troops stand by and watch carnage', *Guardian*, 12 April 1994.

Chapter 3

1. The voting procedure of the Security Council is defined by Article 27: each member of the Council 'shall have one vote' (though in reality this means that Washington has as many votes among allies and clients as it can bribe and coerce). Article 27(3) specifies that decisions made on non-procedural matters require the 'concurring votes of the permanent members'. Thus any Permanent Member can veto non-procedural questions: so authorising a single powerful state to block a resolution that all the rest of the entire UN membership might support. But does an abstention constitute a 'concurring' vote? A literal view of Article 27(3) would require *all* Permanent Members of the Council to vote for a resolution for it to be passed: an interpretation reinforced by the French draft of the text ('Les décisions du Counseil de Sécurité ... sont prises par

un vote affirmatif de neuf ... dans lequel sont comprises les voix de yous les membres permanents').

2. The veto, nominally a simple device, has evolved as a complex phenomenon. In one interpretation the veto has several forms: the open (or real) veto; the double veto; the hidden (or indirect) veto; the artificial and imposed veto; and the veto by proxy (Anjali V. Patil, *The UN Veto in World Affairs 1946–1990*, UNIFO, Florida, 1992, pp. 16–17).

3. Robert W. Tucker and David C. Hendrickson, *The Imperial Temptation: The New World Order and America's Purpose*, Council on Foreign Relations Press, New York, 1992, pp. 14–15.

4. *Ibid.*

5. Abdelrahman Munif, 'The war against a civilisation', *Guardian*, 1 April 1991.

6. James Adams, 'US missiles target Third World', *Sunday Times*, 9 February 1992; Paul Rogers, 'A bomb to blast the bullies', *The Guardian*, 2 July 1992.

7. John Lichfield, 'Sabre-rattling with Stealth: the gunboat diplomacy of our time', *Independent*, 13 September 1996.

8. Martin Walker, 'Master of the universe', *Guardian*, 7 August 1996.

9. Alan Philps, 'Pentagon shows its reach', *Daily Telegraph*, 19 September 1997.

10. Margaret P. Doxey, *International Sanctions in Contemporary Perspective*, Macmillan, London, 1987, pp. 10–12.

11. Based on typology in *ibid.*, pp. 11–12.

12. Barry E. Carter, *International Economic Sanctions*, Cambridge University Press, New York, 1988, p. 32.

13. *Ibid.*, p. 159.

14. Nancy Dunne, 'Sanctions overload', *Financial Times*, 21 July 1998, p. 19.

15. *Ibid.*

16. Quoted in *ibid.*

17. Quoted in *ibid.*

18. *Ibid.*

19. In addition to the comprehensive economic sanctions Washington planned and later launched a series of terrorist campaigns against Cuba. These are profiled in Geoff Simons, *Cuba: from Conquistador to Castro*, Macmillan, 1996, pp. 298–303.

20. Ediciones Obra Pevolucionaria (Revolutionary Works Editions), Number 13, Imprenta Nacional de Cuba, 16 July 1960, pp. 27, 29 and 31, quoted in Nicanor León Cotayo, *Beleaguered Hope: The US Economic Blockade of Cuba*, Editorial Cultura Popular, Havana, 1991, pp. 24–5.

21. The *New York Times* (15 May 1994), for example, commented that this was hardly the way to triumph over Cuba or to portray

the United States as humanitarian. Associated Press (AP) observed that Washington would not gain by making the Cubans hungrier or making them suffer through lack of medicine.

22. A CBS television broadcast (10 June 1977), focusing on 'The CIA's Secret Army', acknowledged that CIA-organised Cuban exile groups had maintained an unbroken series of terrorist attacks on Cuba for 18 years. Castro, interviewed, stated that there had been at least 24 assassination attempts against him and other Cuban leaders over recent years.
23. Mary Murray, *Cruel and Unusual Punishment: The US Blockade Against Cuba*, Ocean Press, Melbourne, Australia, 1993, pp. 15–16.
24. Noll Scott, 'US rules out any relaxation of Cuban trade embargo', *Guardian*, 28 October 1993.
25. Hugh Shaughnessy, 'US Cuba trade ban hits British firms', *Observer*, 14 November 1993.
26. Paul Rodgers, 'Washington takes on the rest of the world', *Independent*, 17 July 1996.
27. 'The blockade is morally crushed', *Granma International*, Havana, 10 May 1998.
28. 'US philosophers against the blockade', *Granma International*, Havana, 19 July 1998.
29. *Convention on the Prevention and Punishment of the Crime of Genocide*, approved and proposed for signature and ratification or accession by General Assembly Resolution 260A(III) of 9 December 1948 (entry into force: 12 January 1951).
30. Murray, *op. cit.*, pp. 59–66.
31. Jonathan Glancey, 'Don't shoot the piano tuner, he's only gone to Cuba', *Independent*, 1 March 1997.
32. Executive Summary, *The Impact of the US Embargo On Health and Nutrition in Cuba*, American Association for World Health, Washington D.C., March 1997, p. 7.
33. *Ibid.*
34. This phase is described in Geoff Simons, *Korea: the Search for Sovereignty*, Macmillan, London, 1995, pp. 14–34.
35. Zalmay M. Khalilzad, 'Should the world take a hard line with North Korea – Yes, threaten sanctions', *International Herald Tribune*, 8 November 1993.
36. Marcus Warren, 'North Korea threat to rejoin nuclear race', *Sunday Telegraph*, 7 June 1998.
37. This process is described in Geoff Simons, *Vietnam Syndrome: Impact on US Foreign Policy*, Macmillan, London, 1998, pp. 314–23.
38. Gary Clyde Hufbauer, Jeffrey J. Schott and Kimberly Ann Elliott, *Economic Sanctions Reconsidered: History and Current Policy*, Volume I, Institute for International Economics, Washington D.C., 1990, p. 162.

39. Nina Burleigh, James Carney, J.F.O. McAllister and Mark Thompson, 'Down goes the deal', *Time*, 27 March 1995.
40. Robin Wright, 'Dubai's wooden hulls will sunder the blockade', *Guardian*, 3 May 1995.

Chapter 4

1. Michael Walzer, *Just and Unjust Wars: A Moral Argument with Historical Illustrations*, Penguin Books, Harmondsworth, 1980, pp. 58–9.
2. A. C. Bell, *A History of the Blockade of Germany*, London, 1937, pp. 213–14, quoted in *ibid.*, p. 171.
3. These elements of the 1977 Protocol 1 Addition (Article 54) to the Geneva Convention should be borne in mind when reading about the years-long sanctions against Iraq (Chapter 5).
4. Marc Weller, 'The Lockerbie case: a premature end to the "New World Order"?', *African Journal of International and Comparative Law*, Number 4, 1992, pp. 1–15.
5. *Ibid.*, p. 15.
6. Washington, keen to protest about Iraq, often shows indifference to international law. More than two dozen US violations of the UN Charter, treaties and international law are listed in Geoff Simons, *Vietnam Syndrome: Impact on US Foreign Policy*, Macmillan, London, 1998, pp. 299–302.
7. Listed in Geoff Simons, *The Scourging of Iraq: Sanctions, Law and Natural Justice*, Macmillan, London, 2nd edition, 1998, pp. 197–8.

Chapter 5

1. Felicity Arbuthnot, 'Zoo animals share the suffering', *Irish Times*, 15 January 1995.
2. Warren A. J. Hamerman, International Progress Organization, presentation (denouncing sanctions against Iraq) to UN Organization Sub-Commission on Prevention of Discrimination and Protection of Minorities, 43rd Session, 13 August 1991.
3. H. V. F. Winstone and Zahra Freeth, *Kuwait: Prospect and Reality*, George Allen and Unwin, London, 1972, p. 111.
4. Described in Geoff Simons, *Iraq: from Sumer to Saddam*, Macmillan, London, 2nd edition, 1996, pp. 345–51.
5. April Glaspie later stated that her remarks (25 July 1990) had been edited by the Iraqis to tone down her warnings to Iraq not to use force. However, when the text of the meeting was released

by the Iraqi government the US State Department described the Iraqi transcript as 'essentially correct'; and has continued to refuse to release Glaspie's own report of the meeting (see Phyllis Bennis and Michel Moushabeck (eds), *Beyond the Storm: A Gulf Crisis Reader*, Canongate Press, Edinburgh, 1992, p. 391).

6. A detailed chronology of the imposition of sanctions on Iraq is given in Geoff Simons, *The Scourging of Iraq: Sanctions, Law and Natural Justice*, Macmillan, London, 2nd edition, 1998, pp. 33–73.
7. *Ibid.*, pp. 73–98.
8. *Ibid.*, pp. 113–22.
9. 'Sanctions against Iraq', *World Chronicle* (recorded 20 May 1992), Information Products Division, Department of Public Information, United Nations, New York; Guest: Ambassador Peter Hohenfellner, Chairman of Committee on Sanctions Against Iraq; journalists: Bruno Franseachi, Raghida Dergham, Ian Williams; Moderator: Michael Littlejohns.
10. First listed in Simons (1998) *op. cit.*, p. 119.
11. Margit Fakhoury, 'A German doctor tells how Iraq's children are being killed', Committee to Save the Children in Iraq, funded by the Schiller Institute, Washington D.C., 1991, pp. 14–18.
12. Felicity Arbuthnot, 'Children condemned to a lingering death', *Asian Times*, 16 March 1993.
13. Miriam Ryle, 'Child victims of the sanctions syndrome', letter, *Guardian*, 15 July 1994.
14. Yves Bonnet (French deputy), 'Sanctions that should shame the UN', *Guardian*, 8 August 1995, reprinted from *Le Monde*.
15. Fakhoury, *op. cit.*, p. 15.
16. The impact of sanctions on the civilian population is described in Simons (1998), *op. cit.*, pp. 122–71, 215–27.
17. Umeed Mubarak, Iraqi Health Minister, Reuters, 12 May 1997.
18. Evidence of this can be found in many relevant documents supplied to the United Nations. See, for example, letter (25 May 1997) from the Minister of Foreign Affairs of Iraq addressed to the Secretary-General, S/1997/402, 27 May 1997; letter (11 June 1997), S/1997/452, 12 June 1997; letter (12 July 1997), S/1997/544, 15 July 1997; letter (16 September 1997), S/1997/717. A report of the Secretary-General (S/1997/419, 2 June 1997) noted (Paragraph 49) 'the slow and partial arrival' of medical supplies that has contributed to 'the continuous degradation' of the Iraqi health sector.
19. *Adverse Consequences of Economic Sanctions on the Enjoyment of Human Rights*, UN Economic and Social Council, Sub-Commission on Prevention of Discrimination and Protection of Minorities, 37th meeting, 29 August 1997.

20. Nutritional Status Survey of Infants in South/Centre Iraq, 27 October to 2 November 1997, Iraqi Ministry of Health and UNICEF, 14 November 1997.
21. 'Nearly one million children malnourished in Iraq, says UNICEF: Surveys reveal deepening crisis', UNICEF, CF/DOC/PR/1997-60, 26 November 1997; see also letter (28 November 1997) from Permanent Representative of Iraq to the United Nations addressed to the President of the Security Council, S/1997/934, 28 November 1997.
22. Survey carried out in March 1998 by UNICEF, WFP and the Iraqi Ministry of Health.
23. Letter dated 27 May 1998 from the Deputy Prime Minister and Acting Minister for Foreign Affairs of Iraq addressed to the Secretary-General, S/1998/452, Paragraph 3.
24. 'Gulf war linked to sixfold rise in Iraqi cancer', Reuters, *Guardian*, 8 August 1998.
25. 'These Iraq talks are achieving nothing', leader, *Independent*, 4 August 1998.
26. Patrick Cockburn, 'Sanctions and heat take toll on Iraq', *Independent*, 8 August 1998.
27. Quoted in *ibid*.
28. Maggie O'Kane, 'Sick and dying in their hospital beds, the pitiful victims of sanctions and Saddam', *Guardian*, 19 February 1998.
29. Geoff Simons, *Iraq: Primus Inter Pariahs: A Crisis Chronology (1997/98)*, Macmillan, London, 1999.
30. Christopher Lockwood, 'Sanctions "to erode" says Saddam as US plots to depose him', *Daily Telegraph*, 18 July 1998; Gary Younge, 'US Saddam base', *Guardian*, 3 August 1998.

Select Bibliography

Bailey, Martin, *Oilgate: The Sanctions Scandal*, Coronet, London, 1979.
Bell, A. C., *A History of the Blockade of Germany*, London, 1937.
Bradbury, Jim, *The Medieval Siege*, The Boydell Press, Suffolk, 1992.
Carter, Barry E., *International Economic Sanctions*, Cambridge University Press, New York, 1988.
Claude, Inis L., *Swords into Plowshares*, University of London Press, London, 1965.
Daoudi, M. S. and Dajani, M. S., *Economic Sanctions: Ideals and Experience*, Routledge and Kegan Paul, London, 1983.
Diggins, John P., *Mussolini and Fascism: The View from America*, Princeton University Press, New Jersey, 1972.
Doxey, Margaret P., *Economic Sanctions and International Enforcement*, Macmillan for The Royal Institute of Economic Affairs, London, 1980.
—— *International Sanctions in Contemporary Perspective*, Macmillan, London, 1987.
Holland, Thomas H., *The Mineral Sanctions as an Aid to International Security*, Oliver and Boyd, London, 1935.
Horne, Alistair, *The Fall of Paris: The Siege and the Commune 1970–71*, Macmillan, London, 1965.
Hufbauer, Gary Clyde; Schott, Jeffrey J. and Elliott, Kimberly Ann, *Economic Sanctions Reconsidered, Volume I, History and Current Policy; Volume II, Supplemental Case Histories*, Institute for International Economics, Washington D.C., 1990.
Leyton-Brown, David (ed.), *The Utility of International Economic Sanctions*, Croom Helm, London, 1987.
Looman, Donald L., *International Economic Sanctions: The Cases of Cuba, Israel and Rhodesia*, University of New Mexico, Albuquerque, 1979.
McPherson, James M., *Battle Cry of Freedom: The American Civil War*, Penguin Books in Association with Oxford University Press, London, 1990.
Medlicott, W. N., *The Economic Blockade*, HMSO and Longmans Green, London, 1952.
Murray, Mary, *Cruel and Unusual Punishment: The US Blockade Against Cuba*, Ocean Press, Melbourne, 1993.
Nincic, Miroslav and Wallensteen, Peter (eds), *Dilemmas of Economic Coercion: Sanctions in World Politics*, Praeger, New York, 1983.

Nogueira, Franco, *The United Nations and Portugal: a Study in Anti-Colonialism*, Sidgwick and Jackson, London, 1963.
Northedge, F. S., *The League of Nations: its Life and Times 1920–1946*, Leicester University Press, 1988.
Salisbury, Harrison E., *The 900 Days: The Siege of Leningrad*, Pan Books, London, 1971.
Scott, George, *The Rise and Fall of the League of Nations*, Hutchinson, London, 1973.
Segal, Ronald (ed.), *Sanctions Against South Africa*, Penguin Books, Harmondsworth, 1964.
Simons, Geoff, *Cuba: From Conquistador to Castro*, Macmillan, London, 1996.
—— *Iraq: From Sumer to Saddam*, Macmillan, London, 2nd edition, 1996.
—— *Korea: The Search for Sovereignty*, Macmillan, London, 1995.
—— *Libya: The Struggle for Survival*, Macmillan, London, 2nd edition, 1996.
—— *The Scourging of Iraq: Sanctions, Law and Natural Justice*, Macmillan, London, 2nd edition, 1998.
—— *The United Nations: A Chronology of Conflict*, Macmillan, London, 1994.
—— *Vietnam Syndrome: Impact on US Foreign Policy*, Macmillan, London, 1998.
Tucker, Robert W. and Hendrickson, David C., *The Imperial Temptation: The New World Order and America's Purpose*, Council on Foreign Relations Press, New York, 1992.
Weintraub, Sidney (ed.), *Economic Coercion and American Foreign Policy: Implications of Case Studies from the Johnson Administration*, Westview Press, Boulder, Colorado, 1982.
Zacklin, Ralph, *The United Nations and Rhodesia*, Praeger, New York, 1974.

Index